THE PATH OF GLORY

Drawn by J. Buchanan. Engraved by W. T. Fry

John Shipp

THE PATH OF GLORY

BEING THE MEMOIRS
OF THE EXTRAORDINARY
MILITARY CAREER OF
JOHN SHIPP
WRITTEN BY HIMSELF

Edited by
C. J. STRANKS

1969
CHATTO & WINDUS
LONDON

Published by
Chatto and Windus Ltd
42 William IV Street
London W.C.2.
*
Clarke, Irwin & Co Ltd
Toronto

SBN 7011 1311 X

Printed in Great Britain by
Alden & Mowbray Ltd
at the Alden Press, Oxford

CONTENTS

CONTENTS

PLATES

Introduction

The Memoirs of John Shipp is an extraordinary book, the work of a most remarkable man whose life was packed with adventures in strange lands among a set of men who were in their own way as unusual as himself. Without money, and without influence, in days when those things counted for almost everything in the army, he pushed his way up from the very bottom by sheer merit. He started his career at the age of nine when, as a troublesome orphan, the parish authorities were glad to get rid of him by sending him for a soldier, and survived the hardships and dangers of his early days to be given a commission for quite fantastic bravery by the time he was twenty. When debt made him sell that, he achieved the even more difficult feat of obtaining a second. All his life he had the gift of making friends, and many people went out of their way to help him, for which he showed gratitude that is quite without humbug or sycophancy. Indeed, while he recognized how much he owed to others he was never shy of pointing out that their kindness was more than justified by his own merit, but he did so with a naïveté which is quite disarming. He may not have been so entirely popular as he makes out, but the people he lived among were not likely to take a man solely at his own valuation, and there is every sign that they did indeed regard him very highly.

They were remarkable men, that handful of soldiers and civilians who, more by force of circumstances than design, spread the British power throughout India. In Shipp's day Kipling's Army of India was in the making. Ortheris, Learoyd and Mulvaney—particularly Mulvaney—were in the ranks already, but their lot was harder than that of their successors. The ordinary soldier, once he arrived in the country, had only a small chance of getting home again. Disease, the climate, battle, and his own habits made such an event extremely unlikely. He was absurdly dressed and fed. Drink, and the dubious pleasures of the bazaar, when he had any money for them, were his only recreations. Yet the men in the ranks seem to have preserved a cheerfulness and courage which would have been remarkable under any circumstances, and was almost miraculous in these. In spite of harsh discipline, a mutual respect grew up between the best officers and their men, which made the most formidable tasks seem easy. As an incentive there was always the chance of prize money, a polite name for loot, and for the exceptional man, on rare occasions, the possibility of a commission. Once an officer, no matter how junior his rank, he might for a time hold some position of great responsibility, for the draining away of able men to political and civil posts frequently left the army short of staff.

Shipp's service brought him into particularly close contact with the Irish, and he pays full tribute to their magnificent qualities as soldiers. The harsh lives of the peasantry, from which they were recruited, made the hardships of army life a little less killing for them than they were for others. They had in addition an élan, and a brotherhood in the regiment, which turned them into an incomparable instrument for war, even if their natural waywardness sometimes made discipline hard to impose. All the fighting men, whether they were the King's troops, the Company's army of part Europeans and part Natives, or even the irregular forces raised in a particular place for a particular purpose, had the habit of victory and should they happen to be beaten showed as much surprise as chagrin at the result. Yet their wars were not easy. Indian soldiers fought with as much valour against the British as they did for them, but European equipment and method were generally superior; though Shipp stresses, again and again, how much better the Indian cavalry was than the British. The rules of Oriental warfare, if they can be called that, were savage in the extreme; and European troops were often shocked at treachery and cruelty so wanton as to pass belief. They were themselves ruthless but always, as they thought, with reason and within the military traditions of their race. Theirs was a world in which hardness was the price of survival, and unchecked pity a burden which few could bear.

Looking back upon it now we can see what an astonishing

thing it was for a few men, from a distant island, dependent on slow and uncertain communications, to spread over a whole sub-continent and in the end to dominate it. That they had a better technique of war, that their leadership was often very good, and they were sustained by a flamboyant patriotism, is only part of the answer. India had known many conquerors, the British were just one more, to be accepted for a time until the chances of history blunted their impact. There was no national feeling, and the smaller powers, which sprang up out of the ruins of the Mogul empire, were willing to utilize the British in the shifting alliances which kept them in being. And so, the territories controlled in one way or another by the East India Company continued to expand; sometimes because safety in one place demanded conquest in another, sometimes because a Governor General had ambitions, sometimes because a state which had accepted British protection called upon them to overthrow some enemy. Yet throughout the early centuries final policy was always in the hands of business men, the Directors of the East India Company in Leadenhall Street; whose ruling desire was to increase their trade, and keep clear of anything which might add to the expense, or responsibility, of government. Shipp's story covers the years when the British were finally establishing themselves. France was no longer any very great threat, and the various Native powers which might have kept the Europeans in check quarrelled among themselves, and were beaten one by one. The ordinary people, who had nothing to gain from the continual wars and plunderings of their own princes, accepted the newcomers for the peace and good order which they brought.

Those who wish to understand the broad outlines of the campaigns in which Shipp fought, will find what they want in volumes five and eleven of Sir John Fortescue's *History of the British Army,* where the confused story is reduced to something like clarity. Fortescue deals with the successes and mistakes of Politicians and Generals, and looks at war through the eyes of those who conduct it. Shipp gives the day-to-day experiences of the men who did the fighting. He tells us what it was like to march and fight for thirty-six hours on end, without sleep, on an empty belly; of the men's reckless courage, of their jokes of what it meant to be left behind wounded on the battlefield, and what the fortress looked like to the soldiers who had to storm it the next day; what it was like to be in the breach, and the death and blood, and wounds, the stench and the destruction which they found when they got inside. All this going on in the torrential rains or searing heat of India. He gives us the raw material of defeat or victory, as he saw it, looking back upon it when his career had come to an end, and he was home in England once more. Every detail may not be correct, but the picture is authentic beyond doubt. Tales like his were the repertoire of the few old soldiers who had the luck to get back to Europe again; and end their days on a trivial pension in the hamlet where they were born, or, worse off still, to beg at street corners, or die in the workhouse. During the nineteenth century all classes in Britain felt the impact of India. It was no longer just the country from which a few, enormously wealthy, nabobs came back to spend their money on country estates and seats in parliament. High and low were all concerned. Men who had served there were in every town and country-side, and there was hardly a village church without its memorials to the younger sons who had died while ruling, or conquering, India. That country has entered into the life blood of our nation more than any other which we have governed, whose people were not of European stock. A long list of Viceroys, Generals, Civil Servants and officials of every kind have written accounts of how they exercised power there. Shipp is one of the very few private soldiers who have put into print what it was like to be one of the valiant, inarticulate, expendable many on whom the whole structure of authority rested.

That of itself was a considerable feat. He did not learn to read and write until long after he had joined the army, and at no time can books have been easy to come by though in a digression on the habits of servants, left out of all editions of his memoirs after the first, he claims to have had a considerable collection. He seems to know Shakespeare and the Bible well, and to be familiar with many of the plays which were popular in his day. These he probably discovered through the amateur theatricals, which whiled away the tedium of peace-time life in a dull contonment. Whether it was the plays, or the "gentleman in every way well qualified for the task" to whom he submitted his manuscript for revision, that determined his style is hard to say, but the book is heavily loaded with high-flown, interminable sentences, repetition of sentiments and descriptions, and a general striving after fine writing which is very tiresome. Yet when he, or his adviser, forgets to be literary the narrative is simple and direct, with the occasional vivid phrase which admirably conveys his soldier's tale.

Among the most popular of stage conventions in Shipp's day was that of the comic Irishman, and this he overworked intolerably. The humour depended on contradictions in thought and language, which were supposed to make the Irish very absurd; but which, in any quantity, must have made them very wearisome. Tales of this sort needed to be severely pruned, only keeping enough of them to show what Shipp, or his men, were capable of. As he came towards the end of his book he began to tire, and fell back on reflections and phrases, which he had used to the full in earlier contexts, and which added nothing fresh to his story. These could be taken out without loss. Several long digressions on separate subjects such as that on servants, already mentioned, on flogging, on the regimental riding school and on new-comers adapting themselves to the Indian climate, had already been removed in the edition of 1843, from which that of 1890 was printed. It looked as if the same process could be continued with advantage. The whole book needed to be worked over again, removing the padding, straightening out what confusion there was and tightening up the narrative. This seemed worth attempting for Shipp's story is too remarkable to be lost sight of. As he had already allowed his work to be revised by another hand there was no reason why this should not be done, and it had the advantage of keeping the good, plain writing which was probably characteristic of Shipp when he let himself be natural; as well as the first-hand observation, and the immediacy, which makes autobiography so much more compelling than any other person's reconstruction of the tale. This has been done and the book reduced by something like twenty thousand words, without losing anything of consequence.

Shipp spelled Indian proper names, and indeed all Indian words, by ear but as he is never very far away from a recognizable form his version could stand. What slight differences there are should give no one any trouble. He claimed to know Hindustani perfectly, and frequently acted as an interpreter for his friends. In all probability his first wife had some native blood, for his mother-in-law stayed behind in India when her husband went back to England. In a book of this kind it is tempting to add almost limitless notes, but these have been kept within bounds, and only inserted where they were necessary to explain, or elaborate, essential points in the text. Chapter headings have also been supplied. In the course of preparing this edition I have received help from many sources. Mr I. J. C. Foster, Keeper of the Oriental Books at the School of Oriental Languages, Durham University, took a great deal of trouble to get me books on Nepal. Dr A. I. Doyle, Keeper of Rare Books at Durham University Library, added to the many kindnesses which I have already received from him. My wife listened patiently to all my enthusiasms and gave advice and help. To these and to the many others who answered letters, or told me where I might obtain information, I offer my sincere thanks.

C. J. STRANKS

I

The Education of a Workhouse Boy

In laying before the public an unreserved account of the many strange incidents and adventures which I have met with during the course of my life I hope I shall not leave myself open to the charge of vanity. Nor, I trust, shall I be accused of any ostentatious display of those gifts which naturally become a soldier. If, in the course of my service, I have shown some daring I am far from claiming any special merit on that account. Any brave officer in His Majesty's service would have done the same in similar circumstances. The high politics which lay behind the battles and sieges in which I played my part are beyond my power to explain. It is the duty of a Subaltern to act rather than to reason, and the necessary duties of my profession kept me too fully occupied to allow leisure for the study of such intricate affairs.

Let me first say a word about my childhood, for even my setting out in the world was different from the common lot. It is recorded in the register book of the parish of Saxmundham,[1] in Suffolk, that I was born on 16th March, 1785, the second son of Thomas and Laetitia Shipp, persons of honest fame indeed but indigent circumstances, who had met with their full share of this world's sorrow. My mother died while I was still an infant, and as my father was a soldier in a foreign land, my brother and I were left to buffet with care and want as best we could, for we were destitute. The advantages which other children derive from the support, and good counsel, of an affectionate father had never blessed us, and now we were suddenly deprived of a fond mother's care, and with it of our humble home. Friends we had few, if any, and those we had were incapacitated by their own distressed circumstances from helping us. Need I feel shame, then, in avowing that there was one place of refuge, and one only, in which two helpless orphans could obtain at once food, clothes, and shelter, and that was the village poorhouse. At the age of nine I lost my brother who was pressed on board a man-of-war. He was a remarkably fine youth of about fourteen, wild and spirited, and being like myself homeless and dependent, he required little pressing, but gladly availed himself of the chance to escape from bondage by becoming a volunteer in the service of his country. Since that time—now upward of thirty years—I have never heard of him.

To return to myself. Now that my brother had left me I was desolate indeed but grief, however poignant, will not dwell long with youth. I was naturally a wild dog of an active, unconquerable, spirit so that, in spite of my friendless situation, I soon contrived to establish in the village a character for mischief, infinitely above that of any other boy of my age. This, however popular it might make me with my fellows, was not likely to increase the number of my real friends. I cannot therefore speak in any rapturous terms of the comforts I enjoyed in my youth. My time was passed in a pretty even routine of planning and executing mischief, and receiving its reward. This however was not to last long. Fortune threw an incident in my way which turned my thoughts into a new channel.

One autumn morning in the year 1794, while I was playing marbles in a lane called Love Lane, the shrill notes of a fife, and the hollow sound of a distant drum, struck on my active ear. I stopped my shot, bagged my marbles, and scampered off to see the soldiers. On arriving at the market place I found them to be a recruiting party of the Royal Artillery, who had already enlisted several likely looking fellows. The pretty little, well-dressed, fifer was the principal object of my notice. His finery and shrill music were sufficient attractions in themselves, but what chiefly caught my fancy was the size of this musical warrior, for he was little bigger than the drum he stood by. "Surely," I thought to myself as I sidled up to him, "I am as tall, if not taller, than this little blade and would make as good a soldier." The portly Sergeant, addressing his words to the gaping rustics by whom he was surrounded, but directing his eyes to the bedroom windows near-by, began a right speech. I swallowed every word of it as eagerly as the Drum-Major's wife would her morning draught. It was all about "Gentlemen soldiers, merry life, muskets rattling, cannon roaring, drums beating, colours flying, regiments charging and shouts of victory! victory!" At these last words the bumpkins who had just enlisted let their flowing locks go free, and waving their tattered hats, gave three cheers for "The King, God Bless Him," in which I joined most heartily. So inspired was I by the word "victory" that it was not until some minutes after the rest had left off that I discovered, by the laughter of those round me, that I was alone in my enthusiasm. However, I put on my hat with a knowing air, and strutting up to the Sergeant, looking as tall as possible, asked him if he "would take I for a sodjer". The Sergeant smiled and patted my head with some condescension, which encouraged me to think that I might do the same to the drum; but I had no sooner touched it than I had a sharp rap over the knuckles from the drummer boy, for the drumhead was as sacred to him as the apple of his eye. Still I pestered the Sergeant to take me, pointing out that I was taller than the little fellow with the drum, which so enraged that hero that he flew at me, kicking and punching in a way that I would soon have returned if fear of affronting His Majesty's uniform had not restrained me. There was nothing for it but to make my way home, but what I had seen and heard possessed me, and from that day onwards a soldier's life was in all my thoughts, and in all my play.

Shortly after this notable adventure I was sent to live with a farmer, whose heart was as cold as the frost that killed his crops. Luckily for me his wife was of a different disposition. She did what she could to shield me from his rage and was, in some ways, a second mother to me; but to tell the truth I was so restless and untoward in my behaviour, and my master so imperious in his commands and unrelenting in his anger, that a day seldom passed without a thrashing. This was little calculated either to conciliate my affection or reform my conduct. I grew more and more stubborn, and more and more resolved to escape from the hardships of my condition. But soldiering possessed me still. All the cats and dogs in the house were made to go through military evolutions. The hoes and the rakes became muskets, the geese and the turkeys were turned into soldiers. This was something my master could not beat out of me. Every time his back was turned I was at my military exercises, and if there was no possibility of that then I was whistling soldier tunes, "God Save the King", "The British Grenadiers", and "See the Conquering Hero Comes". I once got into trouble for whistling the first of these at a funeral service, the churchyard, as the sexton remarked when he laid his cane on my back, being no place to show my loyalty in. Even the old women of the parish could not pass along the lane without hearing me shout some military command or other at them, and as tricks of this sort generally got back to my master, they usually meant another beating.

One December day, when the world was thick with ice and snow, I was standing, half frozen, in a turnip field by the Yarmouth Road, desperately plotting how to escape from the intolerable life I led. I was just blowing on my fingers to blow a little warmth into them, when my ears caught the distant sound of martial music. I jumped over the gate, and was off like a shot towards it. The music stopped, and I stood aching for it to come back again. Then suddenly the whole band struck into "Over the Hills and Far Away" and my heart kindled with an excitement which nothing but death can extinguish. Since that day I have seen my full share of what lies "Over the Hills and Far Away", but the flame that leapt up in me at that moment burns still. On coming up with the party of soldiers I gave the Colonel a military salute, by first slapping my leathers and then bringing my right hand, the wrong one by the way, up to the level of my forehead, and extending the thumb as far as possible from the fingers. There I stood, keeping the elbow parallel with the top of the head, until the Colonel passed; who, noticing how carefully I kept my position said, with a smile, "That's a fine fellow." On that head I quite agreed with the gallant commander, but his compliment so elated me that I hardly knew whether I stood on my head or my heels, and pranced round the soldiers until I ran full tilt into my master; who was following them along mounted on Corporal Dash, a horse of his that I had so named, with his long hunting whip, which was an old acquaintance of mine, in his hand. The instant I recognized them I saw that I had not a moment to lose, and I was off as fast as my legs could carry me. My master rode after me roaring out most lustily "Stop! Stop!" but if, instead of stop, he had shouted halt, it is ten to one that I would have obliged him; for, from constant drills, I responded mechanically to the word of command. As it was I went on until a stile stopped him, and as I was quite out of breath I thought I might as well stop too. So I stood, and had the satisfaction of hearing my master swear roundly that he would kill me when he caught me, but, thank God, I thought to myself, you have not got me yet.

The moment my persecutor rode on I cut across a field and got to the head of the corps of Royal Horse Artillery, which was just entering the village. There I dared not follow until my master's wrath had blown over; so I perched on a gate and yearned after the soldiers, as a wounded man yearns for his comrades in the thick of the battle. But I had something else to think of as well, and that was how to escape the beating I knew the farmer would give me when I got home. I had discovered that the regiment I followed was on its way to Yarmouth, to embark for foreign service, and I had not the least doubt from the kind manner of the Colonel who returned my salute that he would take me for a soldier. Full of these thoughts I loitered about all that day, but dared not venture near the farm until my inside began to express wants that were not to be drilled into obedience. At last, overcome by fatigue and hunger, I marched in, but not until I had seen my master march out. My mistress, who was always willing to play the part of a kind mother toward me, furnished me with a substantial meal to which I did full justice; and, having satisfied my appetite for the present, provided a little for the future by lining my pockets with bread and cheese, for the next day I intended to go off after the soldiers.

When morning came I betook myself to my usual occupation, but I had not been at work more than five minutes when I espied my master reconnoitring me from behind a hedge. Presently he got over a stile, with a large whip in his hand, and I could see that it was his intention to creep up on me unawares. Now and then, in order to lull my suspicions, he would stoop down and pull a turnip but I was already too good a soldier to be outgeneralled in this fashion. I stood back from my work, and kept an eye on the enemy. At last I saw him beginning to get his whip ready for a beating, and I replied by getting my legs ready for a start. Every step he takes now, I thought, is a step nearer my back, but as I have ten yards start there is a chance for me. He saw that I was prepared for a bolt and broke from slow into quick time, and from that into a charge, swearing and threatening, and roaring "Stop him! Stop him!" as he had done before. I turned round to see who there was to stop me, and stumbled against a great clod which threw me head over heels. That finished the chase, for in an instant my tyrant was on me, and snatching hold of the smock frock I wore, started laying into me; but he was so winded with his run that he could not hurt me much. Seeing his condition I showed fight, and caught hold of the whip-lash, which so enraged him that he threw me from him with such violence that my smock was ripped in two; but I had just time to scramble up and get away, leaving him with half my garment as a token of affection. The remaining half I stuck in a hedge, and made off toward the town hoping to see the Colonel, but he was not to be found.

I went from public house to public house in search of the soldiers until night fell, which was no more sombre than my thoughts. Go home I dare not, so after wandering about outside the farmer's house I at length went through the stable, and got into a hay-loft, where I fell asleep and dreamed that I was a General. The harsh voice of my master woke me next morning as he was enquiring of everybody if they had seen me, and vowing that if he caught me he would skin me alive. "Bob," he bellowed at one of his men, "saddle old Corporal Dash, and I'll go and see where he is; and if I catch him I'll put him in the stocks, and see if that can't cool his courage for him. He is the most outdationest lad I have ever seen, and I'll see if the stocks won't cool him." The old Corporal was saddled and led out accordingly. I could distinctly see all that was happening through a small hole in the loft, and watched them trot off toward the market place. Some hard thinking had to be done. What was the best and safest thing to do? Skinning alive I could not bear to contemplate, and as it was freezing hard, and as bitter a morning as ever blew, the stocks were no more attractive.

As soon as Bob had left for his work I reconnoitred, to make sure that the enemy was not lying in ambush, or lurking near my hiding place. Finding all clear I descended to the stable, and soon gained the road. I hoped to catch a sight of my kind mistress but she was nowhere about. I had eaten all my bread and cheese the previous evening and was very hungry, but fear of falling into the hands of the enemy overcame all other considerations; so I satisfied myself with a turnip from a near-by field, and had just finished this chilly repast, when I heard the band strike up the gay notes of "The Girl I Left Behind Me" and felt cheered up a little. Putting myself in marching order I stepped out after the tune, until I arrived at the toll-gate about a quarter of a mile from the town. Here I could not help halting, wondering whether to go on or return, but my master's threats filled my mind and impelled me forward with the men and boys, girls and dogs, that followed the music. I was but a child, cast parentless upon the world into the hands of a cruel master, it was not possible for me to be worse off, so I continued my march towards Yarmouth without a mouthful of bread to eat, or a penny in my pocket. Not a soul did I know in the place to which I was going. My worldly goods consisted of a hat that had once been round, but which from my continually twisting it into the shape of cocked hats, road hats, soldiers' caps and so on was now any shape you wished; a little fustian jacket, with a waistcoat of the same material, a coarse shirt which was completely in rags from being shaken by it so often, a pair of leather breeches intolerably fat and greasy, ribbed worsted stockings, and a thwacking pair of high-lows nailed from heel to toe. These, with a little stick, were my only incumbrances save a gloomy prospect.

Gnawed by bitter hunger, and sadly tired, I went on until we were near Beccles, which is some sixteen miles from home. Here some of the soldiers branched off to go to quarters near the town, but I followed the main body as the best chance of getting something to eat. I made up my mind to accost the Colonel and ask him if he would enlist me for a soldier. He seemed a kind-hearted man, and as modesty was now out of the question I went straight to the head inn, where all the officers were assembled. There, at last, I got shown into the room where they were sitting at a meal. Strutting up to the Colonel, with my hat in my hand, I made him a most obsequious bow; with my foot advanced and my hand on my heart, and then stood as straight as if I had swallowed the Sergeant's pike. Laughing the Colonel said, "Well my fine little rustic what is your pleasure?" I made another bow, and scraping the carpet with my hobnails answered, "Soldiering your honour." At this all the officers burst into a roar of laughter, the Colonel as heartily as any. Thinking this was the fashion of the army I joined in with them, which only made them laugh the louder, so that some of them had to hold their sides at the fun. I soon found that all this merriment was at my expense, and was just about to say what I thought of such behaviour, when the Colonel said in a kindly tone, "My dear child you had better go home to your mother." "Sir," I replied, "my mother is dead." "Could I even take you," he went on, "I should think that I was robbing some fond parent of his child. Besides, we are going on foreign service against the enemy." This news only increased my eagerness to go, and I begged him to have compassion on an orphan. "My dear little fellow," he answered, with all the kindness in the world, "if I was going to stay in England I would take you, but under the present circumstances I cannot." Here I began to cry, and told him that I was sixteen miles from home, and had not got a piece of bread to put in my mouth. When they heard this the officers called the waiter, and vied with one another in ordering him to give me food. I still stuck to my point, but the Colonel told me that it was impossible, he assured me however that I would be taken care of, and desired me to go downstairs and get my breakfast. I did so, and as I passed round the table, where the officers were sitting, on my way out some gave me a shilling, and some sixpence, so that I had more money than I had ever possessed before in my life.

I ate a hearty meal in the kitchen, the servants pestering me with all sorts of questions. When it was over I counted my riches, and found that I had ten shillings, at least, in the pocket of my leather breeches; where every moment I was feeling to make sure that it was all safe. In the afternoon I was given my dinner, and put in charge of a Sergeant with whom I slept.

Early next morning when I awoke, he showed me a note from the good-tempered Colonel to my master, whose name and address he had pumped out of me the night before, in which he begged him most earnestly for his sake not to flog me again. He had also generously given the Sergeant five shillings for me, which he handed over before we started from Beccles. The Sergeant was proceeding to Woodbridge Barracks, and was to deliver me and the Colonel's note, which was open, on the way. We reached the farm at about three o'clock in the afternoon, and found my master at home. He received the Colonel's communication, and faithfully promised the Sergeant that all should be forgiven and forgotten. Encouraged by this I went back to work resolved to do better in the future; thinking that I had not done badly by the adventure, for I still had fifteen shillings and sixpence left, even after treating the Sergeant on the way home. But the sun was scarcely up next day when my tyrannical master seized me by the neck, and dragged the clothes off my back. He had with him one of those fearsome, two-handed, whips which colliers use and with it he lashed me so unmercifully, that I have no hesitation in saying that he would have killed me, if a man who happened to be working in a neighbouring field had not interfered to save my life. He was the most inhuman person I ever saw; and if he were not dead, and his family in abject poverty, I would publish his name, but I have no wish to add to their misery. As it is I will bury my resentment with their father and begin a new chapter with something more interesting to my readers, entreating their indulgence for having dwelt so long on the scenes of my childhood.

2

The Merry Fife and Drum

ABOUT this time, that is 1797, it was decided to form three experimental regiments, which were each to take one thousand boys, between the ages of ten and fifteen, off the hands of the parish authorities, on condition that their expenses were paid to one of the recruiting depots. Their service was to be for life, and it represented a good bargain for the parish overseers, who were thus relieved of all responsibility for these unwanted youngsters. One morning, in about January or February 1797, I was hard at work in a field by my master's house; when who should I see but one of the parish officers making towards me, with a large paper in his hand. Hastily running over my crimes I decided that I had done nothing to warrant the interference of such an exalted personage, so I stood up boldly and faced him. But he was all smiles and began, "Shipp, I have frequently heard of, and observed, your great wish to go for a soldier." He then read me what was on the paper, and asked if I was willing to go, for if I was the parish would rig me out decently, and he himself would take me to Colchester where the 22nd Regiment of Foot was then forming.[1]

My heart leapt into my mouth. Willing to go! Rapture was a poor description of my feelings when I heard his offer. The affair was soon settled, down went my shovel and off I marched whistling "See the Conquering Hero Comes" as I went. By four o'clock of the same day, to the honour and praise of the parish be it spoken, I was rigged out in my new leather tights, new coat, new hat, new shoes, new everything, of which I was not a little proud. I begged as a particular favour that I might sport colours in my hat and even this was permitted to my vanity so long as I remained in the town.[2] I took an affectionate leave of all my playfellows, and of my good mistress, even saying goodbye to my master for I was never of an unforgiving disposition. The next day, by seven o'clock in the morning, I was on my way to Colchester, seated at the front of the coach where I would not have changed places with the Grand Pasha of Egypt or the King of England himself. I whistled merrily enough until, at the well-known turn in the road, I took my last look at Saxmundham which had been all the home I knew and where my mother was buried. Although I was not deserting my family, for I had none to desert, I could not help feeling that I was leaving something behind which clung like a magnet to my heart, but three gentlemen in the coach, who had heard my story from my companion, cheered me up by telling me that they knew the corps to which I was going, and that it was made up of lads like myself. Thus encouraged I forgot my loneliness, and talked away as gaily as any of them until we came to the inn at Colchester where we dined.

After that I was marched off to the Colonel of the corps in which I was to serve, from the Colonel I was sent to the Adjutant, from the Adjutant to the Sergeant-Major, from the Sergeant-Major to the Drum-Major, and from him to his wife, an old drunken Irish woman but as good a creature as ever drank whisky. With her my friend from Saxmundham left me, shaking me by the hand and wishing me every happiness. I must confess that I now felt quite deserted. About twenty boys gathered round poking fun at my new clothes. "Bill twig his leathers!" "Smoke[3] his new coat!" "My eye what a buck!" "Some gemman's son I suppose, run away from his daddy!" "Never mind," said another, "we will soon drill his leathers into hot rolls and butter." But old Maggie came to my help. "Arrah! what are you gazing at you set of spalpeens you. Be off you set of thieves, or I'll be after breaking some of your nasty, dirty mugs for you. Don't mind them, sure they are nothing but a set of monkeys just catched. Come here honey, and let me see who will be after laying a finger on you." She pulled me down to sit beside her and made a fuss of me, stroking my chin and patting my back, but eyeing my coat and breeches all the while; until, at length, she asked if I had any money, because if I had she would get me some hot rolls and butter. I gave her a shilling and she bought me a couple of buttered rolls, the rest I suppose she spent on gin, for she began to give me some of her Irish hugs till I wished myself at a distance. One of the boys called out "Ask for the change! Ask her for the change! Or she'll do you." This so enraged Maggie that, staggering to her feet, she seized a large trencher and hurled it at the boy shouting "You great big blackguard! Do you want to rob me of my name. Take that and bad luck to you." But the effort of throwing was too much for her, and she tumbled over, measuring her vast bulk on the barrack floor while we all roared with laughter. It seemed to me that I had got among a very queer set of people. Just then the Drum-Major came in, and seeing his wife on the floor yelled, "Get up you drunken old hag, or by St Patrick I'll pay you off." Maggie made an effort to rise but the gin was too much for her, so I helped her up and she was put to bed, clothes and all.

The next morning I was taken to the barber's. In a minute I was shorn of my curly brown locks, and left as good as bald, except for a small patch behind which was reserved for a future operation. Next came the tailor's shop, where I was stripped of my new clothes, for which I received in exchange a red jacket, red waistcoat, red pantaloons, and a red foraging cap. The change was now so complete that I could hardly imagine myself to be the same dapper little fellow. I was exceedingly tall for a boy of ten years old, but in spite of this the clothes were much too large, the sleeves being two or three inches beyond the ends of my fingers, and the whole hung on me, to use a well-known expression, like a purser's shirt on a handspike.[4] My pride was humbled and my spirits drooped as, with downcast features, I followed the Drum-Major like a felon going to execution. I asked one little chap what he was staring at. "Ask my eye Johnny Raw," he answered thumbing his nose. The drummers on their way to practise had a lot of fun out of me. "Twig the raw-skin." "Smoke his pantaloons." "Ain't his trousers a knowing cut?" "Look at the sign of the redman," and similar chaff, all the way to the barracks. There I was subjected to the same routine, until I felt that I had put up with them long enough, and told one of the jokers that if he did not stop it I would give him a thrashing. They liked the show of pluck and stopped their chaffing for the time being.

The Drum-Major then went out, first locking my civilian

clothes in his box and pocketing the key. I sat myself down on a stool, and began to wonder whether soldiering was quite as delightful as I had imagined it to be. Still, I resolved to put a brave face on it, and began to mix with my comrades so that in an hour or so I was as free with them as if I had known them all my life. The reason for their friendliness however was soon apparent. One of the clever ones took me aside, and asked me if I knew where to sell my coloured clothes, if not, he would go with me and show me. I told him the Drum-Major had them. "Yes," he said, "I know, but he has no business with them. Them there traps should be sold, and you get the money. If you don't keep your eye on the fugle-man he'll do you out of half of it."[5] He went on to say that, when he enlisted, he got more than five shillings for his things. I told him that I had no doubt that the Drum-Major would sell the things for my benefit or let me do so, if this latter was the case I would be glad of the boy's help. At that moment the Drum-Major came in, and the boy I had been talking to went up to him and said, "That there chap says as how he wants to sell them there things of his in your box, and I am to go with him, and show him the place where I sold mine." This was a lie I could not stomach, so going up to the Drum-Major myself I told him that I had said nothing of the kind. All that I had said was, that I had no doubt that he would either dispose of the things for my benefit, or let me do so. "Yes, yes," said he, "I'll sell them, and you shall have the money." The boy turned away angry enough but the things were put into a handkerchief and carried off to town. As soon as the Drum-Major had left the boy came up to me and called me a liar, and said he had a great mind to thrash me, at the same time trying to lay hold of my nose with his thumb and finger. I got in a rage, and told him that if he touched me I would fell him to the ground. The other boys gathered about us calling, "Well done Johnny Raw! Well done old Leather Breeches! Well done Johnny Wapstraw!" Finding that I was not going to strike him first my antagonist called me a coward, but that I knew I was not. None-the-less, stung by the accusation, I lashed out at him and to it we went in right earnest. After half a dozen rounds my opponent gave in and this, my first victory, established that I was neither a coward nor one that could be imposed upon with impunity. The boys praised me exceedingly, for my adversary was a great bully and always fighting. Just as we had finished, the Drum-Major came in and gave me the money for my clothes—one pound and six—which some said was a fair price, though others thought they were worth thirty shillings. However, I was well satisfied, and stood hot rolls and butter all round, including my adversary, who claimed that this was the first time he had ever been beaten and asked for another bout, a friendly one this time, for which I was willing enough.

After this I went into the town to purchase a few things that I needed such as a powder-bag, puff, soap, candles, grease and so on. As soon as I got back I had to undergo the operation of having my hair tied for the first time, to the no small amusement of the other boys. A large piece of candle-grease was applied first to the sides of my head, and then to the long hair behind. After this, the same operation was gone through with nasty, stinking soap, the man who was dressing me applying his knuckles as often as the soap, to the delight of the surrounding boys who watched the tears roll down my cheeks. That part was bad enough, but the next was worse. A large pad, or bag, filled with sand, was poked into the back of my neck, the hair twisted tightly round it, and the whole tied with a leather thong. When thus dressed for parade, the skin of my face was pulled so tight by the bag stuck at the back of my head, that it was impossible so much as to wink an eyelid. Add to this an enormous high stock, which was pushed under my chin, and I felt as stiff as if I had swallowed a ramrod or the Sergeant's halbert. Shortly after this we were called to dinner, but my poor jaws could hardly move, and at every attempt to do so the pad behind went up and down like a sledge-hammer.

At the evening parade I was inspected by the Colonel, who said that I was a promising lad but as my clothes did not fit, they must be altered. He also gave permission to the band-master to take me into the band, to learn the flute and the triangles. The next day I started my musical education, and in six months had beaten the sides of the triangles nearly as thin as my own, and had also become a tolerable flute-player but, as about that time two excellent performers upon that instrument joined us with the volunteers from the militia, I was sent back to the drummer's room, and put to the fife. In a short time I was made Fife-Major—no small office I assure you. I wore two stripes, and a tremendous long sash which almost touched the ground. I was not a little proud of my new office, and began to ride the high horse among my comrades, making full use of the small cane which I was allowed to carry. When the Drum-Major was away, which was often, I carried the silver-headed stick, about seven feet long, and at the mounting of the general guard astonished the spectators with my double demi-twist of the baton, and began to think myself one of the brightest of the bright.

At this time the regiment moved to Hythe, about a mile from Colchester, and twice a day we beat through the streets followed by all the boys and girls of the town. Sometimes the prettiest of these young women, with beguiling smiles, would beg me to play them some favourite air which I would occasionally do, always however keeping up my dignity and pretending to do so as a great act of condescension. I had grown very tall though somewhat slender. My red coat had been thrown off, and I now wore a splendid white silver-laced jacket, with silver epaulets which could be made to swing to and fro as I walked. And so I swaggered about the town, full of consequence, a great favourite with my officers, and happy and contented. I indulged in a good many rough jokes with my friends, such as filling their pipes with gunpowder, tying their great toes together and crying fire, sewing their shirts to their bedding when asleep, and fifty more; which led me into many a fight, and brought similar tricks upon me in retaliation. But something happened just then which blighted my pride a little. Some of us made a party to go nutting for filberts, which were in season then and we found a place where they were as thick as laurels on a soldier's brow. We had got about a bushel, when three keepers pounced out upon us and carried us back to the barracks, where my three companions got two dozen stripes between them, and I was reduced to my original rank as a fifer. On the whole, we got off fairly well, for we were taken some four miles from the barracks and so might have been classed as deserters, in which case our captors would have got two pounds a man.

Soon after this the regiment was ordered to proceed to Hilsea barracks near Portsmouth. This was soldiering in clover, with fresh scenes and good living conspiring to cheer me for the stripes I had lost. I was not long in learning the tricks of the road, and grew as knowing as the best of them. It was the practice of some landlords, at the inns where we slept, to give us fat pea-soup, or suet dumplings as heavy as lead, to take the edge off our appetites before bringing on the roast and boiled; but I used to claim that such food was bad for my constitution, and forbidden by the doctor, so that I was free, and ready, for the better sort when it arrived. Those who ate the soup, or the dumplings, were as empty as ever in two hours time, but I fed well and kept my own counsel. But it was not always possible to escape. One day, at Chelmsford, we were compelled to submit to dreadfully bad quarters. Even the delicacy of my constitution could not get me out of eating the greasy puddings, and fat stews made of the offal of the house for the past month, with fat an inch thick on the top of it. Finding me so positive in my objections the landlord slipped a shilling into my hand to quiet me, and I was content to be pacified a little; but my companions left a mark of their disapprobation behind them by writing, with a lighted candle on the ceiling, "Damned bad quarters. Pea Soup. Lead Dumplings. Lousy Beds. Dirty Sheets." This was the mildest punishment for such landlords. In addition, it was not too hard to teach some of his ducks and geese to march away with us, and take up final quarters in the cooking pot. Some of these wandering birds would even find their way into the drum.

I was myself once mixed up in a business of this kind, for I was accessory to stealing a fine goose, witnessing what we thought was its death, an assistant in drumming it, and I daresay would have lent a hand in eating it too. We had got the goose and marched off, chuckling to ourselves at our own cleverness, when who should pass us on the road but the landlord of the inn from which we had removed the bird. However, he took no notice of us, and we thought that he might have business at the town where we were going. But when we got there, who should we see in the market place but the landlord, in earnest consultation with our Colonel. We were told that he had complained of a goose being stolen, and suspected us of having it. Our knapsacks were rigorously searched but nothing was found. The landlord was just leaving us expressing his regret at suspecting us so unworthily, we were all grinning with delight at such an escape, when the goose gave a heavy groan, which the landlord at once recognized as the voice of his bird. We were searched again, even our great-coats being turned inside out, but nothing was found. We were all enjoying the fun when the poor goose now near her end, gave her last moan. The landlord, who was standing near the drum, burst out in surprise, "Dang my buttons my old goose is in that there drum!" In an instant the instrument was opened, and sure enough there she was inside, as dead as a herring. The bird was given up to the publican and we were ordered a flogging, but luckily for us the landlord was a kindly man. Taking a closer look at the bird he pretended not to recognize it as his, "Mine was pure white Sir," he said to the Colonel, "and this has black markings. I am sorry to have troubled you Sir", and he marched off muttering "Get a child flogged for a tarnation old goose, no, no." The Colonel saw very clearly how matters were, but he let us off with a lecture.

We were at Hilsea Barracks[6] for nearly a year where we got the name of the red knights from our clothing being all of that colour. Nothing of importance happened to me there, except that I spent a week in the black hole for "eating my shoes." It came about in this way. I had been out to receive my "half-mounting" consisting of a pair of shoes, a shirt, two pairs of stockings, and a stock. On my way back I ran into an old woman who sold plum pudding. I had often had dealings with her before. The pudding was smoking hot, and I was very hungry, but much as I wanted a slice I knew that she was far too old a soldier to trust me until next month's pay day. But the pudding I must have. When, in spite of all my pleading, she still refused me credit I offered to sell her my shoes. She agreed, and after a good deal of haggling I handed them over in return for a quarter of a yard of pudding, and a shilling to be paid down on the spot. Off I went, and had soon made both ends of the pudding meet; but as the last mouthful disappeared, I began to beat my brains for a way of explaining the loss of my new shoes. My first thought was to go back, and beg the old woman to let me have them again but she had disappeared, knowing full well that she was punishable for having bought such things of me. I hated telling lies, but it looked as if I should have to, for I could not face the consequences of telling the truth. In the end I decided on a compromise, which was to say that I had dropped the shoes on my way home. But I might just as well have told the truth for nobody believed me, and I was ordered seven days in the black hole to refresh my memory on how I had lost them. When I heard the cell door creak shut behind me, and the huge key turn in the lock, I began to think that I had parted with my property too cheaply; but I was never of the desponding kind, and considered it better to think of some way to amuse myself during the imprisonment, rather than sit and mope. Seven days and nights seemed a long time to spend in total darkness, and yet there was something soldier-like in the situation. True, I was there for eating my shoes, but might I not imagine myself a prisoner of war? With this fancy strong upon me I dropped into a deep sleep, from which I woke up perished with cold which convinced me that I should have to find a way of comforting my body as well as my mind. So I began to stand on my head, walk on my hands, turn head-over-heels, and indulge in similar exercises. In this way, sleeping and playing by turns, I managed to pass a day and a night by no means unpleasantly. Next morning, at about nine o'clock, I heard the well-known voice of the Drum-Major asking for me, and ordering me to be set free. I thought that the seven days and seven nights had gone at a wonderfully rapid rate, and accounted for it by supposing that I had slept most of the time, and thought that at least I had been free of parades, drills, head-soaping and all the rest of it. When I got out into the daylight I could scarcely open my eyes for the light, but as soon as I was able to endure it I was asked by the Drum-Major how I liked my new abode, and if I was ready to return to it? But I saw from his smile that I had little to fear, and soon understood that I had only spent a day and a night in the black hole. My comrades received me as if I had just escaped from a desert island and, having paved my inside with six penny pies out of the old woman's shilling, I was soon as fit for fun as the best of them.

3

Service in Guernsey

THE regiment was now ordered to embark for Guernsey, and the prospect of leaving for what I took to be foreign parts made my heart leap for joy. We were put aboard a small sloop at about four o'clock in the afternoon, and an hour later got under way. After dark, the wind grew so high that we were forced to put tarpaulins over the hatches, to keep out the great seas that broke over us. The scene was enough to daunt a stouter courage than mine. There were soldiers crying, women screaming, children squalling, sailors swearing, the wind blowing a hurricane and flashes of lightning illuminating the tossing waters and torrential rain. A poor, frightened soldier mustered up enough courage to ask the master of the vessel if there was any danger. "Danger shipmate," said he, "if this storm continues another hour I wouldn't give a rope-yarn for all your lives." I had just squeezed myself up into a small compass, head and knees together, close to the helm, when we shipped another tremendous sea, and the foresail carried away with such a terrific and dreadful noise that it seemed as if the vessel had met her end. Another awful sea swept over us, and carried away three of the deck hands. Just at this crisis a sailor yelled, "Light ahead Sir." "The devil there is! A Frenchman I expect," the ship's master answered. Hearing the word "Frenchman," the officer commanding the soldiers we had on board called out, "What did you say about a Frenchman?" "Why, if we get clear we may have a bit of a fight, for there is a Frenchman ahead." "Then," said the soldier, "I had better get my men ready. Sergeant, get the bugler. Sound to arms! Call the drummer and tell him to beat to arms." But the devil a bugler or drummer was to be had. They were all below and in no condition to come up to scratch, Frenchman or no Frenchman. None-the-less the noble soldier strutted about on deck by himself, sword in hand, and cocked-hat on his head, until a merciless sea swept him into the hold and carried away his gay hat for which he began to call very lustily. "Captain have the goodness to send down my hat. Is my hat on deck? Have you seen my hat?" "Your hat Sir," the seaman answered calmly, "has got under sail and I shouldn't be surprised if it made port before you."

Morning dawned, on what the Captain said was the heaviest sea he had ever seen. We were in sight of port, but the weather was so foul, that we had to tack again and again before we could get in. The Frenchman had sheered off, but what with fear, cold, hunger, want of sleep, and being wet through our poor fellows were completely worn out. I cut as sorry a figure as the rest, though I was not so desperately frightened as some of the others appeared to be. I had hung on to my station all night, more from fear of leaving it than anything else. As soon as we ran into the bay, which was protected from the main ocean by the surrounding heights, we were in a calm, and boats were waiting to take us to dry land. When I set foot on shore I looked for all the world like a squeezed lemon, or the bag of a Scotch pipe without any wind in it; and I should have been glad to take the edge off my appetite, and the dirt off my clothes, before dancing through the town of Guernsey but I had to obey orders. I still led the fifers, and striking up "The Downfall of Paris" found that the march, and the music, did me so much good that by the time we reached the barrack I was in prime order for breakfast.

We were quartered in Fort George, which was an exceedingly good place, though the heavy drawbridges promised an unwelcome restriction to our liberty. Loving to ramble about as I did, and to visit orchards, particularly, for other things than their beauty, I was apprehensive that these drawbridges would get me into trouble as they soon did. Within a very few days I saw my name posted up at the gate, "John Shipp confined to barracks for one week." A week was an age to me, and the outside world looked doubly inviting from the ramparts because I was forbidden to visit it. But when three long days of that week were over, the Drum-Major was taken seriously ill, and the Colonel, seeing my trim, for I was always spotlessly clean, promoted me to act in his place; and at the same time gave me a ticket for the play that was to be acted in the theatre that evening, and put me in charge of several other boys who were also going. So for a brief while I was in favour again, but not for long. Once more I was out of office, and my name up at the drawbridge for another of those interminable seven days. Unobserved by the sentinel I managed to scratch it out from the list, but the Sergeant was not to be deceived, and for this crime I was sentenced to drill three times a day with my musket reversed, and my coat turned inside out. In this condition I was bullied about by the little bandy-legged Drill-Sergeant, who enforced his commands with his cane about my back. That I could put up with, and indeed had to, but the turned coat hung about me as a badge of shame and I imagined every eye was on me. Had I been really depraved this treatment would have hardened me for ever, as it was, I almost determined that the next time I was disgraced in this way it should be for something worthy of the punishment. I am convinced that this method of humiliating a young man, instead of eradicating his faults, only confirms them, whereas kinder treatment might do away with them for ever. The regiment was now ordered to embark for Portsmouth, and I was relieved of my disgrace, which ought never to have been inflicted for what was no more than a schoolboy offence.

4
A Stricken Vessel

FROM Portsmouth we were ordered to embark for the Cape of Good Hope, regimental headquarters going aboard the *Surat Castle*, an East Indiaman of fifteen hundred tons, the rest on other ships that were lying with her at Spithead. The *Surat Castle*, in which I was doomed to go, was most dreadfully overcrowded. Men literally slept upon one another. In the orlop-deck the standing beds were three tiers high, with hammocks slung between. Adding to the misery of this wretched multitude pestilence was already among them. An immense number of Lascars, picked up in every sink of squalor and poverty, had been shipped aboard. Most of them had been living in the most abject want, existing only on what they could pick up in the streets. Many had lost fingers, or toes, from frostbite, others were riddled with disease caught in the filth they lived among. The pestilential smell between decks was beyond description. These circumstances were, I suppose, reported to the authorities before we left, but whether they were or no nothing was done; and these poor wretches, covered with the most frightful sores, and crawling with vermin, were left to die unhelped, unfriended, and the minute the breath was out of their bodies they were tossed overboard to feed the fishes. We could do nothing for them, for there were scarcely enough sound men to work the ship. We weighed anchor with about sixty other vessels bound for all parts of the world. The splendid sight of this great fleet accorded little with the misery of the poor creatures packed below deck.

So great a number of vessels together, caused so much confusion that our Captain decided to steal away from them as soon as night fell, and in three or four hours had quite lost sight of the convoy. Almost immediately we ran into rough weather. The wind and the sea rose in a way to shake the courage of any landsman. I found a place on the poop where I could be alone, and holding on to a hen coop, was melancholy enough as I felt the effects of the storm, and considered that I was leaving my native land perhaps for ever. For a while we were hove to, but then the wind slackened and we went on our way under three top-sails and the fore-storm-staysail. I was dreadfully wet and cold, my teeth chattered most woefully, so I made for the gun-deck, some part of which was given over to the soldiers. There the heat was suffocating, and the stench intolerable. Below, on the orlop-deck, conditions were as horrible; soldiers, their wives and children, groaning together in the extreme of seasickness continually calling for water to relieve their distress. I screwed myself up behind a butt, and fell into that stupor which seasickness will create. When I awoke in the morning I found that the hurricane had returned with full force, and we were running in toward the land for shelter, but the Captain soon changed his mind and we stood out to sea again. By the following day the weather was calm, and we could see a good number of ships, from the fleet to which we belonged, emerging from the sheltered places where they had ridden out the storm; but our Captain was resolved to be alone, and crowding on all sail we were soon out of sight of every other vessel save one small sloop, that was making its way to England.

Three weeks later we again ran into a most dreadful storm, which was far more damaging than the earlier one for the main top-mast and other smaller masts were carried away. But battered as she was outside, the interior of the ship was a scene of even greater desolation. We were far from land, and a pestilence was raging among us with hideous power. Everywhere was the pallid cheek of disease and the sunken eyes of despair. Huge sharks hovered round us waiting for their prey. Their arrival is a sure indication of the presence of death, for they will follow a stricken vessel far out of the way of their usual haunts. To add to the nightmare in which we lived, some ten barrels of ship's paint broke from their lashings and crashed from side to side and from head to stern; smashing, with their enormous weight, everything that lay in their course. So huge were they that we could do nothing to stop them until, eventually, they were all stove in, and the gun-deck was a sticky morass of spilt colour, in which lay the crushed bodies of the dead and dying, white and black together.

It would be difficult to imagine a set of men more hideously situated than we were, but to add yet more to our misery the scurvy broke out in a most frightful manner. Scarcely one escaped the swollen legs, and rotten, distorted gums, which showed the malignancy of the disease. None but the dying were left to bury the dead. Every assistance which humanity could dictate was freely given by the officers on board, who cheerfully gave up their fresh meat, and other comforts, for the relief of the distressed. The skill of our medical attendants was completely baffled. My poor legs were as big as drums, and my gums swollen to an enormous size, and my tongue too big for my mouth. All I could eat was raw potatoes and vinegar; but my kind officers sometimes brought me tea or coffee, in gratitude for which my weakened state would have caused me to burst into tears, had not the fear of being unmanly restrained me. We were all so reduced by suffering that even strong men could not restrain themselves from weeping, they knew not why. And so the time went by, men dying in dozens, and almost before the breath was out of their bodies being thrown into the sea for the sharks to quarrel over. How could we bear to watch what might be our own fate before many hours were over? Nearly every fourth man among the Europeans, and more than two-thirds of the Lascars fell victims to the diseases on board, and it was only by the mercy of Providence that we reached our destination, for there was scarce a seaman fit to work the ship.

Never shall I forget the morning I saw the land. It was a dreary, foggy day but in that moment of joy I forgot all past miseries and thought only of happiness to come. We were too close in to the land for safety, and were in the very act of standing out to sea again when the fog lifted, the wind came fair, and we ran into the mouth of Simon's Bay. Everyone, who could crawl, was on deck to welcome the blessed sight of land, and breathe in its fresh air. Every soul on board was elated with joy, even those whose sickness during the whole voyage had never once let them behold that most magnificent of all sights, the bright sun rising and setting at sea.

The anchor had not long been down, when a boat came from the shore bringing medical men. They questioned us about where we came from, the state of the ship, the diseases we had on board and the number of the dead. This was a finishing blow to our present hopes, and we were bidden to ride at quarantine, but all possible relief was sent to us; fresh meat, bread, tea, sugar, coffee, and fruits of all kinds, and in a few days our legs resumed their proper shape, and the disease died away. As soon as we were out of quarantine the troops landed, and we were marched, or rather carried, to the barracks that stand on the brow of the hill behind Simon's Town. Here every comfort was afforded us and every means adopted by our kind officers that could contribute to our recovery. For the first fortnight drills were out of the question, but by careful treatment we were all soon restored to health again. Only a few of the sick died after we were landed but, if I recollect rightly, our total loss was seventy-two men. We were the first ship to arrive, but none of the others suffered from disease and lost only two men all told.[1]

5

Love and War in Africa

SIMON'S Town is on Simon's Bay, and has many well-built houses. Here we were stationed for a short time, and as we had a good deal of freedom to come and go I soon began to take stock of the neighbourhood. There were some flourishing gardens close to the barracks, which were a welcome sight, for a pound of bad quality meat, and three-quarters of a pound of bread a day, was but a scanty allowance for a growing lad.[1] Indeed, I frequently got through three days' ration of bread in one, but we could get fish for a mere song, and the near-by gardens of the Dutchmen supplied us with potatoes, so we got along tolerably well.

We were next moved to Muisenberg, seven miles nearer to Cape Town, a post defended by a small battery, and a few guns at the vulnerable places along the beach. The road from Simon's Town to Muisenberg runs sometimes along the shore, which is very flat with the sea coming in with gentle undulation; in other places it winds round the base of craggy hills, on whose sides great masses of rock hang fearfully suspended. On these hills whole regiments of baboons assemble, indeed the station is famous for them. They stand six feet high, and are nearer to human beings in appearance than any other animals I have ever seen. They are the most abominable thieves, and were a great nuisance to us all. Our barracks were under the hills, and whenever we went on parade we were forced to leave armed men to protect our property. But in spite of this blankets, greatcoats, and any other articles which could be snapped up, were stolen with great frequency. A poor woman, a soldier's wife, had washed her blanket and hung it out to dry; when some of these miscreants, ever on the watch for an opportunity, stole it and made off to their fastness in the wooded hills. This was too much, and a strong party of us, armed with sticks and stones, set out to recover the property and punish the thieves. I went ahead with about twenty men, and made a detour, to cut the baboons off from the caverns to which they always ran for shelter. This movement round their flank was soon observed, and they detached fifty or so of their number to guard the entrances, while we could distinctly see the rest gathering sticks and stones for ammunition against us. One old, grey-headed baboon who was often seen about the barracks and was known as Father Murphy, was obviously giving his orders and planning the defence like one of our best generals. Finding that my scheme would not succeed I joined the others, and we rushed on to the attack. With a scream of rage old Father Murphy set on his troops, who rolled such enormous stones down on us that we were obliged to withdraw, or be killed. They actually followed us all the way to the barracks, hurling their insults; and spent the whole of that night yelling and screaming outside, so that we really expected them to attack us, but in the morning we could see that all the noise was only about the division of the spoil, for eight or ten of them had pieces of the blanket about their backs, for all the world like old women with cloaks.

Father Murphy grew so bold that one morning he had the impudence to walk straight into the Grenadiers' barracks, and was in the act of stealing a Sergeant's regimental coat, when a Corporal's guard which was being relieved just then, took the liberty of stopping him and putting him under arrest. He was a most powerful brute and I am persuaded that no one man would have been a match for him. In spite of his depredations we had no wish to kill the poor beast; so first we muzzled him, and then shaved his head and face, an operation which he took very well, and then turned him loose, looking in his new guise as handsome as any Bond Street blood. We started him up the hill but he seemed loath to go. His friends on the top came down to meet him; but he was so changed by the barber's art that they never recognized him, and pelted him so unmercifully that poor Father Murphy actually took refuge with us, and in time became quite tame.

Our next station was at Wynberg, where we were for several months. Here the weather was so bad, and we were drilled out of our lives, with brigade field-days from three or four o'clock in the morning until seven or eight at night;

lying then on damp ground, in bell tents, so that we suffered most dreadfully. About this time the Caffres were committing the most dreadful atrocities, robbing and murdering the up-country Dutch farmers, or Boers as they are called.[2] To stop these depredations a rifle company was formed from men of the 8th Dragoons, the 22nd, 34th, 65th, 81st and 91st Regiments, and placed under the command of Captain Effingham Lindsay, one of the bravest soldiers in His Majesty's Army. We were dressed in green, and our pieces browned to prevent them being seen in the woods where the Caffres were congregated. About three months after the company was formed, we were sent up country together with the light company of the 91st Regiment, and a corps of Hottentots. We went on board the *Diamond* frigate, and reached Algoa Bay in fourteen days, having bad weather on the way. From there we marched to Graaf-Reynett, about five or six hundred miles into the interior, and fifteen miles from Cape Town. There we were quartered in a Dutch church. The road from Algoa Bay to Graaf-Reynett is over hill and dale, and infested with lions, tigers, hyenas, wolves and elephants.[3] At a place called Rovee Bank, a day's march on this side of the great pass, we frequently saw eight or ten of these great beasts a day. Here I went out shooting one day with a companion. We came to a pool abounding with wild duck and geese, surrounded by very tall grass, some of it as much as ten feet high. I took aim and fired, and had just time to see at least one bird fall when I heard a most tremendous roar, and the whole pool was immediately in great commotion. I was on the point of plunging into the water after my dead duck, when to my astonishment and alarm, an enormous white elephant rushed from the high grass, trumpeting loudly and striking the growth aside with his trunk. Neither of us had ever seen such a beast before, and we had no wish for a second look, so leaving the ducks to their fate we took to our heels, and never stopped till we were safe in camp.

At every farmhouse on our line of march we found appalling scenes of murder and desolation. Whole families had been savagely massacred by these wild people, whose devastations it was now our duty to check. So ignorant were they, that I am convinced they were unaware that murder is a crime. Beautiful homesteads, still smoking from the fire that had destroyed them, lay deserted by their owners, who were either killed or fled to safety; leaving no living creature in sight save perhaps a dog howling over a dead body, a wounded horse, or a mutilated ox. The savage Caffre exults in these appalling sights. To his bestial mind the groans of the wounded, and the dying, are the greatest of pleasures. When the frenzy of the attack is on him he is wrought up to ecstasy, dancing and jumping about, and hurling his spear at man or beast with a reckless abandon. Money has no attraction for these people, save for its glitter only, while a shining gilt button would be the greatest of treasures. I have seen them with women's gowns, petticoats, shawls and things tied round their legs, and between their toes, capering about the woods in a frenzy of delight. They had got it into their heads that we were their inveterate enemies, come only for the sake of robbing them of their cattle, which they had driven off in vast herds into the safety of the interior. Their main body had withdrawn, leaving only a few stragglers in the neighbourhood to keep an eye on our movements. We had some slight skirmishes with them, but the woods were so thick that we could do little to come at them.

The Caffres are most certainly a formidable enemy. They are inured to war and plunder, and are such expert marksmen with their darts that they can be certain of their aim at sixty, or seventy, paces distance. When you fire at them they throw themselves down on their faces to escape the ball, and the skins they wear are so tough that, even if they are hit, it is doubtful if the bullet can do them much harm. They live in the woods, and when pressed retire to hidden and almost inaccessible places, so that offensive warfare against them is inconceivably difficult. Before they deliver the darts with which they are armed, they run sideways for a little way, the left shoulder forward, and the right considerably lowered, with the right hand extended behind them, the dart lying flat in the palm of the hand, the point of it being near the right eye. When thrown it flies with such speed that you can scarcely see it. They carry about a dozen of these spears slung on their backs, and with them one man alone has been known to kill lions and tigers.

Warfare of this kind, carried on through almost impenetrable forests, over great hills, and through torrential rivers, soon reduced us to rags. We managed to provide a fair substitute for shoes by taking a piece of raw buffalo hide, placing the foot upon it, and cutting it round in the shape of a sole. Thongs of the same material served to provide a means of fastening them on; and in a day or two, when the whole had dried to the shape of the foot, it served very well. When we had been at this station about two years, it was laughable to see what had happened to our once white regimental trousers. Holes in them had been patched with whatever material came to hand, no matter what the texture or colour, so that from a distance we looked like spotted leopards. During these two years I had sprung up at least two inches, outgrowing both my jacket and my trousers; so that when I was in full fig for a parade I must have looked a ridiculous figure indeed. My jacket had literally become a strait-jacket, for I could scarce raise my hand to my head; my trousers had been going up in the world all that time, and now could hardly protect my protruding knees. I was but a novice with the needle, and stuck my patches on, large or small, as it happened. In this predicament I had to march nearly fifteen hundred miles through Africa. The rest of the men were in no better condition, and all of us looked like Falstaff's ragged recruits with which he was ashamed to march through Coventry.

After we had been on this duty upward of two years, to very little purpose, our government, in 1801, ordered the Cape of Good Hope to be given back to the Dutch. The light company and the rifle company of the 91st Foot, were sent in a small vessel from Algoa Bay down to the Cape, where they were to embark for India. I was despatched overland with a Dutch Boer's family, who were travelling to Cape Town, and had the officers' baggage committed to my care, which was a serious responsibility seeing how wild and desolate the country was through which we had to pass. We had to skirt the margin of the territory inhabited by the Caffres, and though the Dutch family I was with had four wagons the savages cared nothing for them, nor for their muskets. Well supplied with powder and shot, we began our march drawn up in battle array. I went ahead, mounted on a horse with a loaded rifle slung at my back and a pistol in my holster, the Dutchman's two sons rode one on either side; after us came four Hottentots armed with muskets, then the old Boer, and following him the four wagons which carried the families and property of us all. The rear-guard consisted of two trusted servants, Hottentots, armed and riding bullocks; then four men on foot with their families, many of the women carrying a couple of children. In this order we could travel twenty miles a day over the most tremendous hills. If we could not get to a farm-house by sunset, which was when we generally halted, we camped in an open spot drawing up the four wagons into a square, with the cattle in the middle, where they fed for the night. Six men were on watch throughout the darkness, each party being relieved every four hours, and I took my full share of this duty. We were so often disturbed, either by Caffres or beasts of prey, that we had practically no rest. The Caffre is a cunning enemy. He usually attacks at night, crawling forward on his hands and knees, and keeping touch with his companions by imitating the cries of animals and birds which are well understood by them. At the smallest noise they will flatten themselves on the ground, so that you can pass close by without seeing them; and then the first indication you have of such dangerous neighbours is the thrust of a spear, or the blow of a club. It was no wonder that we kept a smart watch, but even then it was nothing unusual to see a spear lodged in the top of a wagon next morning, close to the place where a look-out man had stood. Still, we were never tempted away from our possessions, or ever wasted precious powder and ball on slight alarms. To tell of all the trials, watchings, perils and escapes, of this trip would take more room than I can spare, it is enough to say that at last we reached Cape Town in safety.

And yet I must pause to speak of something never to be forgotten, which happened on that long journey through the wilds of Africa. The Dutchman I travelled with had two daughters. The younger was called Sabina. She was a person of exquisite loveliness, tall and rather slim, of a dark complexion, with black hair and eyes; her slender waist and small, light, foot made her every motion entrancing. She had received some education, and was naturally of a vivacious disposition. As we went on our journey I noticed that she seemed to seek my company, as a relief I thought from that of her father, for he was in every way a very gross man.[4] It is not surprising that I was glad to have her with me, or that before very long I found that her charm was stealing away my heart. I would walk by her side, while she rode my horse, for a whole day's march. The burning sky, the rough path, the danger that lurked in every group of trees and behind every rock, was driven from the mind by the delight of her presence. Day after day we spent together, while love grew and blossomed for us on that harsh road in the wilderness. She was a year younger than me, for I was then only sixteen and she fifteen, but in appearance both of us were beyond our years. Love that was at first unspoken found words for itself, and we discovered to our delight, that each returned the affection of the other. And so we journeyed on transported by our new-found love; each day more wonderful than the last, but as the time flew by our destination grew ever nearer, and it was no longer possible to drive from our minds the thought that we must soon part.

Until then all my being had yielded to the fascination of my beloved, from whom it seemed treason to steal even a single thought; but now the time approached when my duty must tear me from her, and when I reflected that there was no possibility of shrinking from that duty without disgrace, the inevitability of the separation from my beloved Sabina made me almost frantic with despair. However much I twisted and turned the matter in my mind, I could see no possibility of escaping from the situation in which I found myself. The more I considered it the more distressed I became. My Commanding Officer would not, for a moment, think of allowing me to marry young as I was, and anything less honourable than marriage I would not contemplate. At last it began to seem as if there was only one, desperate, way out of the difficulties which hemmed us in. I must desert. The very idea of such a thing was terrible. I knew the enormity of the offence and the grave nature of its consequences, but the thought that this was the only thing left to do clung to me night and day like ivy to a ruined tower. It was impossible to settle my mind. At last I broke the difficulties of our situation to Sabina, who in the joy of new-found love had as yet given them never a thought. The minute I hinted at the prospect of parting she turned as pale as death, and burst into tears. It was as if her life had been taken from her. It was then that the devil urged me on and I promised, in that moment of grief and excitement, that I would desert and follow her wherever she might go. Immediately all was changed, and she was overflowing with delight. She kissed me a hundred times saying, "Promise, promise that you will go with me. If you do I shall live, if not I shall die." What could I do in the arms of so much love, but give her the solemn promise she wished for and make up my mind to desert? Her family were willing enough that I should go with them, and spoke of the happiness that would be mine with their beautiful sister.[5] There was no resisting the appeal of such a future, and I again promised to stay with them. But in spite of this the recollection of my native country, my obligation to the regiment, and the disgrace attached to such a crime as desertion, all continually tossed about in my distracted mind. But if I wavered, the thought of Sabina and the bliss that might be mine with her was enough to confirm me in my fatal resolution.

We were now within sight of Cape Town, and the agony of conscience in which I lived grew greater still. Sometimes I gave up all thoughts of desertion, but then the sight of Sabina would call me back to my resolution again, for it was impossible to think of parting from her. I prayed devoutly that the regiment would have sailed before I arrived, and that I would be saved from the shame of desertion in that way, but should it be there I swore to my betrothed and her family that I would leave it, and come back to them. At a spot a hundred miles from Cape Town the old Dutchman tried hard to get me to stay behind, with all the property in my charge, while he and his family went into town and came back again, but this I refused to do. Desertion was bad enough, but I would not add breach of trust to my crime. I handed over everything that was in my keeping. Not a single item had been lost, or damaged, in all that long and arduous journey. My comrades were very glad to see me for they thought that I had been killed by the Caffres, and the officers, whose goods I had taken care of, rewarded me handsomely. The same evening I went to see Sabina and her family at the friend's house where they were staying, and was told that they intended to leave for home the following Monday. I promised to go with them, and when the time came stole out of barracks at night and joined them. They were very glad to see me, for I had kept them waiting an hour longer than had been agreed, so hard was it for me to take the irrevocable step. I was young, and there was great temptation, that is my sole excuse, but I hope that I may not be judged too harshly.

We had gone some thirty miles from Cape Town, and Sabina and I were wrapped up in our visions of bliss, when they were all suddenly dissipated by the Provost Marshal, who thrust his head into the wagon and, pointing a pistol at my head, said he would put a ball into me if I tried to move. There was no disobeying that sort of order, and within ten minutes I was on my way back to Cape Town, leaving for ever the embraces of her for whose sake I was willing to sacrifice all. Sabina and her family would certainly have been punished heavily had I not taken the entire blame upon myself. I was tried by court-martial, for being absent from morning parade and for desertion, and sentenced to receive nine-hundred and ninety-nine lashes, more than fifty for every year of my life. But my Commanding Officer was a kind and compassionate man, who had known me from the day I joined the regiment, and he would not consent to my receiving a single stroke. He sent for me, admonished me like a father, painting the crime of desertion in all its terrible colours, and then dismissed me with the assurance that I had his full forgiveness and friendship, for he was convinced that I had been enticed away by the Dutchman and his family. To that I would never agree until months afterwards, when they were far enough away to be safe.

Some of the Dutch troops which had come from Java and Batavia, and other settlements, to receive the surrender of the Cape came down to the wharf to see us embark, and insult us when they dared. A huge brute sidled up to me and, twisting his greasy moustaches between his thumb and finger, chucked me under the chin, and called me a pretty boy. I gave him a smart kick on the shin, in return for which he tried to pull my ears, but I fixed my bayonet—a weapon which the Dutch greatly dislike—and he marched off. The next morning we sailed for India, and my first introduction to strange lands and peoples and to the scenes of war was over. It was impossible to look back at the last four years of my life without trembling at the dangers I had been carried through in safety, and addressing a prayer of thanksgiving to the Fountain of All Goodness for the unmerited protection which had been granted me.

Our ship was a small American vessel which had lain for a considerable time at the Cape.[6] We had scarcely got to sea before we discovered that it was a hard matter to say which was the more cranky, the ship or the Captain. She took in water in large quantities, he did as much with the grog. She would not go steady, neither could he. She rolled and pitched, and so did he. She shook her head, he did the same, she was often seasick and so was he, they were in fact a cranky pair. Her bottom had grown so foul, with lying so long at the Cape, that she could do no more than four knots an hour even if it blew an hurricane, and then she seemed to tear the very sea apart. And so we prowled about the deep like a nautical Wandering Jew, until our water began to give out, and it looked as if we should suffer considerable hardship, for the sun was burning hot. After about a week of short allowance we stumbled on a piece of land, which our sapient Captain pronounced to be a part of Sumatra. Whatever it was we were glad to see it, but as night was coming on when we first sighted it we had to hold off until morning. At about ten o'clock the clouds thickened, and the wind blew from the shore, increasing in strength until midnight when it had risen to a smart gale, and we had to lie like a log on the water until daybreak. Then we stood in for land which seemed a pleasant place, with fertile valleys and wooded hills, the small bay where we anchored being beautiful in the extreme.

The inhabitants were in a great commotion, many canoes withdrawing up a small creek, and people making off into the woods in apparent alarm. None of this looked very friendly towards us, and it was fortunate that we had the means of taking the fuel and water we required, though we would gladly have paid for it if we could. To convince them, if possible, of our friendliness a small boat was sent ashore, with six or seven men, four of them armed, of whom I was one. We approached with great caution, for we could plainly see people hiding behind trees, and others carrying away their property from the huts which stood about two hundred yards from the shore. We beckoned to them but they were shy and would not come near. As the Captain's servant, a native of Ceylon, could speak several languages we landed him, but he was not willing to go far from the boat. However he managed to make them understand what it was we sought, and that we were willing to pay reasonably for the wood and water we needed. To this they would not agree, but warned us that we must leave their country at once, or suffer the displeasure of their King who had been informed of our intrusion into his territory.

It seemed from this that there was no alternative but to take what we wanted by force and so, disregarding the threats of his Black Majesty, the next morning we sent out the long-boat with all that was needed for getting wood and water. Both were close to hand, for the country was thick with trees which had been blown down, and a stream of crystal-clear water emptied onto the shore near-by. But the minute we started work an enormous number of men, armed with swords, spears and daggers approached us. We formed a line with our pieces primed and loaded, but as we were determined not to be the aggressors we sent the native servant, with a small guard, to reason them into a better mind. After a good deal of bluster they said that they would sell us water at five dollars a butt, and wood in proportion, but this was absurd and we offered them a dollar a butt. They refused with scorn and our negotiator came back, while we went on getting the wood and water we needed, but keeping an eye on them all the time. They now consulted together a good deal and there were messengers coming and going, and a growing excitement, until one of them shot an arrow which fell uncomfortably close to me. Another followed so the officer in charge ordered us to fire over their heads. This sent them off yelling into the woods while we went hard to work. But after about an hour, encouraged by our peaceful appearance, the natives sent a man to tell us that their King was graciously pleased to allow us to "Tread his soil and drink of the water of his mercy," as they put it. We were also told that His Majesty himself would come the next morning, if the day was auspicious, to talk with us in friendship. In the meantime we might take as much wood and water as we wished, but we were not to try and go inland for fear that the King's elephants and bulldogs might get loose and destroy us all, in which case he would not be responsible. There was also a promise to sell us fresh fruits of all kinds at a moderate price. To this we returned a very gracious answer.

At about ten o'clock the next morning a vast number of boats was seen, coming down the creek and concentrating at the village, which stood a little way up the main stream. About thirty of these, with four men to a boat, came out to the ship but we stuck to our rule that no more than ten persons would be allowed on board at a time, and none with arms. Their King was not with them, but excused himself on the ground that his diviners had declared the day to be unlucky. If he was as great a thief as his subjects he ought to have been elevated to a very high place indeed, in fact to the gallows, for such a set of rogues I never did see in all my life. They brought oranges, plantains, and similar things, with a few ducks, chickens, and eggs, for barter; but you could not trust them to handle the goods you offered in exchange, for if you did they were quickly passed from hand to hand until they reached the canoes and then, to use a soldier's phrase, "you might fish for them." There was a very funny scene with one of the sailors over this. Jack offered his blanket for sale, as he was now in a warm climate and no longer needed it. With many an oath he guaranteed the quality of his property, though the purchaser understood not one word of what he was saying. Jack, who had been careful to keep tight hold of one corner, had his attention diverted for a second and the blanket was whisked away into a canoe. Cursing and swearing Jack was on deck, and down into that canoe in an instant; but though he turned over everything it contained there was no trace of his blanket, or of the man who had taken it. Running through the ship like a madman the sailor at last caught sight of the thief, and leaping onto his back crashed him down on the deck, swearing that if he did not "skull over the Whitney" he would tear him into rope yarn. The black man's astonished yelling brought the first officer over, to find out what was the matter. "This here rascal has grappled my blanket, and if he don't shore it out I'll sink him or I'm no sailor." He began hammering his captive's head on the deck, until the fellow said something to one of his countrymen, who put an end to the trouble by running to the canoe and bringing back the Whitney.

We continued our voyage to India the next day with light hearts and cheerful countenances. Soon the pilot was picked up as he cruised off the sand-heads of Saugar, and we were making our way up the river Hoogley. The river is wide, with a strong current, and when you get as far as Fultah the scene on either side is most romantic. On rounding the neck of land on which the Company's botanical gardens are laid out Fort William[7] first appears, and then Calcutta, with its innumerable shipping, bursts into view so that the beholder is transported with the beauty of the fort and the city of palaces. We passed the fort under full sail, and as we went by were greeted by the artillery and part of the 10th Regiment of Foot, then forming the garrison. We returned the welcome with three loud cheers, and in a few minutes dropped anchor off the Esplanade Ghaut (wharfe) after a voyage of five months.

6

I Arrive in India and Fight The Mahrattas

THE instant the anchor was down boats were alongside, to carry the two companies ashore, and in a couple of hours we were safely lodged in our quarters in Fort William. As soon as we were there the five companies of His Majesty's 10th Regiment of Foot, already in occupation, mingled with our lads in a welcoming carouse, drinking, singing, shouting, fighting, with bottles flying in all directions. It was terrific, but too much for me, so I went off to look at the fort, the bazaar, or anything else worth seeing so as to get out of the way. When I returned the men were lying about most filthily drunk, some on the floor, others in cots, some half in and half out of trunks or boxes. I had not then tasted spirits, and did not for years afterwards, consequently instead of joining in scenes like these they only disgusted me. Indeed, the very smell of arrack would at any time drive me from my quarters, and many a night I spent in the open air just to avoid the foul smells and drunken brawls to which its excessive use gave rise.

I was then eighteen years old, healthy and active, a keen though humble member of my profession, and eager for military glory. Remembering that I was in India, and that a wide field of promise was before me, I sought to better my station. I was then fifer and bugler in the light company, and my kind Captain, seeing my desire to get on, generously undertook to assist me in reading and writing of which I then knew but little. After a year's close application I was so much improved that I was able to keep the books of his company, and his own private accounts. I then begged him that I might be removed from being a drummer-boy into the ranks, for I did not like the title drum-boy. Just as I have seen many a man of sixty riding post and still being called a post-boy, so a drummer, even if he is as old as Methuselah, is still called a drum-boy. And there were many other things that I could never bring myself to like about it such as flogging, to say nothing of being flogged, the dancing attendance on a capricious Sergeant-Major, or his even more consequential spouse who is the queen of soldiers' wives and the mother of tippling. An invitation from her to tea and cards is thought to confer a tremendous obligation.

About a week after I had made this request I was transferred from the drummers' room, and promoted to the rank of Corporal. This was advancement indeed! Three steps in one day! From drum-boy to private, from a battalion company to the Light Bobs, from private to Corporal. It was not long before I was off to the tailor's shop, where I tipped the master-snip a rupee to give me a good, neat, cut such as became a full Corporal. By evening my blushing honours came thick upon me. The Captain, coming on parade, read aloud the regimental orders of the day laying great stress upon "To the rank of Corporal, and to be obeyed accordingly." I was the tallest man on parade, and so was on the right of the company, when I was desired by the Captain to fall out and give the time. I did so, and never did a fugleman cut more capers until an unfortunate accident happened. In shouldering arms I lifted my left hand high in the air, and extended my leg in an oblique direction with the point of my toe just touching the ground, but in throwing the musket up the cock caught the bottom of my jacket, and down came Brown Bess flat on my toes, to the great amusement of the company. I must confess that I felt queer but I soon recovered my piece and my composure, and everything went smoothly until I got back into barracks. There I was greeted by a quick hedge-fire from all quarters of "Shoulder Hems", "Shoulder Hems", "Twig the Fugleman", and similar chaff. It went on until I had to exert my new-found authority, and threaten them with the guard house for riotous conduct. But this only amused them the more, so in the end I thought it wise to pocket the affront as the best way out of it all. So ended my first parade as a non-commissioned officer.

There is a good deal of pleasure in being a Corporal. He has to take command of small guards, he may visit the sentinels whenever he pleases, his suggestions are often listened to by his superior officers, and his inferiors must obey his orders promptly. With such authority a man rises in his own esteem, and I now thought a drummer-boy little better than his own drum. Full of the importance of my rank the time passed very quickly, until after about six months, I was advanced to Sergeant, and shortly after to Pay-Sergeant in the same regiment. The post of Pay-Sergeant is certainly one of consequence; and the person who holds it is of no small consideration. He feeds and clothes the men, lends them money at moderate interest on good security, sells them watches and seals, on credit, somewhat above cost price to be sure, but the mere sight of such things dangling from a man's fob has been known to get him the character of a sober, steady fellow, and one that should be set down for promotion. So at least good may sometimes come out of evil. It is not my intention to go into detail about the chicanery which is practised among the lower ranks of the army, it is enough to say that I never served in a company in which any individual in it could not buy, sell, exchange, lend or borrow on terms peculiar to himself.

Shortly after my promotion, the order arrived for the two flank companies of the regiment to join the army in the field with all possible speed. We were to go by land, the distance about twelve hundred miles, and the season winter. Everybody was engaged in making the necessary preparations for the journey, equipping themselves as lightly as possible, when an unfortunate misunderstanding arose, which seemed likely not only to prevent our journey but to put an end to the lives of some of us. It had been the custom when troops arrived at Fort William to stop eight rupees from every man's pay, for what reason no one was ever told. Our two companies suffered this deduction but, as usual, we were not told why. It had always been the custom in our regiment for the officers to explain such things fully, and as we were now going on active service it was only right and proper that we should know. But when asked the officers could give no explanation, they were as much in the dark as everybody else. So the greater part of the two companies then marched in a sober, deliberate, manner to Sir Hugen Bailey's headquarters to seek redress. Here they were told that it was the custom to stop the eight rupees from each man in order to make sure that he got a decent burial.

This explanation only made bad worse, and excited in the hearts of the poor fellows, few of whom ever wanted burial, as the sequel to this narrative will show, the most bitter rancour. When the men returned to barracks drink added to the fury they were already in, until at length they were bent on open rebellion and mutiny. This determination was strongest in the grenadier company. Both companies were doatingly fond of their officers, who took great pains to impress them with the fact that violent measures would never get the wrong put right, but would, in fact, deprive the officers of all chance of interceding for them. This explanation satisfied us of the light company, and we only asked to be led to the enemy that we might wipe out our disobedience, but the grenadiers were more deeply infected and continued to be mutinous; so much so that their officers had to be called in again to deal with them. They loved their Colonel dearly, for he was a father to his men, but the Adjutant they loathed. When the former came in the men grew quiet, but when the latter appeared they all started shouting "Kick him out!" "Turn him out!" and he narrowly escaped with his life. When he left they quieted down again, and went sullenly to their cots. The next morning the eight rupees were refunded.

We left the fort the day after, with the regimental band playing us through the streets of Calcutta, where we were cheered by all the bystanders. Every face was wreathed in smiles, every heart beat high for glory. The country through which we passed seemed fertile and well inhabited, prosperous and contented, British justice prevailed, and the pariah in his reed-thatched hut, and the thrifty farmer with his ripening crops, were equally protected. We lived like fighting cocks, and thought nothing of five or six and twenty miles a day. It was a happy march, with songs and stories to beguile the way, until we were met by Lord Lake the Commander-in-Chief himself[1] some miles from the camp, who told us how delighted he was to see us. We gave him three cheers in which his staff joined. The elation of that moment swept through our souls, leaving us with such mingled emotions that we hardly knew whether to laugh or cry. As we drew near the camp we were met by the whole European army, with

Sketch of the advanced guard of the Mahratta Army, 1791

such shouting and huzzaing that I could never have imagined men were able to work themselves up to such a pitch. On reaching the general hospital it was a most affecting sight to see poor, wounded creatures waving their shattered stumps, and calling up their feeble strength to greet us as we passed along.[2] The scene that followed was indescribable, drinking, dancing, shouting, that made the Byannal Pass[3] ring with the noise. As I have said I never touched spirits at this time, so I left the riot behind and took a look at the camp, which seemed a more interesting thing to do than get drunk. But in three days everybody was back to order and discipline again.

At this time Holkar, a Mahratta chieftain,[4] was out in full force with about sixty thousand horse and twenty-five thousand infantry, and had encamped a short distance away from us, ever on the alert to watch our movements. He was supported by Ameer Khan,[5] and other self-appointed Rajahs. From the very nature of this sort of fighting, against an elusive enemy, thoroughly acquainted with the country, we had little chance of coming up with him. Such armies are careful to avoid a pitched battle, as their only aim is plunder, by which they pay themselves; handing over to their chiefs any article of particular value, if their chiefs happen to know that they have it. Their wives are excellent horse-women, many of them good with sword and matchlock. They are mounted on the best horses, and it is not unusual for them to carry one child in front of them and another behind, while riding at full speed. These Pindaree[6] horsemen, and indeed all Indian horsemen, have a decided advantage over the English. Their steeds are so trained, that they can turn them round fifty times without the animal's hind legs ever leaving the same circle, and even at full speed they can pull them up instantly. Our horses are heavy, fat, and so hard mouthed that no bit can manage them. It takes as long to get one round as it does a ship, and they cannot be pulled up under ten or twenty yards. Some of their horsemen have spears seventeen feet long, which they handle in so masterly a style that singly they are dangerous customers to deal with, though I have frequently seen Lord Lake charge with his bodyguard and put a whole column of them to rout.

A few days after our arrival we moved on towards Jeypore, these plundering rascals manœuvring on our flanks, and giving us a shot now and again just to be neighbourly. One of these occasions nearly cost me my life. We were in column on one side of a field, near some high corn called juwar, about half a mile from our other column on the other side of the field. I had at this time a pony called Apple, the fastest in India, and I rode ahead on him to the furthest end of the field to get a shot at the leaders of their line of march. It nearly cost me my life. When I rounded the corner I was almost on top of about a hundred of the enemy. I wheeled round, and galloped away as fast as my pony could carry me, pursued by fifty or sixty shots not one of which touched me. Ever after that I kept within bounds.

Though we skirmished frequently with detached parties of them, killing many with our six-pounders, we could never come up with the main body. We therefore made our way towards Muttra, a great haunt of the Pindarees, where we hoped that we might surprise them but they were ever on the watch, and the rattling of our swords could be heard a mile off. Tired of this we took possession of the town of Muttra, driving them out and having glorious plunder from their hoards; shawls, silks, satins, money, and other spoils, so that some of the men made a good thing of it. I was not idle, but bad luck hindered me for a time. I was quartered in a Rajah's palace, and had to climb several flights of steps to get at anything worth while. All the way up there were little iron doors, each fastened with several locks. As Paul Pry[7] says I thought this "rather mysterious" so I knocked them all off, and found the rooms full of bales of silks, shawls and embroideries. I had taken the biggest bale from off the top and was walking away with it when, turning round, I found myself watched by one of the most brilliant eyes, set in the most hideous face, that I had ever seen. What the monster was I did not stop to enquire, but made off with my prize as fast as I could go, being more frightened than I cared to admit even to myself. But thinking it over I marched in again with my sword drawn, and having convinced myself by a second look that my friend of the glaring eye was no other then the god Mahadook,[8]

I gave him a cut across the face for disturbing me so, and then made free with all the silks and shawls under his protection.

Early in the following Spring our active enemy moved upon Delhi, where the people were not too friendly to us, and we only had a small force of Native troops. We immediately went by forced marches to their relief, only to find that Holkar had raised his siege a day or two before, and crossed the Jumna for protection against our light cavalry. Colonel Burns, to his praise be it spoken, was marching to the relief of Delhi from the opposite direction with five companies of Native Infantry, when he had the bad luck to encounter the whole body of Holkar's cavalry, but managed to make his retreat to the town of Shamlee, fighting every inch of the way. There he occupied a small gurry, or mud fort, and for six days held out against an immense body of the enemy, suffering most terribly and worn out by continual watching. Our main army crossed the Jumna and rushed to the help of the Colonel and his little body of Native heroes, marching eighty-four miles in two days. Never shall I forget the cheering of that handful of men on the ramparts of their little refuge. Lord Lake himself was overcome with emotion as he rode up, waving his hat to them. I had gone ahead that morning to take up an encampment, and as our advance guard approached some of the enemy were seen still loitering about, though their main body had left early in the day. We had with us two six-pounders, five troops of His Majesty's 8th Light Dragoons, five troops of His Majesty's 24th Dragoons, and a regiment of Native Cavalry, and we succeeded in killing a few of these marauders, who were plundering and laying waste the whole country. You could always tell their line of march by the devastation they left behind. Many of the houses in Shamlee commanded the little fort, and as some of our Sepoys had been killed from them, Lord Lake gave the town up to plunder. Such a scene is inconceivable to those who have not witnessed it, the breaking open of houses, the tearing apart of boxes, and bales of silk, shawls, and satins, the fighting and the tumult.

We marched the following morning close on the tracks of the enemy but they had a day's start of us, and can go fifty to sixty miles a day, so that it was impossible to catch them. The scenes on our road were heart-rending, the poor, naked, plundered creatures, men, women and children; burning cornfields, dead elephants, camels, horses, and bullocks; the road strewn with moah berry with which they drug their horses so that they will go incredible distances, though you can count their ribs a mile off. The enemy's rearguard generally kept an eye on our advance, detaching parties to either flank, and occasionally amusing themselves by giving us a shot. I recollect on one of these occasions a most impudent fellow, on a fine horse, beautifully caparisoned, came within a couple of hundred yards of our column shouting abuse, and now and then firing off his matchlock. At last he wounded one of the Native Cavalry, which so annoyed me that I begged his Lordship to let me deal with the fellow. "O, never mind him Shipp," said his Lordship, "We will catch him before he is a week older." I never in my life felt more inclined to disobey, for the man was still capering about close by. An officer commanding one of the six-pounders came up just then, and told his Lordship that if he gave him leave he would knock the boaster over first shot, or lose his commission. "Well, try," answered his Lordship. The man fired his matchlock at that moment and started to re-load. The six-pounder was unlimbered, laid, fired, and the shot struck the horse's rump, passed through the man's back and out through the poor animal's neck and we said "So much for the Pin."

We marched on an average, twenty-five miles a day, but were compelled to push on even faster, for Holkar was making for Futtyghur, a small military station. It is a rich city, and he no doubt intended to plunder and burn it. He arrived the day before us, and set about extorting money from the Rajah. Our little force there was withdrawn from the barrack, and stationed to protect the mint which had been established a little time before. Holkar's men got there in the evening. On the morning of that same day we marched upward of twenty miles, rested until eight o'clock at night, then, making ourselves as light as possible, we moved on in order to surprise them before daybreak. We had twenty-eight miles to cover before then, but so rapid was our advance that not a man of them would have got away, if a most unfortunate incident had not come near to spoiling all our plans. We were moving at such speed, and the road was so rough, that an ammunition tumbril blew up half a mile short of the enemy, who were sound asleep having just made a forced march to get away from us. The explosion alarmed a few who happened to be awake, but at first they took it for the station gun at Futtyghur, but when that was, in fact, fired some minutes later, some of them were frightened enough to get on the move though thousands were left still sleeping. I would recommend all officers who serve in India always to attack the enemy at night, if it is at all possible, for they eat and smoke such a quantity of opium that their sleep is a profound stupor, from which even a gun fired under their noses would not awaken them. Often there is not a single sentinel on the watch.

When day dawned Holkar's men were surrounded, and a general attack was begun. The slaughter was terrific, some were cut to pieces in their sleep, others as they attempted to escape. The 8th, 24th and 25th Dragoons, with two regiments of Native Cavalry, and a corps of Horse Artillery mowed them down in hundreds with grape shot. About two thousand men were killed,[9] but sad to say there were some poor tradesmen among them from Furrackabad, who had only come to sell their goods. We pursued the enemy for many miles, they burning the barracks and near-by villages in their flight. Sometime that evening, or the following morning at the latest, the enemy reached Mainporee, a distance of seventy-two miles. We had only one Native corps there, but undaunted they took possession of the house belonging to Mr Cunningham, the Judge, and prepared to defend themselves against Holkar's horde of cavalry.

This battle of Furrackabad was on the 16th, or 17th, of November, 1804, after which the enemy moved in the direction of the fort of Deig, which belonged to the Rajah of Bhurtpore.[10] Holkar believed himself to have about twenty-five thousand infantry in that neighbourhood, with upward of a hundred pieces of cannon. He little dreamed that this force had, on the thirteenth of the same month, met with a disaster similar to that which overwhelmed his cavalry, three or four days later. Major-General Frazer, with a small detachment, had completely routed them, taking all their stores and guns. He had so few men that the outcome was often extremely doubtful. The only troops, other than Native, were the Company's[11] European Regiment and the 76th Foot, both corps together numbered no more than six or seven hundred. The enemy took refuge under the walls of the fort, which fired at us, though the Governor was supposed to be an ally of ours. Seeing the risk of defeat General Frazer put himself at the head of his troops, and drove the enemy from their guns and from the shelter of the fort, though in the action he was wounded in the foot, and compelled to retire. He died soon after, but Colonel, the Honourable William Monson, on whom the command devolved, completed the victory. When Holkar learned of this disaster he shifted his course towards Bhurtpore, demanding immense sums of money from the Rajah under threat of laying waste his country, which was the garden of India. He camped under the walls of the fort, leaving about two thousand men to harass and annoy us.

About the 18th of December we took up a position before the fort of Deig, and two days later broke ground against it. The company to which I belonged, was one of the two which led the column, carrying the tools we needed for working. Secrecy was of the greatest importance, so we approached the fort slowly, making towards a small village which had been burned out two days earlier, all its inhabitants having fled to the fort. There we halted under shelter from their guns. Small parties were sent out to find suitable places for trenches within breaking distance. I was dispatched alone, to see what was on the other side of the village. I was but new to soldiering, and had no great fancy for the job, but an order must be obeyed so off I went, my ears sticking out like fans to catch the smallest sound. Turning into a wide street, and moving on tiptoe, I passed two or three solitary bullocks that were dying for want of food. They startled me for a moment, but no other creature could I see. Once I thought I heard voices, and imagined that I could see blue lights burning in the fort, which made me apprehensive lest I was getting too near to it. Just as I had made up my mind that this was so, I distinctly heard a voice call out in the native language "Who is there?" I was riveted to the spot, unable to move until the same voice called again, when I slipped into shelter behind a hut on my right. Soon after I heard the same man say, "I am sure I saw somebody," and another voice reply, "A jackass I suppose," for there were several wandering about. I agreed most heartily with the last speaker, but resolved to prove him wrong by getting away as soon as possible. In moving off, quietly, as I thought, I accidentally trod on some embers which made me jump and caused a noise. One of the voices said. "There certainly is somebody there." To which the other answered, "Why don't you find out then?" Hearing this I dashed into another hut, and squatting down made up my mind to fight for it. Twice a man passed the door but gave it up at last and shouting "It is only a lame bullock," went back to join his friends. It was obvious that I would never get away quietly on so dark a night. I was bound to run into something and be heard. There was nothing left but to make a dash for it, so I bolted off along the road I had just come down, as hard as I could go. A whole volley of matchlock fire was sent after me, but nobody tried to follow, at least as far as I know, for I did not stop to enquire. I got back to the division in safety, but frightened out of my skin. Apart from the elephant affair in Africa I never ran so fast in my life. The enemy turned out to be a strong picquet of cavalry.

We took possession of the village, and established a depot there, and then began to dig ourselves in on a rising ground, about two or three hundred yards away from the houses. As soon as they heard us the enemy started a heavy fire from the fort, but in the wrong direction, however we kept on digging and in about two hours were safe from their shot, and could begin to erect our batteries. By daylight everything was finished, and we were so close to the enemy that we could hear the drums of their revillèe, and English being spoken. We were confident of this, and no doubt the speaker was a drummer who had deserted from the 76th Regiment, and who was afterwards found dead in the fort. On Christmas Eve, as dark and cold a night as ever blew, the breach was reported practicable, and the rising of the moon was to be the sign to begin the assault. Her light fell in splendid radiance over one of the highest bastions, and that was to be ours to storm. In the bright moonbeams we could see spears on the ramparts as thick as plants in a new-set forest. Now and then a solitary gun from the fort saluted us, just to let us know that they were not asleep. Blue-lights were burning among them, and they occasionally sent over a rocket or two, to indulge us with their beauty in the air. The old soldiers, seeing that I was a competitor with them for military glory, and a person of spirit, gave me some good advice. One of them, a veteran of the 76th Foot who had been fighting in the East for twenty years, told me never to pass a man lying down, and supposed to be killed, without giving him the point of a bayonet, or a sword, for it was a common trick of theirs to sham dead, and then cut you down when you were off your guard. He also said that when I saw a rocket, or shell, fall near me it was wise to get as close up to it as possible and lie flat on my face. This was undoubtedly very good advice, but I soon got tired of killing dead men, and flinging myself down every time I saw a rocket, though neglecting to do so once nearly cost me my life as I shall show later on.

There were about seven hundred men in the storming party, made up of two companies of His Majesty's 22nd Regiment, two from the Company's European regiments, and the rest Native troops; the whole under the command of Colonel Ball, as brave an old hero as ever stepped, but so feeble that he was obliged to be pushed up the path of glory. The two flank companies to which I belonged led the column. Sergeant Bury, of the grenadiers, headed the foremost, but was immediately wounded and obliged to leave the battery. I volunteered to take his place. The enemy had strong entrenchments between us and the breach, with innumerable guns so placed as to have a cross fire on the storming party. However we soon fought our way through, led by our gallant Captain Lindsay, who was cheering us on, and in the act of crossing the trenches, when he was cut by a spear in the arm, and also received a severe sabre wound, but so eager was he that he could not be prevailed upon to leave the scene of action. I noticed that a little to our right the enemy were pointing a gun at us, and with two or three comrades rushed over to spike it. Just as I was searching for the touchhole in which to drive the nail, one of the artillery men managed to fire the gun, which blew me flat on my back in the trench, where the same man was about to cut me in pieces, when one of our grenadiers, named Shears, shot him and I escaped once more. Fortunately for us their great guns were elevated too much, and so the shot passed over our heads. If they had been properly handled every man of us must have been wiped out. When I was fifty or sixty paces from the breach, I received a matchlock ball in the head, which dropped me to the ground bleeding profusely. When I came round again I found myself being impelled onward by one of our companies, which was running forward, and stooping to avoid the bullets which were uncomfortably thick now that we were near the breach. However we reached the bastion, and planted the British Flag upon it. Our opponents fought furiously, hurling down huge stones, pieces of trees, burning bundles of straw, spears, great shot and such things upon us as we advanced, but we were not to be repelled for we were determined to conquer. In spite of this laudable resolution however we had our work cut out to make good our footing. The narrow streets of the fort ran across each other, and at every ten yards guns were placed so as to rake their whole length. Added to this, many of the houses were high and well loopholed, so that the occupants could fire down upon us without the possibility of getting at them.

Near the corner of one of these streets, in a kind of nook, I found our dear Captain Lindsay, holding off five or six of the enemy. He was on one knee and weak from loss of blood, because of his previous wounds; but to our great joy we were just in time to save him, and punish some of his attackers. From the intricacy of the place we were afraid of shooting some of our own men, and so were obliged to keep pretty close together. At midnight I met Captain Lindsay again, and he asked me how I felt. I told him that I had a wound in my side but could find no hole, however, this was not a time for talking. In turning sharply into a street, which was rather larger than those we had cleared, we ran into a column of the enemy with a person of rank in a palanquin. It was an open one, and several of us were probing it with our bayonets, when a tremendous fat zemindar (landowner) inside began to roar very loudly, and show fight. He fired a matchlock at me, but the ball only went through the wing of my coat and did not touch my person. Before I could retaliate my comrades had finished him, and we started on the column. I took from the palanquin the weapon which had nearly robbed me of my life. It had a barrel about two feet long with a hook on the end, and a round handle terminating in a very sharp hatchet. I presented this extraordinary instrument to the Commander-in-Chief, but he refused it as a present saying that it was my trophy, though he afterwards consented to buy it for two hundred rupees. About this time, we were told that the five companies which had deserted to the enemy during Colonel Monson's[12] masterly retreat from Jeypore were standing outside the main gate of the fort, with their arms ordered, apparently making no resistance but frequently crying out, "Englishmen! Englishmen! Pray do not kill us. For God's sake do not kill us." As their supplications came more from fear, than penitence for their treacherous desertion, they could expect no mercy. We had positive orders to give them no quarter and most of them were shot.

About three o'clock in the morning, when I was utterly tired and done up, I got under the gable end of a brick building and began to examine my wounds. The one on my head was bad. It went down to the skull and was about two inches long, and one broad. This was alarming. What I had thought was a wound in my side was nothing more than the wind of a cannon ball which must have passed between my arm and my body. It was quite black and much swollen, with red streaks round the edges which convinced the doctors that it must have been caused in the way I have said. I felt it for months afterward. The head wound had been exposed for a long time to the night air, and was in a dangerous state, but with an excellent constitution and youth on my side I soon recovered. When we counted the enemy's dead the next morning they exceeded the number of our storming party. We had a great many injured, but few killed. Poor Sergeant Bury, wounded though he was, found his way in with the rest of the storming party, and fought hard the whole night. Early next morning he was looking over the parapet of the fort when a cannon ball struck him in the back, and killed him instantly. Had it been otherwise he would certainly have been rewarded with a commission, but such is war. The taking of this small redoubt was but a necessary first step, before beginning a regular siege of the strong fort, and equally strong town, but they gave both up being convinced of the impossibility of holding either against us.

7

"Of Hairbreadth Scapes i' the Imminent Deadly Breach"

THE strong fortress of Bhurtpore was to be our next job, I nursed myself in order to be ready for it. I had not been the sole leader of the party into Deig, and as I was eager for such an honour, I volunteered to head the forlorn hope[1] at Bhurtpore. Lord Lake accepted the offer with great praise for my zeal, and promised that if I survived I should have a commission. We got to the place on the 29th of December, encamped about two miles from it and started operations. Under its walls Holkar had an immense body of cavalry, which committed every kind of atrocity upon any of our camp followers who fell into their hands. Some had their noses and ears cut off, others had their hands chopped from their wrists, few were lucky enough to be killed. Our advanced picquets had continual skirmishes with these fellows of Holkar's, who hung about, day and night; so, while the siege was being prepared I went out in search of a little excitement, and nearly paid for the imprudence with my life. There was a fellow showing off his horsemanship, whom I dearly wanted to teach a lesson, and so was tempted too far from our forces. I had a good mount, and was gaining on him fast, when looking round I noticed that several of the enemy had got between me and my friends, and I was in trouble. To run away would only encourage them, so there was nothing for it but to dash through the party that was trying to cut me off. My comrades, seeing the danger I was in, fired a six-pounder at them as they closed in, and while they were in a fright at the shot, and the dust it kicked up near them, I made the best use of my horse's legs and got safely back, never to venture so far out again.

On the 1st of January, 1805, we broke ground against the strong fort and town. As my wound was now nearly closed I was again on the working party. We halted near a wood and, having reconnoitred, started our night's work. We had not been at it ten minutes when they heard the noise of our tools, and began a furious cannonade. We were ordered to stop, and lie down behind what earth we had thrown up, which luckily was thick enough to stop a musket shot, or we should have suffered dreadfully; for their little, rough, iron balls were flying about as thick as bees. Their cannon shot were generally high, and those which fell short and rolled up to us were stopped by our little mound of earth. They kept it up gloriously for half an hour, thinking that we intended to surprise them, but because it was reported that there were one hundred thousand men in the fortress and nineteen crore of rupees,[2] (£19,000,000) we were ordered to approach it with a regular siege. I fear I shall tell an unwelcome tale in relating the disastrous events which took place in this operation, but we must take the gall with the honey. When the firing died down we started work again and were glad to get the blood flowing once more, for the night was bitterly cold and the ground damp. By daylight we had finished our trenches, and set up a four-gun breaching-battery within five hundred yards of the town wall. The moment it was daylight they saw what we had been doing, and the fort was ablaze again. Flags were hoisted, the parapet of the town wall was packed with spears and pennons, as far as the eye could reach, the heads of the soldiers in their brilliant turbans of red, yellow and pink were filling the scene with variegated colours. All this shouting, the roar of the cannon and whistle of shot, rockets grumbling, flags waving, and the flash of spears, made me wonder for the moment if I had not been rash to sell my leathers for the sake of taking part in such a scene, but the thought was soon lost in the shouts of defiance from our trenches. We kept as inconspicuous as possible, though we were anxious to see what sort of place this Bhurtpore was, and took a peep as often as we could. If the firing slackened in the slightest degree we went to our work again, and at length finished the batteries, and magazines, and widened the trenches to seven feet or so, making just room to pass and repass in shelter on the way to and from our main depot. All that day the enemy kept up an incessant fire, both with cannon and small arms, but only a few of our men were wounded. A soldier of the Light Company, an Irishman named Murphy, stood up on the bank, not only exposing himself but drawing fire on us. When he was grumbled at for his foolishness, Paddy coolly replied, "Never fear, Honey, sure I have got my eye on them, and if they kill me bad luck to me if I don't pay them for it when I get into that same fort." He was wounded in the finger that very day but laughed it off, saying that he was looking the other way when it happened.

In the evening we got our guns into the two small batteries of twelves, and sixes, which we had set up. The enemy let us know that they were on the watch all night by a continuous fire, and burning blue lights at intervals. A Mussulman rarely goes to bed until very late, and then only when he is so stupefied by opium that it is impossible to rouse him to active duty. From their constant use of this drug they are dull companions when the spirit is dead within them, but when revived by a renewed application to their intoxicating draught, no people can be more genial and talkative. I have often listened, with great delight, to some old Mussulman who, stimulated with his drug, poured forth his stories and expatiated on his campaigns. We heard drums and music the whole night through, and now and then the hideous roar of their guns. Those made in India by the Natives are of cast iron, but from their beating out the shot, instead of moulding it, the guns labour and bellow most dreadfully, and the rough surface of the balls tears the muzzles to pieces. When morning cast its early light upon the scene, we roused the day by the first salvo from our breaching battery, which was accompanied by such cheering, and shouting, that the sun himself might have been startled as he looked out upon us. After the initial shock the enemy made a tremendous bustle, and their heads were so thick along the ramparts that, had our shelling battery been ready, we might have made huge havoc among them. In an instant the fort was enveloped in smoke, from which issued yells, and shouting, the thunder of their guns, and the whistle of small shot, making a most terrific scene. In the middle of it a soldier called out to me, "Shipp, have you made your will?" "Yes," I said, "it is that I will lead you into that fort in spite of all their smoke and rattle." "Well done Jack! That's a hearty," said my comrade, and joked away at my expense freely enough, though it seemed to me no joking matter and I would have been profoundly glad to say with Macbeth, "I have done the deed." Still, I saw no cause to fret. Without parents, or relative, I could act "As if a man were author of himself, and knew no other kin." My ambition was to make a name for myself in the field, and if I were to fall I could not die in a better cause than fighting for my King and Country. All this lay at the back of my mind, I was too busy to do much thinking, but towards evening we were relieved from the trenches, and got some rest.

The next day I took another peep at the Pins, who were in immense numbers in front of our picquets, and, though I itched to be at them, the memory of my former escape held me back. It was infuriating to see these fellows, galloping their horses within a quarter of a mile of our posts. But what enraged us most was that the miscreants that evening sent into our camp about twenty grass-cutters belonging to the 8th Dragoons, some with their right hands cut off at the wrist, others with the loss of their noses, or ears. There were strict orders against any grass-cutters going out alone, but such is their love of plunder that they will risk their lives for it. English people may be surprised to learn, that for every fighting man in an Indian Army there are at least ten camp-followers. Most of these live by pillaging every hut, field, or village, within ten miles of the camp or line of march. There is no possibility of checking them, or preventing these abuses. Thieves of all descriptions are among them, many of them being consummate in their art. But I shall have more to say about these fellows later on, for I had the bad luck to suffer from them myself more than once. They are a universal nuisance throughout all India.

The next morning I went back to duty in the trenches. We were not actually stationed in them but in a little wood to the rear, from which a path communicated to the forward defences which we could enter at any time. The breaching battery was at some distance from us. A vigorous fire was kept up against the fort, though it was of no great use, for our guns were so weak that they made next to no impression on the mud-built curtains and bastions. Many of the balls we threw were so feeble that they scarcely buried themselves in their object; others, more futile still, merely rolled down harmlessly among the enemy, who very kindly sent them back to us from their own guns. It is hopeless to try and make a breach by means of cannon fire, in a fort made of such materials. The crust you knock off from the walls only adds to the difficulties, for it forms an almost impenetrable barrier between the attackers and any solid footing. Young engineers, inexperienced in this sort of thing, are apt to think from the look of the amount of dry mud they have knocked off that the breach is practicable; but when the storming party takes its first step, they find nothing to bear them, and they are up to their necks in a light dust. I shall have a sad tale to tell of a happening of this kind, but if it proves a warning to inexperienced engineers I shall be rewarded. Stone forts are soon demolished. Undermine them well at the bottom and the top will fall and they cannot be repaired. But mud forts defy all human efforts.

This day we set up howitzer and mortar batteries, which produced consternation among the enemy when they first opened, so that they ran in all directions to get out of the way; but in a few hours they had dug holes in the ramparts to creep into when they saw the shells coming over, so that unless one fell on the top of them they were safe. But our shelling, in those days, was nothing to what it is now. One sent off every five minutes was considered to be enormous then, but twenty a minute in these days is not unusual, and the missiles twice as big as they were at that time. The enemy were fairly quiet all that day, no doubt they were making places of refuge. Any shell which dropped in the town must have caused enormous destruction, for judging by the number of fighting men the population was vast. We could often see houses that had been set on fire, and little explosions took place almost daily, no doubt from blowing up small quantities of ammunition. When anything like that occurred we cheered, and the enemy redoubled their fire. In the course of the day the Rajah himself appeared for the first time. We saw him standing on the royal bastion with his suite about him, looking at us through a spy-glass. The officer in charge of our howitzer battery sent over a shell, especially for him. It struck the very top of the bastion, and scattered his party quickly enough. There was an enormous gun, a seventy-two-pounder at least, on this bastion, which up to then had not been fired, but in revenge for disturbing his highness they began to get it ready for action. Because of its huge size it could not be depressed sufficiently to bear on our batteries, if it could have been it would have torn them to pieces. It went off with a report like an earthquake, but the ball passed a good quarter of a mile over us. They fired it several other times in the course of the day, but not a shot came any nearer. Our men, finding that it did no harm, christened it Civil Tom. The enemy were vastly pleased with the dust it kicked up, but finding that it was doing us no harm they turned its gigantic muzzle towards the camp, and actually landed a ball close by the flagstaff in front of Lord Lake's tent, which was a good two miles away. The only real damage Civil Tom ever did was to knock off a water-carrier's right arm, and kill his bullock, at a distance of about a mile which was uncivil enough it is true.

We kept up a steady fire at night, to prevent the enemy rebuilding during the darkness what we had destroyed during the day. Now and then we sent over a whistling shell or two, to help them keep awake. All of us were impatient to see what was inside this boasting fort, we were familiar enough with its outside. When the breach began to look as if it could be entered, we discovered that they had placed two small guns so as to meet a storming party with a cross-fire, and also to rake the breaching battery. To deal with these we brought up two six-pounders, which had not fired many rounds of ball and shrapnel, before we heard a most tremendous explosion, and that was the end of that nuisance. In the evening, I was standing near to Captain Nelley, who was commanding the breaching battery, when I heard the engineer say to him that in twenty-four hours we would put a stop to the enemy's vaunting. The Captain turned round and said to me, "How do you like that information, Shipp?" I replied, "I wish it was tonight, Sir." This I did wish, most sincerely, for having volunteered for such a dangerous service I felt the sooner it was over the better.

I have heard some men say that they would as soon fight as eat their breakfast, and others that they dearly loved fighting. If this were true, what blood-thirsty dogs they must be! I would not be so mean as to suspect them of lacking ordinary courage, but I will content myself with asking these terrific soldiers, why it is that before storming a fort, or fighting a battle, men are thoughtful, heavy, restless, weighed down with care? Why do men, on these occasions, ask more fervently than usual for the divine guidance and protection in the approaching conflict? Are not feelings such as these the result of reflection, and of man's care for his dearest possession—his life? None will part with that if he can help it. There are times in war which test a man's courage to the full. If, for instance, as was my case then, I knew that I was to lead a forlorn hope on the following evening, innumerable ideas must rush into my mind. For all my poor comprehension can tell tomorrow I may be summoned before my Maker. How have I spent the life he has been pleased to preserve until now? Can I meet his just judgement? A man situated as I was, who did not think in something of that fashion, might have the courage of a lion, but he would be without the feelings of a man. Once in action he is a different being. The softer emotions of an awakened heart are swallowed up in the vortex of danger, and the need for self-preservation. An indescribable elation of spirits possesses the whole being, a frenzied disregard of what is before you, a heroism bordering on ferocity. The nerves become taut, the eyes wild and rolling in their sockets, the nostrils distended, the mouth gasping and the whole head constantly on the move. If an artist could draw the face of a soldier in the heat of battle, and the same man in the calm of domestic life, they would seem to be two different persons. But it is not in the power of art to do so, for in action a soldier's looks vary with the state of the contest; as the battle brightens, so does his face, as it lowers so do his features. I have known men drink enormous quantities of spirituous liquors before going into battle, in order to drive fear from their minds, but the effect is as short-lived as a mayfly. If a man has not natural courage, he may be certain that liquor will deaden, and destroy, what little he has.

Our two companies were relieved for the night, so that we

might rest and prepare for the next evening's attack. It happened that one of our poor fellows was killed by a shot from the fort, and it was ordered that he should be immediately buried. But when we were leaving the trenches we found him still lying there, and the officer in charge asked the Sergeant why the order had not been obeyed. "Faith, Your Honour," said the Sergeant, an Irishman, "he has grown so mighty still since he went dead that he will neither ride nor walk. He threw himself off my back twice, and I am just after ordering a fatigue party to march him there, whether he will or no." This same Sergeant had been reprimanded a short time before for killing an unarmed man. His officer told him that it was cowardly to shoot at a poor fellow without arms. "Arms, Your Honour! Begging your pardon he had two, and fists at the ends of them. He was going to be mighty saucy besides. And didn't a spalpeen shoot and hit me at Deig, without so much as a good morning, or by your leave? Faith they must expect no palaveration or blarney from Dennis Gaffen." This man was one of the jokers of the regiment and tales about him would fill a volume.

Early next morning after a good night's rest, I started cleaning and new-flinting my musket, and sharpening up the point of my bayonet so that it would find its way through the tough, cotton-stuffed, coats of the enemy. These garments are about two inches thick, and in winter all Mussulman soldiers wear them. They hang loose, so that it is difficult to cut through them, and I am persuaded that many are bullet proof. The only weapon which will penetrate is a bayonet or a spear. During the day I walked down to the batteries, and had a good look at the road I was to take to the breaches. Our guns went on working hard, to knock off the defences, and everything looked as if we ought to succeed. My heart was alive all this day, and I wished for the darkness of the night. This was the 9th of January, 1805. The greatest secrecy was observed as to the storming party, no general orders were issued and there was no stir or bustle, until the proper time of nine o'clock. All orders and arrangements were given to the officers commanding regiments and companies, and conveyed to us in the same private manner. The gun was fired at eight o'clock, and this as usual was the signal to move out. I kissed and took leave of my favourite pony Apple, and my dog Wolf, and then went to my post at the head of that little column of heroes—twelve volunteers from each of the different corps of the army. You may believe me when I say that nothing was in my mind but the enthusiasm of the moment, and pride in the post of honour that had been given to me. "What," I thought, "here am I, a mere youth, at the head of an Indian Army!" Could it be presumption when there were so many more experienced soldiers in the ranks behind me? I thought that I was in every-man's eye, and was glad of the pitchy darkness which helped to conceal me from them.

It was as still as the grave when I suddenly heard somebody call, "Sergeant Shipp!" It was Lieutenant-Colonel Salkeld, Adjutant-General of the army, who had brought a deserter, one of the enemy's artillery men, who had offered to betray his countrymen for filthy lucre and lead us into the breach. He was handed over to me, with positive orders to shoot him if he attempted to deceive us or run away. We, then, in solemn silence moved down to the trenches and waited there about half an hour, when we marched out to attack in open column of sections, the two flank companies of the 22nd leading supported by the 75th and 76th European Regiments, and Native Infantry. I took the precaution of tying a rope round the wrist of my guide in case he tried to escape, for shooting him just then would have alarmed the fort. Not a word could be heard, for the roar of the canon drowned every other sound. I was well supported having my own two companies behind me. Colonel Maitland, of His Majesty's 76th Regiment, commanded the storming party, and brave little Major Archibald Campbell the Colonel's corps. Colonel Maitland came in front and pointed out to me the road to glory. Seeing the Native in my charge, he asked who he was. I told him, and he said, "We can find the way without him, let him go about his business." I remonstrated, and repeated the orders I had received, but his answer was, "I don't care. If you don't obey my orders I will send you to the rear." I obeyed, and we moved on to the attack. The pioneers were immediately behind me, carrying gabions and fascines[3] to fill up any holes which might lie in our path. We were not discovered until we were within fifty paces of the ditch, then a tremendous cannonade broke out, with volleys of musketry and rockets in all directions. Blue lights were hoisted, and the fort was stirred to its very foundations. The rampart spouted fire like a vast volcano, while the noise of the guns, and the shrill sound of the trumpets, rent the air asunder. Men were rushing about in the strange light on the tops of the walls as busy as ants. It was an awe-inspiring scene, and one, no doubt, sublimely beautiful to any spectator at a sufficient distance.

We pushed on at speed, but were soon brought to a halt by a ditch about twenty yards wide, and four or five deep, which branched off from the main moat. It was filled with water and surrounded a small island, on which was posted a strong party of the enemy with two guns. Their fire was well directed, so that they punished the head of our column terribly. The gabions and fascines were thrown in, but they were completely swallowed up, and as the fire grew hotter my little band of heroes plunged into the water, followed by our two companies, and part of the 75th Regiment. The middle of the column broke off, and got too far to the left, but the rest of us soon cleared the little island. At this moment Colonel Maitland and Major Campbell joined me, with the officers from the two companies, and many of the other corps. I suggested that we went after the fugitives, but our duty was to gain the breach, since our orders were confined to that. We got there, but imagine our consternation at finding a perpendicular curtain, going down to the water's edge, with no footing on it except here and there pieces of trees, and stones, which had fallen from above. Not more than three men could climb abreast, and if they slipped a watery grave awaited them, for the moat below was very deep. Close on our right was a huge bastion, which the enemy had cleverly hung with dead undergrowth, which, when it was set on fire lit up the breach as clear as day. They soon brought guns to bear on us, firing grape, and with the first burst killed Colonel Maitland, wounded Major Frazer somewhere in the leg, me in the right shoulder, and swept away the remaining few of my little party. We struggled up to the edge of the gap, not more than three abreast, only to find that the enemy had completely repaired it by driving in large pieces of wood, stakes, stones, and pointed bamboos. Through the crevices in this mass a bank of spears jabbed out at us, as if moved by some mechanism. So precarious was our footing that it was impossible to get any closer to these formidable weapons; and all the while darts were hurled at us, stones and lumps of wood, stink-pots, and bundles of flaming straw were thrown down upon us. I managed to get one of my legs through a hole, and put myself into a position where I could see into the fort, which was swarming with people as busy and excited as an angry hive. In a moment I felt someone seize my foot. I pulled with all my might, and managed to get it back again, though the boot was left behind. It was physically impossible for us to establish ourselves upon the breach, so as to deal with the mass of spearmen. Our poor fellows were mowed down like standing corn, without the slightest hope of success. The rear of the column, which was within range of the enemy's shot, suffered terribly. At last a retreat was ordered, and once again we were forced to take to the water; where many an unhappy soldier, weakened by wounds, was unable to struggle through. Not one of our officers escaped without injury, and poor Lieutenant Cresswell was almost cut to pieces. As may be supposed we returned heart-broken at this our first failure in India.

Our losses were bitter, and the thought that so many poor wounded comrades, whom we had been forced to leave behind, would be barbarously tortured, and massacred, incited our brave fellows to beg permission for a second attempt, which was refused. Had it been granted we must have failed again, for there was literally no breach. The enemy exulted exceedingly over our retreat, and their shouts and jeers were daggers in the hearts of our men, who could scarcely be restrained from rushing up to the attack once more. I found that I had a spear wound in the right finger, and several little scratches from the combustibles they fired at us. Pieces of copper coins, as well as bits of stone, iron and glass, were dug out of the wounds of those who were lucky enough to escape. We were relieved during the night, and went back to our lines to brood over our misfortunes. To add to my troubles, I found the next morning that the old gash on my head had opened afresh. The injury to my shoulder went down to the bone and was extremely painful, but the flesh wound on my finger did not trouble me much. General orders on the following day were highly flattering to us, and the blame, if any, was placed where it belonged. Our engineer, finding the spot we had attempted impregnable, changed his position more to the East, where the difficulties were not so great. Our four breaching-guns were sent to the park to be rebushed, for the heat and the constant firing had burned them out. And so ended our first attempt to take Bhurtpore by storm.

8

Commissioned in His Majesty's 65th Regiment

As he had plenty of spare troops on hand, while the rest were getting ready for a second attack on the fort, Lord Lake determined to turn Holkar out of his hiding place, and to effect this sent a party of infantry with four six-pounders. High trees and jungle hid us from the enemy at first, but we soon came in sight of him; and then the fort, observing our movements, began a heavy cannonade. Holkar was greatly alarmed, and getting on the move made for Futtypore Seccrah, one of his old haunts. Once we had prised him away from the walls of the fort, our cavalry soon put his troops to flight and killed great numbers of them. Horses, elephants, camels, spears, matchlocks, colours and a vast quantity of other booty was brought into camp, including Holkar's best elephant, and there was even treasure found on some of the camels. But in spite of this defeat Holkar took up his old ground again, and we went back to camp, having suffered some few men killed and wounded. So far from depressing the enemy this affair seemed to raise their spirits, for they harassed our picquets day and night; hoping to distract them from the main body of their troops, which had been sent to intercept a small detachment coming to us from Muttra. Our spies gave us warning of this, and within ten minutes of receiving their report, three regiments of dragoons were on their way to the rescue, arriving just in time to save both the stores, and the lives of the men who were bringing them. The tale went round that Holkar was killed in this skirmish, but that was afterwards proved to be false. A reward was offered for his head, and a great many gory phizogs were brought in, but none of them belonged to the one-eyed Holkar. Heads with but one eye were indeed tendered, but Chiggram, our best spy, knew the head of that notorious Pin too well to be imposed upon. The time for our next attack drew near, and as my wounds were now pretty nearly well, and I had failed in the first forlorn hope that I led, it seemed my duty to volunteer as leader of the second. That sense of expectancy and anxiety, which is always present at such times, was strong upon me, and I was glad to wander off now and then into a little wood that was near the trenches, in search of a quiet place where I could be out of the way for a while; and have peace in which to think a little, and perhaps say a prayer or two for help in the tremendous ordeal that lay ahead. A feeling of that sort is natural when on the brink of some extraordinary danger, and more have it than will admit to it, for in general soldiers deride religious comrades.

At two o'clock in the afternoon of the 20th of January we were to storm Bhurtpore a second time. To prevent our being held up by the moat, which at the place we were to storm was deep and wide, a bamboo bridge was made which was broad enough to take three files of infantry, advancing abreast of each other. Being constructed of such material it was very light, and the hundred men in charge of it would be able to hurl it forward a considerable distance. It was designed to float upon ghee dubbahs, the skins in which the Natives export their oil and butter, which, when dried, will support a very considerable weight before they sink. We had a number of elephants and camels loaded with old tents; and hackeries, or native bullock carts, filled with bales of cotton, which were all to be tossed into the moat to fill it sufficiently for us to be able to scramble across, and up to the breach.

Once more I took my station, supported by my twelve volunteers, and followed by my two companies as before. A shell sent over from one of the howitzers was to be our signal to move, but when they gave it the missile exploded in the mouth of the mortar, and killed two of our grenadiers, which made but a sad beginning.[1] Behind the forlorn hope came the bamboo bridge I have spoken of, carried on men's shoulders, fifty a side, and looking no doubt to the enemy, who were as yet unacquainted with its use, like some extraordinary monster. We moved on, and before I had got half way down towards the fort six of my men were killed or wounded. The enemy, no doubt greatly encouraged by having beaten us the last time, had doubled their fire power both in guns and men. They had also pushed out an under-work, on the right side of the breach, and put into it several guns and a crowd of matchlock men to catch us on the flank. My men kept being picked off, one by one. When I got to the edge of the moat, which appeared to be terribly deep and wide, and was helping the men behind me with the bridge, I was hit by a matchlock ball, which went in just over the right eye, cut across and out again over the left. This knocked me flat, and tore the skin from my forehead so that it hung down, literally, over my nose, and the wound bled profusely. I happened to be next to our gallant Captain Lindsay at the time, who in the same moment received a ginjall[2] ball in his right knee, which shattered the bone to pieces. As soon as I came round a little, for I had been stunned by the shot, the first thing I saw with the single good eye left to me was the famous bamboo bridge, quietly floating down the stream. It appeared that the enemy had let a great deal more water into their moat, which had widened it considerably so that our calculations were out, and the bridge was some yards too short.

The situation looked desperate. None but the killed and wounded were in sight, and there was still not the remotest chance of getting into the fort. It would have been madness to try and cross that deadly moat. If we had made an effort to get to the water, we should probably have slid down into it, and they had two small guns covering the spot. At last the retreat was sounded, and until it came our poor fellows could do nothing but stand and be shot at, without the remotest chance of success. The camels and the elephants, driven into a panic by the noise of the guns and the shouting, could not be got near the fort. Most of them threw off their loads, and rushed back to camp, some of them escaping altogether to run wild in the woods. We had seven hundred men killed and wounded in this one attempt. Captain Lindsay's injury was so bad that his leg had to be amputated in the battery before he could be got back to the camp. The wound on my head was very dangerous for it went down to the bone. I was at once sent back to the camp, where I lay blind for several days. The pain, and the fret of our defeat threw me into a fever, which threatened my life, but with the help of Providence and a good constitution I soon recovered.

Our engineer now gave up this side of the fort as perfectly hopeless, and moved his efforts to the eastward; but wherever he tried the fort was so built that one part protected another, and however we approached we were certain of a devastating cross-fire. The men were terribly disheartened. There was scarcely one without a wound, and the sad recollection of comrades left behind to be mutilated was a constant topic of conversation; and their misery was increased by seeing the clothing of dead friends, either exhibited on the ramparts, or worn by the enemy. However, we still cherished the hope that our next attempt would be successful. I was soon beginning to get about again, though my wound was by no means healed. It was heart-breaking to go into the men's tents where, a month before, there had been nothing but joking and high spirits, whereas now there were only gloomy faces to be seen, and few of them. Some had lost brothers, others dear comrades. Captain Lindsay's leg had been taken off, and Lieutenant Cresswell cut to pieces. What with killed and wounded our two companies had lost more than half their number, in these two assaults. There was a pause now, to recover a little, and for the guns to be rebushed, but it also gave the enemy time to repair, and reinforce, every point of attack.

By the 18th of February things began to look a little better. The breached bastion seemed definitely weakened, and the 20th was talked of as the day for storming it. The memory of our bitter reverses was still with us, but we hoped that we now had a chance to retaliate upon the enemy some of the things we had suffered. I do not mean to mutilate the helpless; not a single instance of that can be charged upon the Company's armies in the long course of their wars. But we looked forward to pulling the garments of our murdered comrades from the backs of this boasting foe. They were daily, and hourly, insulting us with the sight of the muskets they had taken from us, the ammunition they had captured was turned against us, and so were our shot which they dug out of their walls. Our troops were in good spirits again, and eager to retrieve the British character. The patience, and intrepid bravery, of both officers and men in our army during this siege was not unnoticed by the enemy, and the long friendship between the Rajah of Bhurtpore and the Company which followed, owed much to the admiration which was then aroused.

The day appointed, the 20th of February, began in an unusual way. About four hundred men from the fort, emboldened by their previous success and our apparent tardiness, rushed out upon us just as we were relieving our forward troops, and carried both the batteries and the trenches before we could get back. Every one of them was drugged out of his senses, and fought desperately, but we forced them from the batteries, and then turned the guns upon them, so that the carnage was dreadful. Those in the fort fired indiscriminately at friend and foe alike. Perhaps the attackers were vagabonds they were glad to get rid of. If that was so they had their wish, for few of them got back to brag of their doings. This was the kind of retaliation we longed for. We lost a number of men both killed and wounded in this affair, but the enemy had not the barbarous gratification of cutting them up. Their wounded, which they left behind, were sent to native hospitals where they were well looked after, sharing the same wards as our own men with friendship presiding instead of murder. Had the war been between Native and Native the cruelty would have been the same on both sides.

When this odd affair had died down, the storming party was ordered for twelve o'clock. You can imagine my disappointment, when the doctor absolutely forbade me to serve on this occasion as the wound in my forehead was still in such a state that if I were to get heated, or catch a cold, it might lead to inflammation of the brain. I could have thrown what few brains I had in his face, but there was nothing for it but to obey. The forlorn hope was led this time by Lieutenant Templer, of the 76th Regiment, as brave a little fellow as ever wore a red coat. I watched the struggle from a short distance away, and a desperate hard affair it was too. No sooner did our brave fellows get to the top of the breach, than a well directed fire swept them off. Footing they had none, they literally hung on to the bosom of the bastion. A third retreat was unavoidable, leaving behind upward of five hundred dead and wounded. Death was inevitable for any poor wretch abandoned there.

Again the enemy manned the breach in swarms, shouting victory. I would have been better off if I had been in the fighting, for I am sure that I was as excited as those that were. I cannot describe my feelings, or those of the rest of us who were looking on at this dreadful scene. What can eight or ten men abreast do against a legion posted above them, protected by walls and bastions, and where every possible engine of destruction is brought to bear upon the attackers? Exposed like that there was never a chance of success. The size of the bastion was such that fifteen or twenty men abreast were the most that it could hold, and the entire destructive power of the fort was directed onto this small space, to the certain annihilation of all who were on it. Everything that brave men could was done by our troops, but in vain.

The storming party was ordered again for the following day. I had an excruciating headache, but I said nothing about that or the state of my wound, bad though it was, for I was determined to die rather than give up the post of honour. I assured the doctors that I was well, and quite able to take my station, and entreated them not to stand between me and glory. So they consented at last, and I made the most of the short time between then and beginning the attack by writing a letter to my only relative about my affairs, and in supplicating the divine protection. I had made up my mind that the chances were all against my coming through with my life a third time, and yet I knew that he who created life can also preserve it. As on a former occasion I left my tent that evening to seek religious consolation in peace and quiet. It is with gratitude that I mention the name of Captain Effingham Lindsay, of the 22nd Regiment, now a Colonel on half pay, for in addition to many other kindnesses he imparted to me, while I was still a youth, those religious feelings by which I have endeavoured to regulate my conduct; and which have brought me inexpressible consolation in every kind of danger, and difficulty. With a view, then, to thought and prayer, I withdrew that evening before leading the third forlorn hope against Bhurtpore. The moon shone brightly through the branches of a tree I was standing by, and in its light I was startled to see a European soldier, lying prostrate on the ground, dead as I believed. I bent over him, but there was no sign of life. His breath was still, and his cheek cold to the touch. But when I took hold of his hand he sat up quickly, and said, "What did you disturb me for? I have just had a sweet sleep." Then, as he woke up, he recognized me and said, "Is that you, Shipp?" "Yes. What brought you here?" I said. "The same that made you come I imagine," he answered. "And what do you think that is?" "To give some thought to what is likely to happen tomorrow, and, if you must know, to spend an hour or so alone in prayer, which has lifted such a burden from my heart that I fell asleep, and now I wake up and find a friend here." We spent some time in prayer together before we separated. It was the will of God that my comrade should be killed the next day, and for me, mercifully, to be spared.

Two o'clock was the time set for the assault. I forgot the pain of my wound, and was at my old post. Lieutenant Templer, of His Majesty's 76th Regiment, went with me on this occasion, with a small Union Jack which he was determined to plant on the enemy's bastion. He was a little man, but he had the heart of a lion. Giving me his hand, he said with a smile, "Shipp, I have come to rob you of some of your glory. You must not monopolize the whole of it. I will put Old England's banner on that bastion or die in the attempt." He did put it there, and he was killed while doing so. On the way down from the camp we met His Excellency, the Commander-in-Chief, and his suite, and his Lordship stopped to speak to us. "Sergeant," he said, "it is with sincere regret that I see you again wounded at the head of your little band of heroes. I will not check your praiseworthy zeal. Go into glory lads, and may heaven prosper you and crown you with triumph." His Lordship addressed every corps that passed him, but when the 22nd Regiment, or the remnant of it, marched by he turned from them with a tear, but anxious lest his grief might be seen he took off his hat and cheered them. It was no Judas tear, for he was always the soldier's friend, and as careful of their lives as he was of his own.

The storming party marched out in its usual steady order, but our calamitous defeats had robbed the men of the spirit they had possessed on former occasions. We had already been disastrously repulsed from the fort three times, and I have no hesitation in saying that most of us felt that the fourth assault would end in the same way. When we approached the breach, the scene was enough to overwhelm men who were already dispirited and disappointed. Those who had been wounded in our previous attacks lay there, some stripped naked, some without heads, some without arms or legs, others with their bodies slashed about in the most hideous fashion. Instinctively one turned from such an appalling sight. Those who stopped to help were added to the number of the slain, for the spot was exposed to a devastating cross-fire. Could anything be more distressing for affectionate comrades to look upon? I say affectionate, for soldiers living together in tents, or barracks, in daily familiar intercourse, get to know each other's qualities, good or bad, and the hardships of the service bind them together in a way unknown to more casual acquaintances. Many of these mutilated objects were still alive. We could see their agonized breathing. Some raised their heads clotted with blood, others the stumps of arms, or legs, and faintly cried for help and pity. It was a sight to turn the blood and melt hearts of stone. After the first shock, every man of us was roused to a passionate desire for vengeance on those who had committed such hideous barbarities. If mortal men could have found their way into that fort, these would have done it, none braver or more loyal ever left England, but for the fourth time the assault was found to be impossible. It was certain death to show oneself. The defenders were in full armour—a coat, breastplate, shoulder plates and armlets, with a helmet and chain face-guard—so that bullets had little effect. I myself fired at a man in the bastion three times, and he was not above six yards from me but he did not even bob his head.

Before I had been on the breach five minutes I was hit by a large shot in the back, which threw me down from the bastion, toppled me over and over, and sent me rolling sideways down the steep slope; until one of our grenadiers brought me up with his bayonet which he jabbed through my shoe, injuring the fleshy part of the foot under the great toe. The man who helped me get up was shot dead that minute. His name was Courtenay, of the 22nd Light Company. I got back to my place in time to see poor Lieutenant Templer, who had planted his flag on the top of the bastion as he said he would, cut to pieces by one of the enemy, who rushed out upon him as he lay prone at the top of the breach. His killer was immediately shot dead, and rolled to the bottom of the ditch. Before I had been back long a stinkpot, or earthen jar of some combustible material, fell on my pouch, in which I had fifty rounds of ball cartridge. The whole lot blew up. I never saw the pouch again, and I was hurled from the top to the bottom of the bastion. How I got there I never knew, but when I came round I was lying below the breach with my legs in the water, my clothes burned, my face severely scorched and all the hair burned off the back of my head. For a while I was too dazed to know where I was, then I managed to crawl to the other side of the bank, and sit down by a soldier of the same company who could not recognize me. Here I stayed, unable to move, until a casual ball landed in the ditch and threw mud all over me; which added greatly to the elegance of my appearance, and stimulated me to struggle out of the way. At that moment the retreat was sounded, after all that could be done had been done, though in vain.

The taking of Bhurtpore now seemed hopeless, and we were obliged to give up the attempt, having lost before that fort upward of three thousand of the bravest men that ever lived. Of the twelve gallant fellows who made up the third forlorn hope I led, not one lived to claim the Commander-in-Chief's reward. Added to that was the loss of one of the best officers in the army, Captain Menzies of the 22nd Grenadier Company, Aide-de-Camp to Lord Lake. He was trying to rally some Native troops who were tempted to give way under a particularly galling fire, and in doing so lost his life. Scarce a man of our two companies escaped uninjured. Had not a small party successfully stormed an eleven-gun battery few, if any, would have escaped the carnage. Here my personal service at Bhurtpore ended, leaving impressions both on mind and body that can never be obliterated. In the course of the siege frequent overtures were made from the fort, what their content was I never knew, but in the end its defenders were compelled to pay all our expenses[3] before we would consent to end the fighting, and return to camp. Their losses must have been immense, report put it down as five thousand men, women, and children, and this does not appear improbable when we remember the huge numbers that were in the town. Certainly they were as tired of the fighting as we were.

There can be no doubt that our sad failures were due to an entire want of means to achieve success.[4] What were four breaching-guns against such a fort as Bhurtpore, when forty would not have been too many? This is proved by the fact, that when Lord Combermere did eventually take it, he had ten guns for our one. It is impossible to think that it could have been subdued with fewer, or carried by assault, when you reflect that it was originally garrisoned by as many as one hundred thousand men. With such means as we had, the ditch surrounding the fort was an insuperable obstacle. Sapping and mining, the only way into such a place, were unknown when we made our attempt, and shelling was in its infancy. When it was eventually taken it was by the use of these means; shelling, for instance, was then so improved that it was ten times more effective than in our day.

After the last failure everything was done to encourage the disheartened troops, and after a few days, though they could ill bear the stigma of defeat, they began to cheer up a little. And then an incident occurred which might have had the most terrible consequences. After the peace had been ratified, the garrison of the fort had permission to visit our camp; but imagine the fury of our men when some of our late enemies had the effrontery to appear among us wearing the coats, sashes and weapons they had torn from the dead bodies of our comrades. The whole army was in a boiling rage and threatening immediate vengeance, but by the timely interference of the Commander-in-Chief, and the officers, the men were calmed and the mischief stopped.

In the next general orders my name appeared as Ensign[5] in His Majesty's 65th Regiment, with many flattering observations by the Commander-in-Chief. From the whole of this regiment I received the kindest attentions during the short time I served with it, and have never met it since without being given proofs of the most disinterested friendship. On the day of my appointment I was metamorphosed into a gentleman. I had a new coat, my hair was cut and curled, and I was invited to dine with the Commander-in-Chief, but I was careful to keep myself in the background. The gentleman did not sit on me very easily, for I was young and modest then, but the extreme kindness of both his Lordship and his son helped to take away my shyness. On hearing that I had arrived, his Lordship approached me with an outstretched hand, and shaking mine most cordially said, "I congratulate you as a brave young fellow, and I shall not lose sight of your merit." He placed me next to him at dinner, and when the cloth was removed made me fight the battles of the forlorn hopes over again, at which he was much affected. The next day his Lordship sent for me again and said, "Shipp, I have been thinking about your case. You have not much money. I know your generous Lindsay will do everything to serve you, but he must really leave a little for me to do. You may draw on me through the field-paymaster for what you want." He afterwards sent me a tent, two camels and a horse as presents. The rest of my outfit was generously given me by my excellent patron Captain Lindsay.

Lord Lake was truly my friend, as he was of every soldier in the army. He was munificent in his gifts, being the first to subscribe to any case of distress. Let me mention only one instance of his generosity. A very old Lieutenant had given up all hope of getting a company that was vacant, knowing full well that he could not afford to buy it.[6] I was standing with him when the orderly book, showing his promotion by purchase, was put in his hands. He looked at it and said "There must be some mistake. I have not a rupee I can call my own." Just then Colonel Lake, his Lordship's son, came up and wished him joy of his promotion. "There must be some mistake," the man answered, "I cannot purchase." "My father knows you cannot," said the Colonel, "so he has lent you the money which he never intends to take back." It was acts like this which made him beloved by the army, and admired wherever he came.

About three weeks after I had been appointed ensign in the 65th Regiment, his Lordship promoted me to Lieutenant in His Majesty's 76th Regiment, thus faithfully keeping his

Officers in the King's Army about 1811: from right to left a Staff Officer, a Captain of Infantry, a Heavy Dragoon off duty, and an Assistant Surgeon. From Luard's *History of the Dress of the British Soldier* (London 1852)

promise that he would lose no opportunity of serving me. There I soon became a great favourite with the Colonel, the Honourable William Monson, Brigadier-General of the army. One of the articles of our treaty with Bhurtpore was that Holkar should not be allowed to shelter under the walls of its fort. This had not been carried out, and he still hung about the neighbourhood, harrying our forage parties and any small escort which came into camp with supplies. A few days after I had joined the 76th I was appointed an extra Aide to the Brigadier, to go on a foraging party consisting of a regiment of

Native Infantry and Irregular Horse, from Luard's *History of the Dress of the British Soldier* (London 1852)

Native Cavalry and four six-pounders, with five hundred Irregular or Native Horse. We had not gone many miles from camp when we saw an immense body of Holkar's troops posted on an eminence, and showing signs of fight. We left our elephants, camels and bullocks in charge of the Irregular Horse, and placing two of the six-pounders behind the Native Cavalry went slowly on until we were within two or three hundred yards of the enemy, when we gave them about twenty rounds of grape, killing great numbers of them. We then charged and cut up a great many more. I had a narrow escape in this action, for my horse was killed under me by a spear thrust through his heart, and the enemy was about to give me the same treatment, as I lay pinned down beneath my charger, when the Brigadier cut him down. I rode my adversary's horse back to camp, though I was a good deal shaken by the fall. This, with one or two men wounded, and some horses killed, were our only casualties.

Holkar, finding that we now had leisure to attend to him properly, made towards Jeypore; and we crossed the river Chumlah near Daulpore, in pursuit of him, but he retired to his old haunts with his colleague Ameer Khan, and we went back to our quarters in Futtypore Seccrah. As everything now looked peaceful, and there was hardly a sound man in my regiment, it was thought that both officers and men deserved some rest. They had been twenty-four years in India, and borne the weight of all Lord Lake's conquests, as well as those on the coast, and were literally cut to pieces. When I was with the regiment in 1805, I believe that Lieutenant Montgomery, and Quarter-Master Hopkins, were the only persons remaining of the original corps. So we now embarked for Calcutta, and I went ahead in charge of the invalids. They were in a terrible condition, many without arms or legs, some so dreadfully disfigured that they seemed hardly human. Many died. My wounds by the blessing of Providence continued to heal, but I had the most excruciating headaches and dizziness from the one on my forehead. The terrible memory of what I had seen at our last storming of the breach haunted me continually and gave me such hideous nightmares that I could not sleep. Even the single report of a gun would startle me most dreadfully. But with care, a good constitution, and keeping clear of drink, I soon recovered, though the wound in my forehead has permanently injured my sight. Twelve splinters of bone came away from the upper part of it, leaving the skull so thin that if you touch it you can feel the pulsation like the pendulum of a clock. To this day the place swells on any change of weather, or variation in the atmosphere, so that my wounds are a pretty sure weather glass.

9

Gay Doings and an Odd Duel in Wakefield

We were given a splendid welcome in Calcutta. Every house was open to us, and every table groaned with hospitality, to which we were invited with the most pressing warmth. Everybody wanted to hear about the war, and it was considered ill-natured not to fight all one's battles over again as often as asked. But our stay in the city was short, for we were bound for home. We embarked at Balloh Ghaut on small sloops, which in three days ferried us down to our transport, the *Lord Duncan,* Captain Bradford, in safety. There were a great many passengers on board, and about two hundred invalids under the command of my old patron Captain Lindsay. Two days afterward we said goodbye to India, all of us leaving dear friends behind. We were then at war with France, and their cruisers kept a close watch on the Indian Ocean. Our fleet consisted of thirteen first-rate Indiamen, convoyed by the *Tremendous* and the *Hindoostan*, both seventy-fours. We sailed in two lines, headed by the men-of-war. Everything was done with order and discipline, and we thought ourselves a match for any French ship we might meet. With such good arrangements, and fine weather, the voyage went very smoothly. There was gun drill once a week, and a constant lookout was kept for the enemy. Early one morning, when we were off the coast of Madagascar, we saw a ship standing right down on us. As it was a single vessel we thought it must be one of our cruisers from the Cape of Good Hope, but when she was within a mile and a half of us she failed to answer our signals, and ran for the land which was to the windward of us. As the *Tremendous* was a good sailer she went in chase, and the Frenchman learned what he had run into. He had no doubt taken us for a French fleet which was known to be in those waters, and trusted to his speed to get away should he be mistaken. But our Commodore overhauled him, hand over hand, tack, twist and turn as he might. Still, he had another trick in store. He shortened sail, and waited until the Englishman was within pistol shot. The Commodore, thinking that the enemy was about to strike, did not wish to injure her and held his fire. The Frenchman suddenly gave the *Tremendous* a terrific broadside, and left her so disabled that she was little better than a log upon the water, while he put up his helm and made off. The Commodore however managed to get his guns to bear, and nearly tore her out of the water, but not so as to stop her getting away, for with the *Tremendous* disabled she was the fastest ship in sight. We were all greatly mortified by this affair, all of us except Captain Brusée, a French prisoner of war, who happened to be on our ship, and who positively danced with delight. It was all very well for him, but certainly was not a pleasure for an Englishman.

The following day we were overtaken by a terrific hurricane, which blew for two days without a pause. During the course of it the *Lady Castlereagh* seemed certain to be lost. She was about a quarter of a mile from us, and we watched her as she heeled over so violently that at one time we could see the whole of her keel. There was a shout of horror from all of us at the sight of it, and our Captain said that she would never right herself. But the next wave brought her up, and though she rolled, and pitched, and laboured dreadfully she kept afloat. Some of her masts were carried away, but which I do not now recollect. She was the only vessel in the fleet to suffer much damage. Three of our ships separated from the rest of us, and we feared lest they should fall into the hands of the French, but they turned up at St Helena the day after we arrived. They had sighted the French fleet the night after the duel between the *Tremendous* and *Le Cannonier*, which turned out to have been a sixty-four from the Isle of France, which was so badly damaged in her encounter that she put into Simon's Bay not knowing that it was once more in the hands of the English, though she managed to get clear as soon as she found out. Our ships got away from the French in the dark, or they would certainly have been taken, for there were five or six sail of the enemy. Governor Brooke gave us a splendid reception at St Helena, but we only stayed eight or ten days and then left for home.

We arrived in England some time in October 1807, landing at Long Reach, and going from there to Dartford in Kent. From that place I marched my invalids, or rather had them carried, to Chelsea Hospital. The journey took us three full days. On the fourth we reached our destination, where I made my report to the Commandant of Chelsea and returned to my regiment at Dartford. We stayed there a few days, being treated with the greatest kindness by the gentlemen of that town, and neighbourhood. From there we moved to Nottingham, and I got leave to go home.

My primary object in coming to England was the hope of seeing my father, but I also looked forward eagerly to telling my adventures to all who knew me. The coach, which was to carry me to Saxmundham, had not gone many miles when something happened which was so odd that I might be accused of inventing it, though I solemnly declare it to be true. A pilot from Aldborough, who sat next to me in the coach, suddenly said, "Sir, you have such an extraordinary resemblance to a person I once knew that I think you must be his son." The words "once knew" seemed so ominous, that it was a minute or two before I could ask the name of the person he referred to. "Shipp," he replied. "Is he then dead, Sir?" I asked, though I was convinced that it was my father he spoke of. "I regret to say that he is," he replied, with obvious sympathy. "You must be his son John. I thought I could not be mistaken." The coach stopped to change horses, and leaving the passengers to sup by themselves, I took a solitary walk to wrestle with my grief and disappointment. I had left India at a great sacrifice to my prospects. There were all my friends and all my interest. I might have made a very advantageous exchange, and stayed on in the country, but I was irresistibly drawn to England by the wish to meet my father, whom I had not seen since infancy. Now I heard in this strange and sudden manner of his death.[1] But not to dwell on this too long, I was still determined to go on to Saxmundham. There I found my father's two brothers, and my mother's sister, and with her I spent a most happy fortnight. I will not weary the reader by telling him of all the changes that had taken place, or of the congratulations which poured in upon me.

GAY DOINGS AND AN ODD DUEL

After I had rejoined my regiment at Nottingham, which I soon did, I was ordered to Wakefield, in Yorkshire, on a recruiting trip. The town was very gay, and for some time I was the only officer in the place, so there was nothing but invitations to dinners, balls, and suppers. To tell the truth I rather thought myself somebody, which perhaps was true as I was now in a grenadier company. While I was there I was called upon to act as second in a duel, between a little military officer and a hulking great civilian. The quarrel arose at a ball in the town, where a very pretty girl, with whom the tall gentleman was in love, and wished to keep to himself, was none-the-less happy to dance with the dashing little warrior who, though small, was a dapper, good-looking little fellow. This preference for the soldier so irritated the huge civilian that he determined to pick a quarrel. He found himself a partner, and as soon as the dance began contrived to stamp on the little officer's toes. In dancing down a second time he played the same trick again. The soldier did not think it much of a joke to have a fat gentleman of six-foot-three on his toes twice, in a few minutes, but as the civilian apologized profusely each time, he thought it best to let the matter go. His little rustic beauty, who understood what was happening better than he did, and had watched more closely, whispered to him, "A pointed insult, Sir." This aroused the little man's wrath in an instant, and just as the toe-treading swain was coming down a third time to repeat the trick, he jumped onto a chair, and from that onto the back of his adversary, and then reached round and tweaked his nose most unmercifully until he cried for help. The master of ceremonies separated them at last, but of course a challenge was the result of this ridiculous incident, and, as the insult was given in the presence of practically the whole town, the civilian was compelled to fight or quit society.

Mortal combat was arranged for the next morning. The seconds decided that the combatants should be placed back to back, each man was then to advance six paces, turn and fire at the same instant, on the signal. The parties met punctually at the appointed spot, and were duly placed back to back. In courage they were as disproportionate as in size, for my little man was cool as a cucumber, and seeing his opponent's fright said to me, just loud enough for the other to hear, "Where shall I hit him, Shipp? Shall I wing him?" On hearing this the big man's knees, which were knocking already, became quite furious in their trembling. When his second gave him the pistol, he was so stupefied by fear that he grasped it by the muzzle, as if it were something strange to him, a mistake which I duly rectified for I love fair-play. The word was given to march. Away went long-legs, covering at least three yards at each stride. If we had let him go on like that one of them might as well have shot from the top of St Paul's and the other from Table Mountain, so we saved him trouble by measuring twelve paces. The signal to fire having been given the little man's ball cut through the collar of his terrified opponent's coat, while the big man nearly shot his own toes off. He was crouched down, and trembling to such an extent that we thought he would fall flat at any moment. His second tried to encourage him saying, cheerfully, "Come, Sir, we must have another shot." "I will see you damned first," his principal replied, throwing down his pistol. "He has put a ball through my coat already. Next time it may be where the tailor can't mend it. I am perfectly satisfied. Good morning!" And off he went at a good round pace, much to our amusement, and that of the country bumpkins who were grinning at the whole business from behind a hedge nearby, and who roared at my man, "Well done little un. Well done robin redbreast." The result of this affair was that the big gentleman lost his honour, as well as his lady love, and had many a song made about him in those parts for years after.

But the life I was living at Wakefield was expensive, and I was spending more than my income. This, added to the loss of fifty pounds of which I was robbed by my servant, and the tricks of a designing Sergeant, ran me into debt.[2] There was nothing for it but to apply for permission to sell my commission, which was granted in consideration of my former services. I paid every shilling of what I owed, and with what was left went down to London where, in six months, I found myself without a home, without a friend, and without a penny. In this condition I turned to the army again. There seemed no earthly reason why I should not rise in that profession again, as I had risen before. So I enlisted at Westminster in His Majesty's 24th Dragoons, and a few days after left with the Recruiting Sergeant for the cavalry depot at Maidstone then commanded by Major-General George Hay. I had not been there long before I was recognized by an officer who had known me in India, who told my story to the Commander-in-Chief, and I was made a Sergeant. After three months at the depot we were ordered to India, and embarked on the *New Warren Hastings*, Captain Larkins, and sailed from Spithead on the 8th of January, 1808. I was then Acting Quarter-Master.

We met with such a terrific gale in the channel that we were obliged to run for Torbay, where we brought up near the place where the East Indiaman, *Abergaveny*, was lost. Close by lay a ship of war, from which a boat with an officer and six men put off, at the imminent hazard of their lives. But they reached us in safety, and ordered us in the most authoritative tones to throw out a rope. There was a general whispering among the tars, who were clustered at the leeward side. "Start me but it looks like a press," said one. "So it does!" said another. The officer in charge, who was no bigger than a "Quaker"[3] with a sword as long as himself, came up the side in an instant, and sweeping off his vast cocked hat saluted the quarter deck, and approaching the Captain, demanded, with the authority of an Admiral of the Red at least, to see the ship's books. It was ludicrous to watch the sailors as they twisted up their features, and contorted their limbs, in the effort to appear as decrepit as possible. The Captain argued, pointed out that the ship might go ashore at any moment, that she was already dragging both anchors, that there were many lives, and a vast amount of property, in danger, but it was no use; the little officer was set on obeying his orders, and walked off with six of our best seamen. This doubled the danger we were in, for these were the ablest hands in the ship. Whether all this was justified I know not, but it seemed sadly against the principles of humanity. But, fortunately for us, the storm died down and next morning early we were on our way. The vessel was uninjured, and sailed well, but the voyage was long and tedious, and made hell for the troops by the conduct of our Commanding Officer. He is dead now, so I will not mention his name, or detail his conduct which I have long tried to forget. It is enough to say that the cat-o-nine-tails was for ever at work, until Captain Larkins interfered and stopped it; saying that he would not have his quarter deck turned into a slaughter house, or the ladies disgusted every time they came on deck with the bloody back of some poor screaming soldier.[4]

The sight of birds, and a distant line on the horizon, cheered us with the thought that we were getting close to land. But the wind was contrary, and night was falling, so we were obliged to stand out to sea again in order to escape the dangerous currents of that coast. The next morning was dark and hazy, but the weather cleared about ten, the sun shone brightly, and the birds were once more flying out from land. All the passengers were now on deck, some admiring the scenery, others whispering sad farewells, but all anxious to disembark. Every sail was set to carry the ship safely into the river by nightfall. Nothing could seem more perfect; the wind fair, the sky cloudless, except for some little white puffs which danced above us. Suddenly a terrific force threw the ship on her beam ends, the gunwale was underwater, and the passengers hurled about the deck. The crew had to struggle frantically to keep her afloat. All on board were aghast. Every sail had been stripped from the masts by the fury of the blow, except the mizzen, and that was much injured. In that one moment all our delight at nearing the end of our voyage was swept away, as the ship wallowed, helpless and stricken, upon the water. Immediately the crew were set to work to clear the wreckage, and the hold was sounded to see if any water was coming in, for it was feared that we had struck a rock. But on trying the pumps the ship was found to be quite dry, and it was decided that we must have been hit by what they call in those seas "a white squall." These come on suddenly, and though short, are so destructive that no vessel under full sail can stand against them. They are most frequent when there are those pretty little puffs of white cloud about, and some think that they contain them. Certainly they hover above the ship, as if waiting to catch the seaman off his guard.

We were forced to stand away from shore while the wreckage was cleared up, but we were soon able to turn back towards land again.

It changed to a rainy, hazy, day but to our joy we discovered a sail nearing us in the mirk, and found it to be the Calcutta pilot come to take us in. Our main top mast was too damaged to bear sail, and had to be put in splints, and as the wind blew strongly we anchored for the night, though the weather had brightened up by then. The next morning we found that we were so close to shore that we could see people walking on the beach, and houses in the distance. We had a good deal of trouble in getting in to Saugar, and at one time were so close to the breakers that we expected to be cast ashore every minute. Indeed, at one time, we shipped such a tremendous sea that it swept over the poop and into the cabin, carrying boxes, and beds, and everything before it. I was on deck at the time, and the ship trembled so much beneath me that I was certain we had run aground, in fact I think we must have done, but we suffered no harm except for the soaking of a few boxes and beds. There was another extraordinary incident at the end of this strange voyage. As we went into Saugar, Captain Larkins was standing on the poop, looking through his glass at the shipping in the harbour. I was standing close by him, and suddenly heard him say, "Surely I know that ship. My eyes can't deceive me. It's my old ship, the *Warren Hastings*." The pilot was asked to take us close up. The Captain got out his long range speaking trumpet, and bellowed, "What ship ahoy?" "The *Warren Hastings*," came the answer, "What ship are you?" "The *New Warren Hastings*," was the reply.[5] The shouts of the crew were deafening. The Captain could not utter another syllable. He was completely overcome at meeting his old ship again, which he had manfully defended against a Frenchman but lost in the end, and which had now been retaken by some of our cruisers. The rest of us were almost as excited as he was, at so odd and happy a meeting.

Our ship anchored a little above Saugar, and we were embarked on sloops to sail up the Hoogley, which took us above a week. We stayed at Fort William another week, while boats were got ready to take us up the Ganges to our respective regiments, and we thoroughly enjoyed ourselves during that time. The rainy season was just beginning when we left Calcutta. My party was under the command of Colonel Wade,[6] and our destination was Cawnpore, which we reached in about three months with the loss of seven or eight drowned, and a few who died from eating unripe fruit.

10

In the Ranks Once More but Start to Climb Again

On the day before we reached Cawnpore, Colonel Wade sent for me and gave me a handsome letter of recommendation couched in the strongest terms. On the next evening we marched to the tents which had been pitched for our reception, and found two officers of our regiment waiting to receive us, one of whom I had often dined with in the days when I myself held a commission. Here we were refitted, and started on the road to Meerut which was about three hundred miles away. We were commanded by two gentlemen who took the greatest care of their men, and I do not know that I ever spent a happier time. The march was always over by nine o'clock, and then we pitched our tents for the remainder of the day under some shady and often scented trees. This pleasant journey came to an end on the 9th of November, 1809, when we reached Meerut, having been eleven months and one day on the route from England. As soon as I arrived I was warmly welcomed by all my old comrades, and was made a full Sergeant in Captain Beattie's troop. I was kindly received by the officers, and in fact by everybody, except one or two Corporals whose hopes of promotion had been upset by my arrival. With them I was certainly in no great favour, and one or two attempts were made to try my courage, but I knew my rank too well to let myself be imposed upon or annoyed. As soon as they found this out they forgot their grievances.

We were inspected on arrival by the Commanding Officer now Major-General Need, who called me on one side and said, "I am much grieved to see you in your present situation after all the laurels you have gained in India, but I feel pleasure in being able to promote you to the rank of Sergeant, and be assured if you behave well I shall not lose sight of you." Once more I had to go through the regular drills, both on foot and on horseback, like a raw recruit, but as I knew them well already I was soon dismissed. Before a year was over a Colonel I knew, who had the command of a regiment of the Company's Native Cavalry, offered me the post of riding master which was equal to being an Ensign. I was elated with the idea. It was a situation I fancied above all others, so I dressed myself up in my best, and marched off with the Colonel's invitation in my hand to ask my own Commanding Officer's leave to accept the post. Considering how often he had professed an interest in my welfare, there was not the least doubt in my mind that he would consent. I presented my letter, and asked his permission to accept the offer. He read it, paused, knotted his dark eyebrows, and made his displeasure so plain that I reviewed my misdemeanours but could think of nothing in which I had offended him. To my surprise and mortification he gave me back the letter, saying brusquely, "I shall not recommend you for any such thing," and turned away to leave the room. I ventured to remonstrate on his cruelty in denying me the chance of such a respectable situation, and asked him if he felt me unworthy of it or if I had displeased him in anything. He said, "No, but don't you think I like good men in my regiment as well as Colonel K——? Besides, what am I to do for a Sergeant-Major if you leave the regiment, or an Adjutant if anything should happen to those we have?" This seemed an odd remark to me, for both of them were younger than I was, and bursting with health. I was bitterly hurt, and could not help saying so, and we parted in enmity. That was the death blow to my present hopes. I made what excuses I could to the Colonel who had offered me the post, and as I was soon made Drill-Corporal, and then Drill-Sergeant, I had something else to think about. The job of Drill-Sergeant was one I liked, and as it was preparatory to that of Sergeant-Major it was all the more agreeable. It is better to drill than be drilled any day, but the duties were very laborious.

I went on tolerably well with the hard work of my office when, one fine morning, the news went through the lines that the Sergeant-Major was dead in hospital. Everybody thought I was certain to get this post, and I was congratulated on all sides. Every minute I expected to be sent for by the Commanding Officer. In fact, I was so sure of it myself, that I ordered my traps to be got ready for a move, when lo and behold another Sergeant got the promotion and I was left to be the butt of the whole corps. It was impossible to imagine the reason for this strange appointment. I say strange, because it had been promised to me, and the man who got it was as unfit for the work as he could be. I was hurt beyond words, but too proud to ask for an explanation, so I put up with things as well as I could, fagged away at the drill, and perhaps took a little of my disappointment out on the poor fellows under me, for I had them out early and late. I mentioned what had happened to my Captain, and told him that I would resign all my stripes, but he had more sense than his Sergeant, and advised me to keep quiet; saying that no doubt the Colonel had something better in store for me. This soothed me a little, and I tried to make myself a better Drill-Sergeant, and in a little while the incident faded away. None the less I always avoided the Colonel if I could, and when I had to meet him saluted formally, but with enough black looks to let him know the state of my gratitude.

And so I went on, chewing the cud of disappointment, when one morning, as I was going down a narrow lane brooding gloomily on all possible reasons why I had been passed over, rounding a corner I ran straight into the Colonel. I gave him a most formal salute, one which was as stiff as my feelings towards him; and with a very black look passed on with one eye over my shoulder, turning round completely as soon as I had got by to have a good look at him. Much to my surprise he had done the same thing. We were now face to face, and as retreat would have been unsoldier-like I went towards him, making as if I was going back to the barracks. As I passed him I saluted again, a little more smoothly this time, hoping that because of this amendment in my behaviour he would speak to me, for I had a speech ready for him as long as my sabre. In fact I had hardly got by, when he called, "Halloa! Shipp! Come here." I returned, and saluted more civilly still this time, and was just about to open my battery on him, when he said in a kind, and friendly, way, "Well, Shipp. How do you get on?" Here was a pretty preface to my intended speech. I stood at attention, knowing the respect due to my Commanding Officer, and replied, "I get on badly, Sir." "How is that?" he asked. I said that I had but little encouragement to get on well, seeing that he had passed me over for promotion. "Why then," said he, "did you not come and ask me for it?" This nettled me, and I replied, no doubt impetuously, that if he did not think me worthy of it unsolicited I would never ask for it. This did not please him, and he replied shortly, "Then you will never get it." I gave him another salute, bordering on impudence, and was just in the act of facing about, when he turned his displeasure into kindness again, and said, "Stop, Sergeant! Suppose I have something better for you than what I have taken from you, and which you did not think worth soliciting?" There was a note of inquiry in his voice, and I answered that all my prospects in life depended on his friendship for me, and if he withheld that I had nothing to hope for. He answered, "My good will and friendship you have, but you must get rid of your impetuosity of temper. Go home and keep quiet." That was just the balm I wanted to calm and soothe me, for what with my disappointment, and the trouble I had with obstinate young soldiers and drunken old ones, my patience was worn out, and all that bellowing at drills had made my voice as loud as a church organ. But whatever state of mind I was in I never failed in respect to my superior officers, or in my duty, knowing that neglect there would lose me everything. I was always first on parade and last off, and had risen through all the ranks from Lance-Corporal to Troop Sergeant-Major without once being confined or reprimanded by a superior officer.

In the year 1813 another Regimental Sergeant-Major stepped backward into his grave, but I still could not bring myself to beg the Commanding Officer for his post, though I saw several other Sergeants running for it. However, I kept myself at home properly dressed, and expected every minute to be sent for by the Colonel who, I thought, would surely never pass me over again. Here I waited, looking out of the barrack window for the messenger who did not come. I began to think that for a second time somebody else had robbed me. Pride said, "Don't go!" Self-interest answered, "Go, or you will get nothing." And pride won the day. That evening I was early at drill, and going through the usual evolutions, when the Adjutant rode up and said abruptly, "Why don't you go and ask the Commanding Officer for the vacancy?" "Sir," I answered, "I would think myself unworthy of the situation if I had to beg or cringe for it. If my Commanding Officer thinks me fit for it he will give it me, and if he shows me that kindness he can rely on me performing the duties to the best of my power, and showing my gratitude that way, but ask for it I never can." After this fine speech I went on with my drill. The Adjutant paused a few seconds, and then said, "Well if you are too proud to ask for it I am not," and galloped off. In a quarter of an hour he was back and said, "You are appointed Sergeant-Major." I thanked him warmly, and promised that he would never regret his kindness. He replied, "Shipp, I admire your proper spirit in not begging for the post and the Commanding Officer does not think any the worse of you either. You will move into the Sergeant-Major's bungalow immediately and take up his duties. I need not tell you what they are." The next morning I moved into my new house, and published my appointment.

Now all my cares were forgotten. The very idea of having the whole regiment under me at drill was delightful, and I looked forward to it as the height of military glory. As the basis for all success in my new post, I established a proper distance between my rank and that of all the other non-commissioned officers; giving them all the respect due to them, but emphasizing that they must keep a proper distance between themselves and the private soldiers. I let them know that I must have prompt obedience from them, and that they must have the same from those under them. They thought that this was pride at first, but they soon saw the point of it and obeyed with pleasure; those who did not were removed, and more amenable people promoted in their place. So things went on smoothly, and pleasantly. I could leave them to do their duty with confidence, and they soon found how far they could go with me. Over me was a strict and vigilant Adjutant, and he made a strict and vigilant Sergeant-Major. I made good non-commissioned officers, and they made good privates. So discipline and goodwill went hand in hand. My situation was a respectable one, and what was equally pleasant, profitable as well. I had as many titles as a peer of the realm. J. Shipp, R.S.M—Regimental Sergeant-Major, J. Shipp, G.K.—Gaol Keeper. J. Shipp, U.T.—Undertaker. J. Shipp, L.M.—Log Maker. The perquisites of all these posts brought me in a good income. I was respected by the officers and loved by the men, and scarcely had a wish ungratified.

All the year round there were pretty much the same people in the Congee House. One fine young fellow was never off my gaol book. The minute he was out he was in the guard room again, and from there to his old abode. I once asked him how he could put up with that sort of thing, month after month, and he answered, "Habit is second nature. In gaol I can be alone and brood over my melancholy career." He concluded in a most pathetic manner. "Sergeant-Major I have never done any good since your predecessor got me flogged. I have tried all I can to forget it, but I cannot. It crushes me to the ground. That day's work has ruined me. I am of a good family, but I never will go back to disgrace them by these scars on my back." He died about three months afterward, in a sad state of drunkenness. But life had its humorous side as well. Twice a day I visited the Congee House with the Orderly Officer. He was famous for his keen nose, and could smell a cigar a mile off. In going round the yard, which is enclosed by a tremendously high wall, he found a large beef bone, recently dropped. The Sergeant was asked to account for this suspicious object, but he was a shrewd fellow and said, without turning a hair, "The pelicans must have dropped it, Sir." This was not unlikely, for those birds will carry enormous bones, and when fighting over them drop them sometimes, and that might have happened in this case. We had not gone much further round when the officer spotted a bundle of cigars, which he picked up, and with a knowing look, said, "Sergeant what luxurious dogs these pelicans are! We have seen beef, pork, and mutton bones, and now a bundle of cigars. I shouldn't be surprised if we come across a bottle of brandy next." Even the Sergeant had no answer to that, but the truth was obvious enough. All the stuff had been thrown over the wall for the prisoners by some of their friends. They were not punished in any way,

Calcutta from the Esplanade

though the Sergeant was severely admonished for neglect of duty.

Those pelicans were extraordinary birds. The minute the dinner trumpet sounded flocks of them gathered round the barrack doors, waiting for anything the soldiers might throw them. No matter how many times they were tricked, they still came. Some of the more mischievous boys would tie two large bones together, with a length of string. One bird would pick up one bone, and another the other. Then, with the bones in their crops, they would soar round and round the barracks; pulling and tugging at one another, attended by a flock of crows and kites which would peck and harry them unmercifully. Sometimes, to add to the fun, a boy would tie a large piece of rag, or a paper kite, to a bone with a long piece of string. A pelican having swallowed the bone, would fly round with the rag or the kite trailing behind him, and hundreds of his own tribe after him as well, in the hopes that he would throw up the bone, which these birds can do very easily. By and by, the whole crowd, whirling and squabbling, would be lost in the distance, but the same gentleman would be back again next day and probably with a bit of the string still hanging from him. Pelicans grow so tame that they will eat out of your hand. At night they roost on the roof of the barracks, or in near-by trees. Early in the morning they pay their respects to the riverside, in search of any dead bodies which may have been washed ashore, and it is a most horrible sight to see these ravenous creatures, with hundreds of huge vultures, tearing some corpse to pieces. If you live on the banks of the Ganges it is common enough to see crows, kites and vultures riding down the river on the bloated remains of some poor soul, and feeding on it as they sail along. The reason is obvious. Hindoos who can afford it burn their dead, but the poor just scorch the hair off the body, and then commit it to Holy Gunga, as they call the Ganges.

I was walking one day along the bank of that river, when I saw a group of people sitting together, and mumbling among themselves. Near-by was a corpse, wrapped in a white sheet with its feet in the water. A few minutes later a young man of about twenty shouldered the body, and walking slowly to a high bank pitched it into the stream as if it were a log of wood. He then plunged in after it and took away the winding sheet, leaving the dead to float down the river stark naked. When he got back I asked him who it was that he had thrown away like that, and he answered, with a kind of grin, "My wife." I said, "You don't seem very sorry about her." "No," he said, "it was God's pleasure." I asked him how old she was, and he said, "Thirteen years." I then inquired if he had any family, "Not now," he said, "but she had one, a little girl. The Gunga got her yesterday." I asked him how long his wife had been dead, and he said that she died just as I came up. The father and mother of the poor girl were both there, and seemed as indifferent as the rocks on which they squatted to watch her float away, down that sad stream which is the only grave of millions.

II

I Fall in Love and Become an Ensign in the Old Fogs

As I now had a good home and a satisfactory income, I began to look around for a wife to share my fortunes. For some time I had been intimately acquainted with a most respectable family, the father of which was a Conductor[1] to the commissariat department. He had three daughters, whom he took great pains to bring up well, and who were in every way a credit to him, for their home was a place full of domestic comfort and affection. I fell in love with the eldest of these three daughters, and asked permission to marry her, which was granted on condition that the marriage should not take place for a couple of years, as she was very young. Meanwhile we could make preparation for our future happiness. And so things went on, until my good friend the Colonel, for so he had proved himself to be, was promoted Major-General and said goodbye to the 24th Dragoons, a regiment in which he had been both respected and loved. Scarcely had he gone before I drew up a short memorial to the Marquis of Hastings, then Governor-General of India, which my new Commanding Officer, Lieutenant-Colonel Philpot, immediately sent to headquarters in Calcutta with a handsome supporting letter from himself. When I first showed him the memorial he said, "Shipp, I am glad you have done this. I was speaking to your friend, Major Covell, yesterday about you. I will send it on with pleasure, and hope you may succeed." About twenty days after this I was sent for in a great hurry to the riding school, where the Colonel was looking at some young stud horses. When I went in he was standing with his back to the riding school door, so I waited at a little distance. The Adjutant said, "Here is the Sergeant-Major." The Colonel came straight up to me, took me by the arm and led me from the school. As soon as we were out of sight he pulled out a letter, and I shall never forget his delight as he shook me by the hand and said, "Shipp, I sincerely congratulate you on your appointment. The Marquis of Hastings has been pleased to meet your wishes, and mine. You have been given an Ensigncy in His Majesty's 87th Regiment, and are ordered to join that corps immediately. But promise me to keep the affair secret until tomorrow, or I shall be teased out of my life for your appointment. If it were not for that I would ask you to dine with me today, but I shall have that pleasure another time." I thanked him most sincerely, then he gave me the letter and went to his horses again, and I to evening parade.

When that was over I went down to see the girl I was engaged to, so that I could tell her and her family my good news. On the way down a most curious feeling came over me. So far from being elated, as I should have been, I felt depressed and miserable. This mood took possession of me so completely, that I reached the house before I was aware that I was even getting near to it. In fact I would have passed her father by, if he had not called out as usual, "Ah, John, is that you? How are you?" His voice roused me from my reverie, and putting on an air I said, "Come, Sir, be a little more respectful to your superior officer, or you will find yourself in the Congee House," and in high spirits again, burst into laughter. The old gentleman did not know what to make of this, but had some sort of an idea that I might be drunk, so he said, "What is the matter, John? You are not yourself tonight." I took him by the arm and walked with him to the house, telling him on the way of my good luck. When he heard of it he said, a little sadly, "So I suppose you will break off your match with my poor Ann. You will look higher now." I contradicted him warmly, saying that he was mistaken, and that having won the affection of a woman I would not forsake her, and that in fact I was on the way to assure her of my unalterable love. He gave me his hand and we went into the house together, where all the family were seated round the table at work, as was usual with them in the evening.

As soon as we got inside, the father jokingly called to the family, "Mrs H and girls, allow me to introduce to you Ensign John Shipp, of the Horse Marines, I mean of His

Majesty's Own Irish Regiment of Foot." I made the most elaborate bow I could think of, in honour of my new commission and the corps to which I was appointed. This only set the children laughing, and the youngest had the impudence to say, "He an Ensign! So's my cat," and started dancing her kitten round the table on his hind legs, and calling him Ensign Shipp. Sitting down beside my future bride I told her what had happened, but instead of being glad she turned pale and depressed, and at last said, slowly, "I am sorry for it. I suppose you won't want to marry a Conductor's daughter now." This made me angrier than I had ever been with her before. "What the devil do you take me for, man or beast? No, no, Ann, have a better opinion of me than that." We clasped hands in unalterable affection, and she burst into tears. Just to cheer things up a little, I pretended to give the child with the cat a tremendous scolding for her impudence, but remembering that I had seen less sagacious animals holding commissions, I kissed her and forgave her. The next day I had my hair cut à la Ensign, and ordered my new regimentals. On the third day I dined in the mess of my old corps, who overwhelmed me with kindness. Invitations flooded in, and much of my time was taken up in making excuses. The generosity with which I was treated by the 24th is something that I shall never forget.

I left Cawnpore for Dinapore on the 1st of January, 1816, having arranged to marry as soon as I was settled in my regiment. It took me five days to cover the four hundred miles to my new quarters. I arrived on the 5th, and went to report my presence to my Commanding Officer. After wandering about the station for some time, without seeing a single European, I ran into an old, half-drunken, Irish woman, and asked her if she could tell me where I could find the 87th Regiment. "What! The old Fogs?"[2] said she. "Fogs?", I said. "No, I mean the 87th Regiment." "Is it making fun of me you are?" "No, my good woman," I said, "I just want to find out where the 87th are." "Sure they have gone away these three days," she replied. "Gone?" I said with surprise, "Where?" "Faith! To fight against Paul." "Paul? Who the devil is he?" She took this very badly, and squared up to me as if she was going to fight, but I assured her that I was an officer of the 87th, and seeking the regiment. She burst into a horse-laugh, and slapping her legs shouted, "You an officer of the old Fogs! None of your blarney Honey." "You can laugh," I said, "but I am an officer of the old Fogs, as you call them, and I have come to join them." "Then," said she, "you could have saved yourself the trouble, Joy, for devil a one is here, except the Quarter-Master and I couldn't find him this morning. But does Your Honour really belong to the old Fogaboloughs?" I pledged my word that I did, and she took my hand in her brawny paw saying, "Give us your daddle, Your Honour. Sure I am always glad to see any of the old corps here." She showed every sign of kissing me, but I warded her off, so she started praising the regiment. "There is devil a better corps in a day's march. They are a credit to Your Honour. Och! They are the boys for fighting." Here she hauled her petticoats up to her knees, and started capering about with the skill of a dancing master. When she had pretty well winded herself she seized my hand again, and asked for something to drink my health, and the health of the regiment. I told her that if she could let me know where I could find anybody belonging to the regiment I would give her something. "Thank Your Honour," she said. "Sure then, the Adjutant and Captain Bell are both left behind." "The Adjutant here?" I said in some surprise. "Is he sick, or here on duty?" "Neither, Your Honour. He is as snug as a bug in his own room, and a prisoner besides. There has been a mighty hubbub between him and that same Captain Bell." I asked what had been the matter. "Murder is the matter. Bloody murder, Your Honour. There is no end to the murders in this regiment." "What! have they been fighting?" I said, meaning had there been a duel. "Fighting sure enough." "Is the Captain a prisoner as well?" "Snug enough, Joy." "Well, will you be kind enough to show me where the Adjutant's quarters are?" "To be sure Honey, he lives just over against the corner house, by the side of the chapel, and forenent the main guard room. Anybody will show you that knows." Finding that I should never get any intelligible directions out of her, and that the more she tried to explain the more muddled she got, I gave her a rupee and took my leave, with her calling after me, "God bless Your Honour!

May Your Honour never die till the side of an old house falls on you, and kills you.''

After parting with this pretty specimen of my new regiment I found the Adjutant's quarters, where the soldier on duty outside his door told me that he had just gone out. But he was back in about five minutes, and gave me a hearty welcome and a good breakfast, and I stayed with him for the two days that I was at the station. From him I learned that the regiment had gone out, two days before, against the Nepaulese.[3] This news delighted me, although I had not got a single thing prepared for such a campaign, and it was very unlikely that I would get any, for the whole countryside had been drained to supply the army. However, in two days I was ready as far as transport was concerned, but I could not, by any possibility, get a tent; so I was obliged to make one something like that which English gypsies use, out of an Indian cotton carpet. Thus provided I set out to join the old Fogs, who were ahead of me some five marches. The first day I covered a distance equal to two days' march for the regiment. The next I covered two more, and stayed the night with an indigo planter of Tirhoot, who treated me handsomely, for their liberality is proverbial. I sent on my things the next morning with orders to carry them twenty miles, and to go on for another twenty if I did not reach them that night. All that day I spent with my liberal host the planter, and after a hearty breakfast set out next morning on horseback, my host having provided relays for me along the road. I overtook my things about two miles from their destination, and stayed that night at another indigo planter's house.

Here I met a young officer who was on his way to join the same division, and as it turned out the same regiment. He was very young, and appeared to be quite delicate, utterly unsuited as it seemed to me for such a campaign as we had in prospect. We regaled ourselves there that night, and the next morning went our way. This was the last of the indigo factories on our road, and from there on we were in danger. Caution had to be our watchword, for we were without protection, and the low-lands are notorious for robbery and murder. If we rested during the day we kept to our tents, at night we sheltered in some hut or temple. But neither tent nor mud hut was any safeguard against the desperate thieves of that area; or against the bears, tigers and other wild animals which abounded throughout the district. These creatures were unused to Europeans, and we could not tell how far they would venture for such a delicacy. So safety was the word. On our first march I taught my young friend how to be his own butcher and cook, for I killed and skinned a fine kid, part of which I made into a curry and the rest grilled, both dishes he thoroughly enjoyed. After tea we moved into a village for the night, for there were some very suspicious looking fellows loitering around. It is always wise when travelling like this, to show one's firearms, and to shoot them off at dusk. The dacoits, or low thieves, of India, though desperate rascals, have a great dread of guns, and will seldom molest those who possess them though bold enough otherwise. Often when coming home down the Hoogley at night, or on the Ganges, in a lonely boat, I have got through safely by letting off my pistols at intervals; while others who have neglected these precautions have been robbed, or even murdered, in spite of the police on those two rivers.

The regiment was only twenty miles ahead of us; so we went to bed early, intending to start in time to catch up with them next day. We had not been asleep more than an hour or so, when sounds like the crowing of a cock, and the barking of a dog woke me up. I had been in the country long enough, to know that noises of that sort generally meant that thieves were about. I siezed my pistol, determined to have a shot at anything that might turn up. For a time all was quiet. The hut we were in had two doorways, and we each lay across one. I was awake, but my companion was dozing, when he suddenly sprang up as if a snake had bitten him, and bellowed so that the hut rang, "Who is that?" I leapt up too, and asked what was the matter. He said, "Somebody's hand touched my face." "You must be dreaming," I replied. "No", he answered, "I am sure of it." "Well," I said, "don't be afraid." This nettled him and he said, "I'm not as easily frightened as all that," and I thought he was going to pick a quarrel with me, just to show his courage. However, we lay down again, and I thought to myself we shall see how brave you are by and by my lad. I pretended to be asleep, but soon heard the thieves on the move again, so I stole silently out of bed, and fired both my pistols into the air crying, "Choor! Choor! Choor!" which my companion understood well enough meant, "Thieves! Thieves! Thieves!" Hearing this he made a desperate jump over my bed, and was outside with me in an instant. He afterward confessed that he was most dreadfully frightened. Once more we lay down, but in a little while I felt a hand move softly over my face. I grabbed the fellow, but he was so oiled that he slipped out of my hands like an eel, and though I rushed after him he was gone like a whisper on the breeze. My companion was crying out, "Where are you, Sir? Where are you, Mr Shipp! Don't leave me!," in great alarm, and I must admit that I did not half like it myself. These night thieves go stark naked, oiled from head to foot, and with all their hair shaved off. They must have been very set on robbing us, for it is rare for them to come back after hearing shots. I reloaded my pistols, and said, "Now, Sir, I think we can sleep till morning." "Sleep!," he said, "I don't think I shall sleep again this week." "Nonsense!," I said, "soldiers have to put up with such things, they happen every day. If there was nothing worse than that soldiering would be delightful indeed. The great thing is to keep a good watch, and never to be taken by surprise."

12

A Midnight March through the Mountains of Nepaul

We started betimes the next morning, so as to be with the regiment as soon as possible. It was nine o'clock when we overtook them, and they had just crossed a nullah and halted on the other side. I immediately delivered my credentials to the Acting Adjutant, who took me straight away to the Commanding Officer, Lieutenant-Colonel Miller C.B. He received me very kindly, congratulated me on my appointment, and said that he was pleased to have me in the regiment. All the other officers were equally friendly, and every one of them invited me to breakfast,[1] but I was already engaged to that meal with the Commanding Officer. This generous welcome was the more gratifying because I did not in the least expect it. Officers promoted from the ranks are generally received with some caution, and perhaps a little prejudice, but there was nothing like that with this distinguished regiment. If I had been the son of a Duke I could not have been better treated. It is true that I had some flattering letters of introduction from my last Commanding Officer, but I had not delivered them yet. The welcome I received was wholly spontaneous, and they accepted my young companion just as well. The jacket I had ordered when told to join the corps was widely different from their proper uniform, and I apologized for this to the Colonel at breakfast, but he put me at my ease, saying, "It will do very well for fighting in. We expect pretty hard service."

On the following day the regiment reached the ground on which the army was directed to form, for the arduous campaign in Nepaul during the years 1815 and 1816. We were commanded by Major-General Sir David Ochterlony,[2] a name our Irishmen found hard to their tongues, so it was generally turned into David Malony. The place was called Ammowah. It was about thirty-five miles from the great forest of Nepaul. Behind this wild region were the stockades, and strong forts, of the enemy in the foothills, and in the distance beyond them lay a vast range of loftier mountains still. The army was slow in forming, and though we amused ourselves with hunting, shooting and racing, the time hung heavy on our hands. We were not in this wild country just for sport. We were there to conquer an artful and warlike people, whose triumphs over us the year before had made them overbearing in the extreme. They laughed at any idea of a settlement, and trusted, with good reason, to the almost inaccessible nature of their country; which they had defended still further with fortifications and stockades, on the high hills. Safely behind them they looked down on us with contempt. But our preparations were finished at last, and we began to move into that vast forest which had guarded Nepaul for centuries.

Our advance was slow, but in three days we reached a place called Summarabassah, at the edge of the forest. I was in the rear guard for the final march, and we did not get into camp until late at night, though we only had ten miles to cover. The road was no better than a bog, traversed by deep ravines, with steep banks of clay. We had to get the heavy guns over by using men and drag-ropes; for the bullocks had no footing, and only hurt themselves in the effort to pull. It was three hours from the time we sighted camp till we reached it. The men had begun their march about four o'clock in the morning without breakfast, expecting to arrive at the ground by nine, which was the usual time; instead they were not in until four o'clock in the afternoon, and were half famished. When we at last reached camp we found that in front of it, in a kind of inlet to the forest, stood a large square building two storeys high. It was stone built and tiled, with only one small door for greater safety against robbers and wild beasts. It was said to have been the residence of the collector for these lowlands and valleys. Here we established a strong depot, to serve as a communications post, and where we could leave our heavy, or superfluous, stores in safety. We erected a strong stockade on the forest side, with a wide deep ditch, and embrasures for guns, I forget how many but I believe four.

The following day five of us, Captain Gully, Lieutenants Masterton, Lee and Bowes, with Ensign Shipp, must needs take a morning ride to look at this terrifying forest, the dread of men and the haunt of wild beasts. We had not gone far when we saw several bears near a brook, out for a swim as the weather was warm. Further on we found a path about a yard wide, which we agreed to explore. There was thick undergrowth on either side, and trees of an enormous size. At every hundred yards or so the jungle had been burned back, and great trees felled across the path to keep out intruders. We rode on until it would have been prudent to go no further, but we were still very curious and agreed to venture about another couple of miles. At the end of this distance we were close to the hills, and could see men moving about on them. There was still about another mile of this frightful forest which, a year before, had kept five thousand men at bay. Beyond it was an open space, with large clumps of bamboos, and pebbly ground all round them, which indicated that the area was covered with water in the monsoon. Riding on a little further we saw men run across the road, and decided that it was high time to turn back for our curiosity was satisfied, and we were risking our lives. It was possible that we had been seen, and a detachment might be sent to cut off our retreat. Still, it was too late to repent and so we pushed on back to camp, and arrived safely, thanking our lucky stars. We had gone about thirteen miles, which, doubled by the journey home, made a good morning's ride. In the course of it we must have leapt over at least a hundred large trees. We were severely admonished for this piece of foolhardiness and we deserved to be, still, the information gained was acceptable.

The following day we began our march, taking the road we had so rashly explored. The pioneers went ahead, and soon made a good carriage road of it. We had scarcely any stoppages, and saw not a single one of the enemy. If they had thrown up small stockades across the path we must have lost great numbers of our men, but the supposed inaccessible nature of their mountains made the enemy careless. Soon we were through the forest, and across the pebbly ground referred to. About a mile beyond this there was a small plain, studded with little bushes, at the further end of which the dry ravine took a direction to the left. The scene here was most magnificent; the hills rising like stairs, summit above summit, in beautiful succession, all of them wooded with the most gloriously variegated trees and shrubs. Among them majestic rocks lifted up their heads, as if in proud defiance of the attacker. At the foot of these hills, two strong picquets of the enemy were posted; one of them on a hill to the right, in a house similar to that described at Summarabassah. On our approach they withdrew to the nearby hills without a shot. This silence on the part of a brave, and subtle, foe let us know in plain terms that something was brewing for us. They seemed to be inviting us to advance, and take a look at their beautiful country.

It was necessary to establish a base for supplies here, so the house just spoken of was fortified, and a depot set up, and we waited until this was done. During this pause the Quarter-Master-General's department was busily occupied reconnoitring the surrounding country, but the terrain was so difficult that very little certain information was to be had. At last, when our patience was about worn out with the delay, the Quarter-Master-General announced that the reports his spies had brought in made it seem certain disaster to try and force an entrance at this point. In the direction we had thought of taking there was nothing but stockade upon stockade, fort upon fort. To risk failure at the beginning of a war, against such an enemy, would be to lay the basis of ultimate defeat and destruction. To go on along this route would be like knocking our heads on the rocks, or giving our bodies to fill up the trenches before their stockades. We had more than fifty years dear-bought experience on our side, in the person of an officer seventy years old, who was our guide. The younger men, in all the ardour of youth and inexperience, felt mortified at the information, and would have rushed on to their graves. The wiser men, who had seen more fighting, thought that if, after the information we had, we pushed ourselves into disaster all the opprobium of it would fall on the head of our General, with the consequent displeasure of the government. But we had at our head a Commander with just the right gifts for such a campaign, and he now began to seek a more practicable route.

Everybody eagerly set themselves to find this new road. Some of our spies had been absent two days, and we were getting anxious about them, well knowing the barbarity of the enemy they were among; but they came back and the information they brought was kept so secret that not a whisper of it could be gleaned from the Quarter-Master's department. There were plenty of rumours flying about, but the common opinion was that we should have to give up the campaign, as it was impossible to penetrate the enemy's country. A small ravine branched off from the dry river bed in which our encampment lay, but it looked as if it could lead to nothing better than some gloomy cavern, yet it was down this that our spies returned. The moon had just risen, flooding the countryside with glory, when a whisper of command stole through the quiet. "Prepare to move." One hour later we entered the little ravine, leaving the greater part of the army to guard the standing tents and the baggage. We were equipped as lightly as possible, but had with us elephants carrying two six-pounders. The path lay along the rocky bed of the ravine, down which a small stream tumbled. We could not go faster than one or two hundred yards in an hour, climbing up and down all the while. Sometimes we were hidden at the bottom of a deep pit, at others perched on the top of a great rock, but luckily the sound of the many waterfalls drowned the noise of our approach. The night was cold, but in the brilliant moonlight as bright as midday; not a cloud was to be seen in the sky, which was one sheet of beautiful blue. At the bottom of the deepest hollows, where the light did not fall, we had to grope our way forward in utter darkness. The water there was deep and cold, but even in such places there were sudden glimpses of beauty as, through some abrupt fissure in the rock, we caught sight of the distant landscape filled with moonlight, and looking as if we were watching it through a telescope. If the enemy had been aware of our advance that night they could have annihilated us at any moment, simply by rolling down stones upon us, but they slept on in fancied security.

What with the falling and slipping about we were soon wet

to the skin, but I had the honour of carrying the colours that night, and there was no time for me to think of personal comfort or discomfort. If I bore them through with honour I should be happy. My Covering Sergeant once had the temerity to ask if he could relieve me of the "incumbrance." "Incumbrance!" I replied, indignantly, "how dare you call England's pride an incumbrance! Whoever takes these colours from me in front of the enemy takes my life as well." "I beg pardon, Sir. I did not mean to offend you, or reflect upon the flag under which I have fought and bled." "No, Sergeant. I know you did not," I answered. "But if I were to give it up to you, and you should lose it or be killed, and anything can happen in war, how should I excuse myself to my superiors? It would not be enough to say I gave it to the Sergeant to carry. I should deserve to be hung!" I gave him my little pistol, or brandy flask, and said, "Come! Let us drink prosperity to the flag." He took it, and said in a most impressive manner, "God bless and prosper the old banner, Sir. Before tomorrow morning may you wave it over a conquered foe!" I took a drop myself, and said, "Amen." The young officer who had travelled with me from Dinapore, and was now my friend, had the honour of carrying the other flag, and gloried in the distinction. Though he had many heavy falls, and sprained his thumb badly, he would not give it up.

The march now became slower and slower, and the ups and downs of the road more difficult. In some places huge rocks hung poised above our heads. The increasingly precipitous nature of the path made it certain that we had not much further to go. We were well into the high hills, the last of them in fact being so steep that it was barely accessible. The soles of my boots had long since parted company with the uppers, but I pushed resolutely on. Morning began to break in the blue sky, where the last moonlight still lingered. We halted for a while until broad daylight, and then I could see from my station in the middle of the regiment, the advance guard hauling themselves up that terrific mountainside hand over hand, and from shrub to shrub. We were in a basin, entirely surrounded by high hills. In about a couple of hours the whole of the 87th Regiment, including our gallant general and his suite, climbed this seemingly impossible height. From the top we could see a great distance, and on every hill observed signals passing from one summit to another. We guessed from this that the enemy had learned of our approach. I do not think that they quite knew where we were, but were pretty sure that some of our troops had moved from their old ground. That night proved how valuable a good example is with soldiers, for our gallant General walked every yard of this critical approach with his men encouraging them as he went, and that sort of thing works wonders.

The question now was how to get the guns up, and the powder and shot, but those who are accustomed to war in India are never at loss for an expedient. As soon as all the men were up, except for the rearguard, the pioneers went to work with their pickaxes felling trees and making some sort of a road. The roughest parts of the way were smoothed out, and the trees laid across it for a kind of foothold, and then the elephants were made to approach. The first did so with some reluctance. He looked up, shook his head, and when forced on by his driver trumpeted piteously. There is no doubt that he knew how risky some of the steps were, that had just been made. But after a few of them had been altered a little, he seemed willing to try. The first was a tree which he carefully examined with his trunk, then, tentatively, put on a forefoot and gently eased his weight onto the log. As soon as he was sure of that step he moved on to the next, which happened to be cut out of the rock. He made the same careful examination before trusting it, keeping his flank pressed against the hillside. The next was a tree, which he carefully tested as before but did not like, and refused to budge; though his driver called him, "Wonderful, My Life, My Dear, My Dove, My Son, My Wife," and all those endearing names which elephants delight in. They tried to force him on, and though he roared terrifically he would not move. Some alteration was at last made which satisfied him, so that he went on, and at last reached the top of the mountain. When he got there he was perfectly delighted, caressing his keeper and throwing dirt about in the most playful manner.

The other elephant, a younger one, was now to follow. He

The Old Fort at Muttra

Gateway to the Palace of the Mogul Emperors,
Futtypore

had watched his companion's climb with intense interest, making motions all the while as if he was helping him up, the kind of involuntary gestures which I have seen spectators make at gymnastic games. When he saw his friend at the top he saluted him with tremendous trumpeting. But when his own turn came, he was frightened to death, and would not move at all without force. At the third step he slipped, but recovered himself by digging in his toes. With this exception he went up easily enough. As he got near the top, the one who was already up reached out with his trunk to give him a pull, which the other accepted with his own trunk, and so got safely up. Having both accomplished their task they greeted each other as if they had been separated for years, and had gone through indescribable perils. They embraced each other with great affection, and for a long time stood face to face as if whispering congratulations to each other on having survived their ordeal. Their drivers made them salaam to the General, who gave them five rupees to buy sweetmeats, for which they thanked him by another salaam.

At the top of the ghaut (pass) we left five companies of Native Infantry to protect our baggage, which would have to follow us along the pass, and some pioneers to make a practicable road so that men could drag up the heavy guns. We then pushed on for a couple of miles. Our route lay as before, along a river bed dry now, but judging from the huge trees which lay stranded there, a raging torrent in the rainy season. I do not believe that we covered more than five miles, the whole way, but we were on the move sixteen hours. By evening the enemy knew that we were among them in force, with elephants and guns, and this alarmed them so much that they were frightened to take a look at us. They thought us to be devils rather than men, who had dropped down upon them from the skies. Some of them even believed that we had been seen passing through the air in flying carriages, drawn by celestial elephants; until a few, who were braver than the rest, had a look at us and exploded the superstition. They were astounded that we had climbed that terrific mountain, indeed, looking at it afterwards, we wondered ourselves how we had managed to get an army up it, equipped too with twenty-four pounder guns. Our next object was to keep safely what we had so hardly got. Accordingly picquets were established on a small hill near-by, from which they could observe the surrounding country, but not an enemy was to be seen. They had withdrawn into the shelter of their woods and hills.

The sun, which had mercifully dried out our wet clothing, set in such a riot of crimson that it was like a blood-red banner flung across the sky. When it had wholly retired behind the hills its last rays lit up a scene of the most ravishing beauty. The mountains in the distance were so lofty that their tops seemed to touch the clear blue above them, and they stood so thick together that it looked as though the smaller ones were being jostled in our direction, so that they might be the first to crush our advance. When night fell we could see fires in all directions. They were alarm signals calling for a desperate effort to drive us down the ghaut. We needed to take every precaution. There had been an order that every man should take three days' rations with him, but the order had not been properly made known. However, the expectation that we should be fully occupied during the night made us forget hunger and cold. An additional picquet was thrown out two hundred yards in front of the other, and I was in charge of it. We were there for reconnaisance mainly, and in case of trouble could fall back upon the main line of picquets, which lay in a semicircle before the body of the army.

It was now twenty hours since I had eaten, and I was in good watching condition for there is nothing like an empty belly to make Englishmen peevish. I had no bedding and could not sleep, so I took care to see that the men did not either. There was plenty of clear water in a brook close by, but we were cold enough without that. It was dark and lonely. Fires were forbidden for the picquets, but the men on the hill had huge ones. We were also forbidden to speak louder than a whisper, for we fully expected to be attacked as the enemy were famous for night work. I visited my sentinels every quarter of an hour, and could find them easily enough by their teeth chattering. I forbade them to challenge me, saying that I would whistle as I approached, so that if the enemy attacked they would stumble on us without knowing, and if we were overpowered we would have time enough to fall back on the stronger line. It was more cheerful when the moon rose, for her light was so brilliant that we could see a great distance. All was quiet, save for the crackling of the wood on those great fires, and the sound of wild beasts in the forest. Suddenly two of my sentinels bellowed fit to wake the dead, "Who comes there? Who comes there?" Bang, bang, went both their muskets at once, and my entire picquet was on the spot in an instant. The men in the line behind us were ferreted out of their beds of dried leaves, the guns were loaded, and matches lit, all ready for instant battle. But it turned out that it was some bear, or tiger, approaching the post which alarmed the men. Probably he would have got one of them if they had not been alert. An Aide-de-Camp turned up to see what was the matter, things were explained to him, and everything dropped back into quiet. The two sentinels got finely abused by their comrades, who had been obliged to turn out of their nests, especially those who had lost some specially warm spot. So passed the night, and a bitterly cold night it was for it was January 1815.

Next morning it was very laughable to see the men crawling out of a huge heap of dried leaves, for all the world like pigs out of straw, but they had at any rate managed to keep warm during the night. Liquor and biscuits had arrived for some companies, and soon after daylight I and my men got a bite to eat, which helped us to forget the hard service we were on for a while; for myself I had some tea which was very reviving. I must confess, I love to be on service with the Irish. There is a promptness to obey, a hilarity, a cheerful obedience, and willingness to act, which I have rarely met with in any other body of men. Whether, in this case, it was due to the rigid discipline imposed on them I do not know, it may be characteristic of the Irish as a people. I observed in this corps, I mean the 87th Regiment or Prince's Own Foot, a generosity of spirit which I have never known in any other set of men. They were willing to share their last drop, and last crust, with a comrade; and would go to any lengths to oblige, or cover up, for one another. There was a unity among them that excelled anything I have ever met and for fighting they were absolute demons. During the Peninsular War, a General Officer remarked to the Duke of Wellington on how unsteadily the men marched. "Yes, General, they do indeed," said the Duke, "but they fight like devils." And so they always will, while they are Irish. They are said to be too impetuous in some situations, but that is a fault on the right side, and has gained England many a victory.

There was still not a single one of the enemy to be seen. Daylight revealed nature's masterpiece of scenery. It was a little world of golden woods, which would have defied the skill of any artist to depict. The hills glittered in the rising sun, clear brooks fell from rock to rock, among great pines; the water, sometimes a cataract, sometimes no more than a gentle stream. Weeping willows leaned over the pools, with multitudes of fish playing in their shadow. All along the banks were roses, tulips, violets, and the air was filled with the song of birds. It was tragic that human blood should be shed there, and those fertile valleys despoiled by war. But the people who inhabit this paradise are proverbial for their cruelty, cold-hearted and cunning, powerful in war, and active as the goats that live on their mountains. We were obliged to advance cautiously, our eyes wide open at every step. Our first intention had been to stay on the mountain all day, to allow supplies to come up, but, these having arrived early, we started our march again along the same river bed. We had not been moving above an hour, before the enemy lighted his signal fires again, to pass on the news of our advance. The way was difficult, for we had to cut a path through the undergrowth, and ford freezing rivers fed from the waterfalls above, and all this held us up. It was clear that the enemy had been watching us during the night, for, every quarter of a mile or so, we came upon fires still burning, and earthen pots in which they had recently cooked their rice. After about a mile there was an abrupt turn in the river bed, where it swept round the base of a little hill, and before us was a small plain. It was covered with a kind of yellow grass, which gave off a scent like sandalwood. We were told afterwards that this grass was a deadly poison. Here we halted, for our spies came back and told us that we were not far from a strong post of the enemy. Immediately everybody was on the alert. Flints were adjusted, bayonets fixed, cartridges arranged, everybody was glad to come to grips with the foe at last.

I did not much like my position in the centre of the regiment, it was not what I was used to, but I was the junior Ensign, and had to do as I was told. The Light Company was busy all the time, probing the country on our left and right, to make sure that we were not hemmed in. This is very necessary in a mountainous country, where the enemy may, so to speak, open the door and then shut it behind you beyond hope of escape. It is always wise to make sure that you have that last extremity, a good retreat. I watched the light bobs on the surrounding hills, and wished I was with them. This was a critical campaign, and needed more caution than I have ever had in my life. At any time the next step might be into a cannon's mouth. I was thinking like this when I saw the Adjutant running toward the centre of the regiment, and shouting, "Pass the word for Mr Shipp! Pass the word for Mr Shipp!" "Hullo," I thought, "what is all this about?" He came up to me, and said that I was to join the Light Company immediately. Handing the colour over to the Sergeant, and thinking that this might be the last time I should ever see it, I kissed the standard as I did so. After all I was a soldier, and that often blood-stained banner was my pride. Soon I was among the light bobs, for I could run and jump with the best of them. The fine Light Company of the 25th Bengal Native Infantry was with us, and between us and them there was more intimacy and good fellowship than I have seen between different regiments in all my service in India. We climbed a small hill, and saw at the bottom several men running away. Our soldiers were not cruel, nor did they ever waste ammunition, in fact a soldier ought to guard every round as the apple of his eye. Many a brave man has lost his life for want of one, which perhaps he wasted in the beginning. To squander powder and shot is worse than folly, it is a crime. I took about ten men with me, and the Acting-Adjutant, and we soon came up with the poor frightened creatures. They flung themselves down on the ground, but did not beg for mercy, that is unknown among them. They seemed rather to meet the bayonet than run from it, but when they saw that we were not going to hurt them they kissed our feet, and the earth beneath us, in token of their gratitude. They were not soldiers, but poor, oppressed villagers who had been sent for rice; of which they carry great quantities on their backs, in willow baskets supported by a strap over their foreheads. We were ordered to let them go, so that they might tell their friends that we were not bloodthirsty murderers. When we let them know that through one of their countrymen, their eyes lighted up with joy, and they prostrated themselves before us abjectly, a hundred times, before setting out for their village with all their fear forgotten. I daresay they would rather have stayed with us than return to slavery under their tyrants.

We now came to a wider river, with a rocky bed and a strong post higher up. The ends of houses, standing back some thirty yards from the steep bank of the river, could be clearly seen; we therefore crossed a little lower down, and the 87th Light Company was pushed on at a good round trot. The first house we came to was a square building, like that I have described at Summarabassah but much larger and stronger. This we surrounded and entered. There were about fifty men inside, who ran out of the opposite door when they saw Europeans come in. Many escaped, some who showed fight were killed. The house was empty except that there was some unshelled rice and saltpetre lying about. Now we saw another house of a similar kind, hidden in the wood about three hundred yards off, at the end of a small path. We struck into this expecting every moment to be saluted with a shower of grape, or a volley of musketry, for the road was commanded by two or three hundred loopholes in the building. But we pushed into the place, and found near the door a dead man, most dreadfully mutilated. The few soldiers in the house escaped into the woods, except those who were shot by our best marksmen. All there was in this place also was a little grain scattered about, and their cooking pots, well filled, were boiling on the fire. These we smashed for fear of poison, a crime they are well capable of committing. The poor, mutilated man turned out to be one of our spies, whom the

Quarter-Master-General had been anxious about. He had been appallingly treated; among other monstrosities his arms had been cut off between the elbow and the shoulder, and thrust into two deep gashes in his body, just above the hips. Spies are always punished severely, but in Europe never except publicly, and by proper authority. When I say that these were a barbarous and cruel people, the accusation is not unfounded. Our men were so enraged at the monstrous sight that I, and the Captain, had great difficulty in preventing them from rushing headlong into the woods in search of the torturers. When the pioneers came up they made haste to bury the poor man's body, for the sight was too horrible to endure.

This place was called Ettoondah, and is one of the loveliest in the world. We had some very good fishing in this place, by tying horse-blankets together and then dragging the stream. Here we remained some days in order to set up a depot. For this we used the lower house which was better situated, and not so near the woods. Round it we built a large stockade, with six embrasures for guns, and turned the house into a store room for superfluous baggage. Not that I had much, one on and one off was always enough for me; but I often wished that the officers carried knapsacks, like the men, so as to have things safe and handy. Many of the chickens kept by the natives had gone wild, and roosted in the trees round about. We were forbidden to shoot at them for fear of wasting ammunition and alarming the camp, but we managed to get a few for the pot none-the-less.

13

Hard Fighting on the Hill of Muckwanpore

After we had rested here for three or four days we moved on again. The 87th, being the only European regiment with this part of the force, always formed the advanced guard. We groped our way on through a thick wood, rather wishing that we could see the route a little better, though there was a tolerable road which made movement easy. At the end of two miles we came to an open space, with fires alight, and the usual earthen cooking pots scattered about. A river, near to knee deep, ran through this open space; and on the further bank we could see people moving about among the trees, peering out at us from the nearer foliage. We went on through this wood, and came to the edge of another river which the road did not cross, but turned alongside the stream which swung left. On one side of us was a steep cutting, where the mountain had been pared away, and on the other the river itself. This looked dangerous. We should have an abrupt height, impossible to climb, on one hand and deep water on the other. The enemy could wait until we were well in, and then pour a devastating fire upon us, from which we could neither escape nor defend ourselves. But Major-General Sir David Ochterlony was not to be caught in that way. Every point of danger was always scrupulously explored before we were allowed to approach it. When we were safely through, we came to an extensive valley with small, straggling clumps of huts about, though few people were to be seen and those only poor peasants. But, half a mile or so further on, we noticed a sizable village to our left; and on the hills behind it an immense number of people who looked like soldiers, for we could see spears and colours among them. There seemed to be a good deal of activity going on up there, so we turned toward the place, going in at double quick time, and then separating into files with our pieces loaded. I searched several huts, but could find nobody save decrepit old people.

Further on was a two-storey house, probably the zemindar's, for I could see no other like it, and I noticed several prosperous looking fellows run in and shut the door. With the help of some of my men I broke it open, but, going suddenly into the dark interior from the bright outside, I could scarcely see; though I just made out several men on the lower floor, and one of them sitting. I picked my way in, with my old dragoon sabre in my hand, and got accustomed to the gloom just in time to see a man fitting an arrow to the string to shoot at me. I struck at it, for he was very close, but owing to the poor light I missed, and he let fly. The arrow passed hardly a hair's breadth from my head, and stuck in the door post, and then a soldier of the company, called Quanbury, finished the archery practice by shooting the archer, for daring to attack an officer. The rest begged for mercy, which was granted readily enough. I never, at any time, saw a soldier of the 87th commit an act of wanton cruelty. We took them prisoners, but they were soon turned loose and allowed to go back to their villages.

Continuing our march we came in sight of the Muckwanpore valley, and an immense line of huts, which we were told were the summer quarters of the Goorka army. We still had on our left the line of hills I have mentioned, covered with variegated shrubs and trees, and filled with the enemy's soldiers in great force; but they did not attempt to interfere with our line of march, though we must often have been within range of their ginjalls. They seemed to be solely on the defensive, and there were many guesses why they were allowing us to overrun their country in this way. When we reached the line of huts, or cantonments, we could see the fort of Muckwanpore, and innumerable stockades on the hills behind the rising ground which faced the huts. The fort itself appeared to be some miles off, and looked a mere speck in the sky. It was well protected by stockades, and looked dangerous to approach. We encamped here, in what had been the enemy's lines; and though we cannot have been more than a mile and a half from our adversaries they made no attempt to attack, but sat cross-legged and watched us. Our position was a strong one, with a deep nullah on two sides, and a pleasant stream for our refreshment.

Next morning we had a look round the encampment, and explored the woods a little, but found nothing except a few partridges and woodcock, which we could not shoot for they were too near our quarters. The camp stood in a most romantic situation. A mile or so distant from it, craggy mountains began to lift their white heads to the clouds, and high among these hills stood the fort itself, seemingly inaccessible to human endeavour. For the first time in ten nights I got some sleep, having no responsibility, and nothing on my mind. Sleeping in my clothes was no hardship, and I stayed soundly off till daylight woke me. A change into dry linen was a great treat, and so, feeling a new man, refreshed and fit for anything, I made a round of calls on my brother officers, and finally on my Commanding Officer on whom I never failed to call each day as an act of respect for his rank. He invited me to breakfast, and afterwards, as we stood looking at the enemy's positions, we were surprised to find that a strong picquet of theirs, which had been posted on the hill before our encampment, had been withdrawn. At that moment two of our men were brought before the Commanding Officer for having gone beyond our outlying picquets. After admonishing them for their imprudence and disobedience, the Commanding Officer asked one of them what he had seen. "Nothing at all, Your Honour, but a great big picquet and they had gone." "Well, what did you see on the other side of the hill?" said the Colonel smiling. "Nothing, Your Honour." "What! Are there not hills and valleys on the other side?" "Neither, Your Honour, save a mighty big mountain as big as the Hill of Louth." "Did you see any men?" "Devil a one, Your Honour, save a poor old woman in one of the huts, and she was after going when she saw me and Pat Logan come near." "What took you there?" "Faith we wanted a good walk, for we were tired of doing nothing. I hope no offence, Your Honour."

Suddenly we heard "Fall in the Light Company," bellowed and repeated throughout the camp. The Colonel flew one way, the Adjutant another, and each of us in his own direction to respond to the call. I had scarcely reached the parade ground before three quarters of the men were under arms, with our noble General at the head, getting the men together. Within five minutes of the first call we marched off with not a soldier absent. We found, by the direction of our march, that we were setting out to take the hill their picquet had abandoned. The ascent was steep and winding, and it was a good half mile to the top, so our progress was slow. Our lads were as merry as crickets. We heard some firing from the top of the hill towards the right. This came from a small reconnaissance party under Lieutenant Lee of the 87th Regiment, and Lieutenant Turrell of the 20th Native Infantry. He was a brave young volunteer who fell in the execution of his duty. Their object was to protect some operations which had been undertaken by the Quarter-Master-General, and the fort of Muckwanpore over-looked the area they were reconnoitring. The large enemy picquet, which had withdrawn from their position the night before, was now sent to occupy it once more, and in returning they fell in with our reconnoitring party, which they hopelessly overwhelmed, driving them back down the hill. Poor Lieutenant Turrell and several others were cut to pieces. As they were retreating down the hill, we were making the best of our way up, supported by our old friends the 25th Native Infantry. The path was so narrow that we had to struggle along it almost one by one.

There was a small, flat spot a good part of the way up, and here our Captain brought the men together. We could see the enemy creeping about like ants from stone to stone using all the cover they could find. I ventured to suggest to the Captain that our forming in a body would expose us to a destructive fire, and that we had better fight them on their own system; taking advantage of rocks and trees to shelter behind, and to steady our muskets upon. He readily saw the danger, and ordered the extend to be sounded and then the advance. The fighting soon became very warm, for the enemy maintained their ground manfully. I hate a runaway foe, for there is no credit in beating him, but these were no flinchers. I never saw a steadier bravery than they showed in all my life. Run they would not, death held no terrors for them, though we were so near that every shot told. At last some of their men began to give way, and, as we were pushing on quickly, one of their principal officers made desperate efforts to rally them. He succeeded for a minute, and then turned on me. He was a big, powerful fellow and I did not like the look of him at all. Protected by two shields, one tied round his waist and reaching down to his knees, the other, a much larger one, on his left arm, he was hard to come at. From this gentleman there was no escape, but luckily I had my old sabre with me, which I had put in good shaving order a day or two before. With this I was obliged to act on the defensive until I could catch him off his guard. He cut, I warded off, he thrust, I parried, until he lost his temper and set to work on me hammer and tongs. So furious were his blows that he nearly battered my sabre to pieces. At last he seemed winded, but I could see nothing of the fellow save his black face, peeping above one shield, and his feet below the other. I tried to give him a cut across his extremities, but he would not stand still a moment and capered about like a French dancing master. At length I made a feint at his toes, down went his shield to protect them, and up swept the edge of my sword under his chin, and his head nearly fell off, for he had thrown it back to avoid the blow. I was not sorry to see him fall, for he was a most unsociable neighbour. Whether I did right or not I do not know, but I took his sword, gold crescent, turban, chain, and large shield; this last I sported on my arm for the rest of the action, and it was lucky I did so, for it was bullet proof and saved me a severe wound.

The Captain and his men were a credit even to the Old Fogs, the noise they made would have frightened the devil himself. Slowly the enemy, fighting desperately, were being forced off the hill, some of them flinging themselves on our bayonets in the most frantic manner. As they were compelled to give way some withdrew to the near-by hills, others into the gullies and ravines below, from whence they kept up a destructive fire. We had now taken the hill and fulfilled our orders. Reinforcements were rushed up to our assistance, and two six-pounders which followed them began to spray grape onto the poor brave fellows in the ravines; but though the havoc they suffered was dreadful, they scorned to flee. During our ascent some howitzers, in front of our camp, began to shell an immense force of the enemy which had gathered to help their defeated comrades. These reinforcements had with them a three-pounder gun, about a yard long, which one man could carry, intending to use it against our advance; but one of the shells from our howitzers found the ammunition they had brought for this, and the rest of their firearms, and blew up the whole in an explosion which killed and wounded great numbers. When they no longer had powder for their gun they rolled it down the hill, where we found it when the action was over.

Our troops were now scattered over the hills, and frequently killed or wounded each other by firing at random, wherever they heard a shot. The cease fire was frequently sounded, but to no purpose. It was indeed tantalizing to see thousands of the enemy under our very noses, and not be able to shoot at them; but we were hidden from our own men on the near-by hills, and feared we might draw their fire. The Colonel had come up with the reinforcements, and repeatedly ordered the cease fire, but there were still some pot shots being taken by the Native troops. When he came to the Light Company I could see how delighted he was, but there was no time for compliments. He ordered us on no account to go ahead, but to find what cover there was and cut down the first man who disobeyed the cease fire. At this moment one of the enemy, who had been annoying us from a thicket about thirty yards off, moved out of his hiding place; and one of our company, finding the chance irresistible, fired and killed the fellow. The Colonel in a tearing passion rushed at the man, and struck him across the nose with his walking stick, and it was a sizable nose too, shouting, "You rascal! I've a good mind to have you shot for pointed disobedience of my orders." But the enemy, secreted in the brushwood, were now being ferreted out by our shells, and the men, if they died for it, could not resist having a shot at them. This infuriated the Colonel who was a little lion when roused. He picked out an offender from the 25th Light Company, and ordered him to be shot at once, which would infallibly have been done had not the Adjutant arrived at that moment, with orders which took off the Colonel's attention. Seeing his chance the offender slipped away, and escaped the punishment he justly deserved. Implicit obedience is the great principle of military discipline. Any officer would have been perfectly justified in shooting, or cutting down, a man who disobeyed in this way. Encourage a breach of orders and there is an end of discipline at once. The soldier who was struck was well aware of his crime, and quietly put up with the penalty, thinking himself lucky that he had not been deprived of his life.

Nothing was heard now but the roar of the two six-pounders, and the whistle of shells. The wounded and the dying lay in masses in the ravines below. In our company we had, I think, eleven killed and twenty wounded, out of a total number of no more than eighty. I say again I never saw such soldiers as ours, they made me feel a novice. Soon night mercifully hid the scene; but as long as it was light we could plainly see the struggles of the dying. Some were moving convulsively, others forced themselves to their feet. I saw one poor fellow just manage to get up, put his hand to his bleeding head, then fall and roll down the mountainside out of sight. Dark clouds overhead promised a coming storm. I have been told that any loud noise, particularly the roar of cannon, in mountain country will bring on rain. A gentleman explained it once by saying that the dark clouds are reservoirs of water, and the noise brings them down low, where the attractive power of the earth causes them to discharge their contents. However that may be I do not know, but if noise can bring on a deluge we had noise enough. Night closed down in pitchy blackness.

The pioneers were sent up, and started entrenching and stockading the hill round the huts, in number about twenty. Food had come up for both officers and men, so we had a meal, and my Captain and I decided to watch four hours in turn, he to begin. So he posted his men, and I, with some more soldiers, took possession of a hut full of good straw and lay down to sleep. Scarcely had I shut my eyes when I heard the shout of, "Pass the word for Mr Shipp! Send Mr Shipp to me!" It was the Colonel's voice, so I presented myself in a hurry. "That's right," said he, "I want you to go on duty." He then took me by the hand, and said, "Shipp, you have verified the recommendation you received from your late Commanding Officer of the 24th Dragoons. I shall not lose sight of your conduct. Our spies say that the enemy will try to retake this hill, under cover of darkness. It is of more value to them than to us, so we must meet them with determined force. Take a steady Sergeant and twelve men, and go down by the reservoir of water but stay on this side. See that your sentinels form a link with those on the right, and on the left, and don't let them go to sleep or lie down. They must be on the alert. I need not explain anything more. Your Captain is in a similar situation." I did as I was told. The rain fell in torrents, the thunder rolled, and the lightning flashed in massive sheets along the mountain top, lighting up the corpse-strewn battle-field. I cannot think of a more uncomfortable situation than the one we were in just then, in the midst of this furious storm, surrounded by the dead and dying, and expecting to be attacked at any moment by a cruel and merciless foe. Only a sense of duty can offer much support at such a time. That, and his pride as a soldier, will enable a man to do with comparative cheerfulness what he would otherwise revolt from. The enemy was notoriously cunning, and the danger of surprise great. All stratagems are justifiable in war it is true, but it is impossible to do other than pity them for their cruelty. They are taught the art of war from infancy, they fight under the banner of a gloomy superstition. Cruelty is their creed, the murder of their foes their glory. But let us not condemn them too severely, they are what they are taught to be.[1]

In spite of my forebodings the night passed quietly enough. Towards morning the rain stopped, and when the sun rose only the scene of death below marred the glory of the prospect. Our lower picquet was withdrawn after daylight. On going over the hill afterwards the number of the dead astonished me, it was impossible to walk without treading on them. I paid a visit to the body of my antagonist of the day before. His head was almost off, he had a deep wound in the abdomen, and a bullet in the fleshy part of his thigh, though whether he got this before or after he fell I could not say; from its direction I should say before. He was a fine looking man, dressed in the uniform of an English General of twenty years earlier; with old, frog-lace both on skirts and sleeves, though without epaulets. I had not noticed this earlier because, when I was fighting him, I dared not take my eyes off his. If I had not been thoroughly practised in the exercise I must have fallen, for he was a very expert swordsman. In a letter he afterwards addressed to me, the Quarter-Master-General, Captain Pickersgill, congratulated me warmly on the death of this distinguished chieftain. His name, the letter said, was Khissna Rhannah Bahader, and he was the identical officer who had planned, and carried out, the massacres at Summanpore and Persah[2] the previous season. Both the Quarter-Master-General, and Sir David Ochterlony himself, thought that the death of this chieftain contributed greatly to turning the current of events in the Nepaul campaign.

An enormous working party was employed to take the wounded to hospital and bury the dead. In two days eleven hundred of the fallen were put into the grave, having almost one general tomb. It might have edified those babblers, who rail so much at soldier's cruelty, to see how deeply moved both Natives and Europeans were on this occasion. Having performed our sad duty we were relieved at midday, and returned to our lines being warmly greeted by our comrades at the foot of the hill. The orders of the day were complimentary, even flattering, to all engaged, and this was a trophy gained that no man could rob us of. As soon as I was washed and dressed I went to the hospital, to visit my friends and those who, a day before, had been my mortal enemies. It had been some time before our wounded could be moved from the hill, and then bringing them down shook so many of the poor fellows that inflammation set in, and they were in the most excruciating pain. Every comfort that liberality could purchase was afforded to the sufferers. It gladdened my heart when I went into the tents where the enemy wounded were housed, to see some of our Native soldiers waiting on the poor wretches in the most devoted manner; speaking to them in their own language, comforting them, and calming their fears, which was the more necessary as some of them thought that their lives were only being prolonged for a more cruel and lingering death. One

View of Delhi from the River showing the King's Palace

of these Goorka soldiers was in such a bad state that his leg had to be amputated. He submitted almost without a struggle; but when it was all over, the leg off, and the stump dressed, he was convinced that all white men were cannibals as he had always been taught. He asked a countryman, who was lying by him, when he thought the other leg would be taken off for if it was going to be a long time he would destroy himself. This was understood by one of the hospital attendants, and to ease his mind it was explained to him that the act was one of kindness, not of cruelty, and done simply to save his life. He refused to believe it, and only the sight of the same operation performed on one of our soldiers convinced him that we were not the barbarians he supposed us to be.

Our General had ordered that the wounded prisoners of war should be attended to by men of their own caste, and there was an abundance of volunteers for this humane work. It was delightful to see men who, the day before, had been bitter enemies, showing the deepest kindness to each other. In the hurry of my narrative I have left out a circumstance which does great honour to the soldier concerned.

In the heat of the action on the top of the hill, one of the enemy was particularly conspicuous, fighting like a hero. He had just shot one of our men, and I was making towards him with one of our fellows, called Quanbury, who, finding that the man was drawing away from us and reloading, fired, and the man fell to his knees. Quanbury ran up to him, for he was still holding his firelock, and was about to thrust him through, when the man threw down his arms. Seeing this the brave Irishman stayed his finishing blow, saying, "It is well you did that, my fine fellow, for if you had shot me as you did the other man I would have blown your brains out, so I would." At this point the Quarter-Master-General came up, and took charge of the prisoner, and we passed on to clear the hill of others who were still keeping up a heavy fire.

14

A Man and His Dog. The War is Over

IN SPITE of our little victory[1] we were still facing a fierce and determined foe which obliged us to exercise the keenest vigilance. Everyone eagerly scanned the hill in front of us, and many and ludicrous were the comments on what we imagined we saw. Fallen trees were magnified into guns and mortars; the many-coloured bushes into soldiers, shafts of light which fell between the trees into flags; the *ignis fatuus*, roaming through the night, was taken for enemy torches, and every rustle of the leaves for the beginning of an attack. If one of our Captains, whose spyglass was never away from his eye, had got his way we should no doubt have been in Khatmandoo in half the time; for he would first have blown up everything on the hill, and then attacked while the enemy were asleep, the only drawback to the plan was that the Nepaulese never sleep; or rather, such is their watchfulness that they never seem to do so. How preposterous it is to hear some men boast of what they would do if they had the command. A soldier's duty is to obey his superiors, not to criticize them. If this particular kill-devil of a Captain had been as expert with his sword as he was with his tongue, two companies of men like him would conquer the universe.

But the army had men of another quality. On parade one evening an officer noticed a man who looked very ill, and asked what was the matter. "Nothing at all, Your Honour," he replied, "except a little scratch I got on the hill yesterday." The surgeon was standing near, and asked to look at the man, who was told to show his "scratch" as he called it. He was taken into a tent and examined, when it was found that a ball had carried away the point of his lowest rib, and as the wound looked neglected the surgeon thought that the bullet might still be in the man's body. "I beg your pardon, Sir," the patient answered, "that is a mistake, for here it is, beat as flat as a crown piece." He was ordered to go to the hospital and almost had to be dragged there, bellowing out as he went about the satisfaction he wanted of the enemy for his wound. He had to wait for that, however, as he was out of action for the rest of the campaign.

I was on duty just then with a picquet, at a point where a small path led from the enemy's position into ours, and which on that account had to be most carefully watched. It was then, I think, that I came across such a remarkable instance of sagacity in a dog that it is worth recording. When passing one of the sentries, I frequently had to admonish him for not challenging in a louder voice. To my surprise he answered that he did not wish to wake his dog, which was asleep under a bush near-by. "What!" I said, "I suppose you take nap and nap with him do you?" "Why, yes," said the man innocently enough, "I do, sometimes, and to tell you the truth I only relieved him five minutes ago." "Very candid, my good fellow," I said, "but don't you know that you could be shot for sleeping at your post?" He admitted that he knew it well enough, but insisted that he could rely on the dog to jump on him, and wake him up at the slightest noise. I found that this clever creature, when his master was on watch, would regularly stand his hour and walk his round, without ever leaving the post. It was even said, that on dark nights he would put his ear to the ground and listen. The man told me many stories about this dog, among them how he had once been drinking, and fell asleep some miles from the camp. When he woke up he found that his clothes were torn, and that he had been dragged three or four yards away from the bush he had lain down under. Near-by was a great snake, almost torn to pieces by the dog. He was a powerful animal, a kind of Persian hill-greyhound, that could kill a wolf single-handed.[2]

Our batteries were now playing on a stockade that stood on the hill between us and Muckwanpore. We could not get the guns nearer than eight hundred, or a thousand, yards because of a deep ravine that lay between us and them. At this range we could not be very effective. The stockade was alive with men. There was a tent set up inside, and colours flying, but a few shells, beautifully pitched into the place, soon cleared everything away, except for the occasional hero who peeped out to see what we were doing. I am positive that cannon balls have no power at all to damage these stockades. They build them of green bamboo, so skilfully interwoven that they are very elastic, and well able to resist a bombardment from such a distance. We frequently saw men run out and collect something from outside the stockade, and as we could not believe that they were just picking up stones, it must have been spent balls that they were after.

During this day we were ordered to admit a Native emissary with his six attendants into the camp. "Hallo," we said, "they have had a sickener of it have they?" There were plenty of guesses about it all, and everybody had a different opinion. The Captain with the spyglass, whom I have mentioned, excelled himself and saw the messenger coming on horseback, in a palanquin with a troop of followers, on a milk-white steed; but was always of the opinion that however he came he would not be allowed to set a foot in the camp. But when the envoy did come it was in something like a sailor's hammock—a dirty, ill-looking fellow, thickset, with small eyes, wide face, low forehead and only one follower.[3] In spite of his dingy appearance he had all the consequence of a nabob. He was highly offended when we began to search his hammock, and person, to make sure that he carried no hidden weapons; and protested that so holy a being as himself, for he was a priest, could never allow himself to be contaminated by the touch of a christian. In a great rage he threatened that if we persisted he would go back to the Rajah, and tell him how he had been insulted. We soon let him know that if he did not submit to what was always expected in the East, on these occasions, he could go back and do as he liked. He was actually getting into his hammock when he gave in, and said, sullenly, "Well, you may examine." As I searched the long cloth wound round his waist as a cummerbund, he shrank away from my touch as he would from a serpent, but I gave his holiness such a twirl that I thought he would never stop spinning. He was so furious that he foamed at the mouth, and I thought he would strike me, but he restrained himself. We found no weapons and let him pass, but the precaution was very necessary, for these people are treacherous and cruel beyond measure. It was his kind that had tortured the poor spy at Ettoondah. We passed him on, but he was back within an hour, his sallow face distorted with malice and fury. He went by in sullen silence, no doubt vowing vengeance within himself at the failure of his mission. Two more days went by quietly, and then a second ambassador came, who might not have been so holy but was certainly more of a statesman. He stayed a considerable time in conversation with our General, who though the service had deprived him of one eye could see as far as most folks. At last the envoy left, beaming with delight, smiling and bowing as he passed. Our infallible Captain was of the opinion that this meant peace, and for once he was right.

Our batteries ceased firing the next day, and the uncle of the Rajah, who acted as Regent during his nephew's minority, was said to be coming to our camp. To do him honour the two flank companies of the 25th Native Infantry, and the two flank companies of the 87th Regiment, lined up on either side of the approach to the General's tent, where every preparation was made to receive him. He kept us waiting two hours beyond the set time, and Sir David, who was beginning to get nettled, was about to withdraw the guard of honour and set the batteries to work again, when the sound of a trumpet and the roll of drums let us know that the Regent was on the move. Shortly afterwards we saw him coming down the hill, in a superb palanquin attended by about twenty armed footmen. He was met at the entrance to the double line of soldiers by the Adjutant-General, the Quarter-Master-General, and several other staff officers who, after a little hugging, led him by the hand as a token of friendship, towards the General's magnificent tent. As he passed the soldiers presented arms, a compliment which he perfectly understood, and to which he bowed in a most majestic fashion. He was a most noble and venerable looking personage, superbly dressed, with numberless daggers stuck in his cummerbund, his sword studded with diamonds and all sorts of precious stones, his neck, turban, and hands one mass of jewels. The Envoy and our General met at the tent door where they exchanged a mass of oriental compliments, for all the world like those between Doodle and Noodle in

Tom Thumb.[4] Our visitor was a perfect courtier, but free, affable, and jocular none the less. In two hours after the customary sprinkling of scents, the treaty of peace was ratified, and he returned home obviously pleased with what had been done.

Thus ended the fighting in this second campaign, in what has been called the Goorka War.[5] It was lucky for us that it ended when it did, for that very morning seventy men of the 87th had gone to hospital with dysentery, a complaint that was raging among us from the dampness of the valley in which we lay, and the fogs that rarely cleared till nearly midday. Guns were ordered down, and we began to prepare for quarters. None of us were sorry, for our clothes were in rags and our toes sticking out of our shoes. We were told by the Quarter-Master-General that the hill we took had been vacated by the enemy without permission, and they had been sent back with reinforcements, and ordered to take it again or pay for the loss with their heads. That accounted for the desperation with which they fought on that spot.

Our enemies having now become our friends, for they were freely in and out of our camp buying things in our bazaars, three or four of us made up a party to visit their stockade and the fort. We set off after breakfast, and reached their advanced posts easily enough; but there we were stopped, and told that we could go no further without the permission of the Keeledar, or Governor of the fort, and they would send a man to see if he would give it. So we waited, and in about half an hour the man came back with two others, and said that the Keeledar would allow us to enter, but we must go unarmed leaving our weapons at the last stockade. It was a difficult climb up to the fort, and every turn in the road was guarded by a strong stockade and guns. If we had tried to take the place our losses would have been enormous, for there was hardly any footing. At last we reached the grand fort of Muckwanpore, if it can be called that. It was very high, built of brick and stone, but a dozen shots from our twenty-four-pounders would have tumbled it down, indeed one bastion already gave notice of its intention to collapse, for the tempests which rage in those parts had loosened its foundations. The gate was strong but the hinges small. As we entered a small guard presented arms, and a drum and fife played "The British Grenadiers". Both these instruments were English made. The tent we had seen in the stockade was still there, or at least a part of it, for it had been riddled by our shells and the top torn to ribbons. We were introduced to the Keeledar, who was seated on some greasy cushions which had once been white, but were now the colour of his face. He shook hands most heartily, and was really a very jolly old fellow, twenty to twenty-three stones in weight I should say, with the fat hanging in great flaps over his hips, which shook tremendously whenever we made him laugh. He complimented us highly on our fighting and system of warfare, and wanted to know how many of us they had killed. We told him not more than forty, and he laughed, and said we meant forty hundred for they had lost more than that. We spent a pleasant hour with this very well-fed Governor, who let us look round the fort, and was so polite as to parade his regiment for our inspection. You could not wish to see a finer body of men, and they were in every respect as well armed and equipped as our own Native troops. We went back to camp, and the next morning marched towards cantonments.

We had to keep a sharp eye on our new acquaintances, for in India only time makes treaties valid, and many massacres have been perpetrated under the cloak of friendship. Often negotiations are spun out, solely to allow the enemy more time to prepare their next blow. One of the points in the settlement between us was that a British Resident and the usual escort should stay at Khatmandoo. This escort set out for the capital on the same day that we began our journey back to India. I was in the rearguard the morning we left Muckwanpore, and the enemy, or perhaps I should say our friends, flocked round in great numbers to see us go. Some of their soldiers were gathered round the guard, asking all sorts of questions; when one of them, a most respectable young man wearing the dress of an officer, came up to me and said, "Were you not in the action on the hill of Muckwanpore?" I answered, "Yes, I had that honour." "So was I," he replied, "and fired three shots at you from behind a tree. Are you not wounded?" I told him "No." "Well," he said in surprise, "I never missed a man before in my life." I asked him just when it was that he aimed at me, and he answered that it was when I was fighting with the Sobah Khissna Rhannah. "Then you nearly got your man," I said, "for one of your shots hit the peak of my cap." He laughed at this, and then complimented me on my swordsmanship, for he said few could touch the Sobah at that exercise. He borrowed a musket from one of our men, and put himself through the drill, giving the words of command in English. I asked him where he had learned all that, and he answered that a man of the name of Bell, a deserter from the Company's foot artillery, had taught him, and a man called Browne had instructed him in English. Bell, he said, had been made Colonel of artillery, and Browne schoolmaster, but both had left the service at the beginning of the war. As we moved off this young stranger shook me warmly by the hand, saying, "I love a brave soldier, and all white men are brave." He was, it appeared, the Adjutant of the corps in which Khissna Rhannah, the man I killed, was Colonel.

Our first march on the road back to India was fairly easy, winding along under a hill so that we nearly reached the top of the pass before we encamped. The next morning we sent our things on very early, to prevent them being looted should the Natives prove treacherous, which was not at all unlikely. The road, which at the start was wide and tolerably good, narrowed off as we went along, and dropped down between two huge mountains. Here the path was so contracted that there was hardly room for a loaded elephant to pass along it. Above, on either side of us, great stones were piled up for our destruction, many of them so delicately balanced that the least touch would have sent them hurtling down. I could not but reflect upon the folly of those young officers who, at the outset of the campaign, would have had us try to force this pass of Cheriagotte.[6] There was stockade upon stockade, all commanding the narrow slit of a road along which we had to pass. In the middle of this route, the sheer mountain wall on either side must have been at least five hundred feet high; all the enemy need have done would have been to roll down rocks and stones upon us, and our annihilation would have been complete. We could not possibly have escaped. When we reached the other side of this pass nothing was to be seen but stockades, and fortified hills, in all directions. The road was nothing but a dry river bed, but it grew a little wider as we went along, though it had strong breastworks thrown across it, and was commanded by numberless little sugar-loaf hills, each one fortified and reached by ladders only.

To complete the destruction which these hills must have poured upon us they had poisoned the stream, either before the campaign or possibly even after the peace was signed. Some of the deadly yellow grass which I mentioned earlier, had been sunk in a kind of natural basin, about twenty yards round, and two deep, which was filled continually by water falling into it from the rocks behind. An elephant belonging to Lieutenant-Colonel Rose of the Company's army, and a horse of his, went on ahead of the main body one morning and came to this basin. The elephant stood with his forefeet in the water, and drank a little, but did not relish it much; the horse tasted it, but could not be forced to take any more, nor would the elephant touch it again. His mahout, puzzled at what was happening, got down to see for himself, and noticed a yellowish colour rising to the surface of the water, apparently from the poison grass, which the elephant had trampled on when he stepped into the pool. The man pulled it out at once, and the incident was reported to our Commander. I shall never forget how angry he was when he heard it. Our medical department examined the water, and as the elephant and the horse both died a little while after, there was not much doubt about what had happened. Sir David peremptorily called upon the Nepaul Government for an explanation of such a diabolical action, but they denied all knowledge of it, and pretended that it must have sprung from private revenge for some injury in the war. If they could find the culprit, they said, his head should pay for his crime, and they promised the strictest search, but we heard no more of it. A guard was set on the poisoned water until our pioneers could fill up the basin, to prevent it ever being used for such a purpose again.

As we happened to be near the place we went to visit the still exposed bones of those poor creatures who had been murdered at Summanpore and Persah. Skulls, and even whole bodies were lying about in all directions, and there was scarcely a tree which had not forty or fifty shots in it. We buried their tragic remains, and pitied their fate. At the end of our journey we settled down in cantonments by a beautiful lake, which abounded in fish and wild fowl. The year before some temporary barracks had been put up, to house two regiments at this spot, and we added some more huts for ourselves, not knowing how long the truce would last and we should be at war again. But the peace endured, and I should say that from the long, and uninterrupted, friendship which has continued between us and the Goorkas, it is essential always to make a strong impression from the beginning. It is folly to risk failure at the start of a campaign. Our complete victory at Muckwanpore beat some new principles into our foes, but they remain very wary of admitting strangers, and it is only with the greatest difficulty that passports may be had to visit any part of their beautiful country. In March we finished our huts, with two or three rooms in each, but we had no sooner got them done than we were ordered to proceed to Cawnpore by water, which is a long and tedious journey at that time of the year. I was sick of war just then, and was more and more occupied with the thought of the girl I loved, and whose letters had cheered me all that campaign. Ready permission was granted me to go by land to Cawnpore, so I set out alone, to cover the four hundred and thirty miles of the journey.

15

The Taking of Huttras

AFTER twelve days of very hard travel I arrived at Cawnpore, worn out and ill. None-the-less, affectionate nursing and the kind attentions of my betrothed and her family soon put me on my feet again, and we were married on the 4th April, 1816. My old regiment received me in the most generous manner, and showered politeness on me and my young wife. No stranger ever passed through the station without liberal hospitality from the 24th Light Dragoons, and I was no stranger. When my own regiment arrived there was a great welcome from everybody, and for the next eighteen months I was happy in domestic affection, and the companionship of my friends. At the end of that time we were called upon to march again, our objective being Huttras, Cummoun, and some other refractory dependences of the Huttras Rajah.[1] Huttras is about thirty miles from Agra, and twelve from Muttra. It is a mud fort, immensely strong, standing in the midst of some of the most fertile country in Bengal. Round about the fort is an enormous ditch, eighty feet wide and seventy to seventy-five deep, crossed only by two small bridges which the defenders could destroy in an instant. As soon as we arrived before the place our political agent began negotiations with an Envoy from the fort, but we went actively on with our military preparations none-the-less. Our only chance of success lay in a steady, progressive, siege, for we should first have to take the walled town before we could get near enough to the fort to mine or breach it. Just to show that we were in earnest we continued setting up our batteries against the town, while the parley was going on. The siege operations were commanded by Major-General Sir Dyson Marshall K.C.B.

Whether the future held peace or war was to be finally decided by midday, and the Envoy had been in our camp all the morning bargaining for more time to consider the proposals, or what was more likely, to increase their preparations for the struggle. This sort of trick has often been resorted to, and I have known emissaries swear by all their gods and goddesses, kiss the earth, and call upon all that is dear to them to witness that they desire nothing but peace, beat their breasts and vow eternal love and friendship, just in order to gain another minute or two in which to complete their preparations for battle. In this case the Vakeel (Envoy) swore most earnestly that his master, the Rajah, would be in camp on a certain day to sign a treaty on the proffered terms, and, half believing him, our General ordered that the batteries should not open fire until noon on that day. Ten o'clock came, but no Rajah, eleven and half past eleven, but still no Rajah. At about a quarter to twelve the Vakeel came out of our political agent's tent looking very worried, and getting into his carriage set off at speed, with me riding beside him as far as our grand battery, still protesting as he went along that the Rajah would be in camp before noon. That fateful hour struck, and exactly upon it our guns opened fire. As they did so the Vakeel leapt from his carriage, and dashed for the fort, screaming like an angry tiger, and I took the liberty of returning to camp with his horse and carriage as prize. Whether he ever got into the fort or not I do not know, we never heard of him again, but the minute our guns opened fire theirs replied, which proved just how honest his vows and promises were.

We went steadily on with the siege, keeping in view the main point in all these affairs, that of never wasting men's lives, and of going to work with our eyes open. Our heavy guns were only about four hundred yards from the town wall, and if we wanted to take a peep at what was going on we were forced to do so on the sly, for we were within half a musket shot of the enemy. We were, in fact, so close that we were forced to set up screens at the embrasures, to protect our men as they worked the guns. The firing was directed at two extreme corners of the wall. When we began the town was full of men, but we sent them a little shrapnel, and a few rockets which played beautifully along the tops of the houses and along the narrow streets, and cleared the ramparts in no time. We could hear the enemy digging, and found afterwards that they had made holes to hide in, and covered them with old doors, and bits of plank, in the effort to get away from the shellfire, but some of it found them out just the same. A Congreve-rocket[2] is a most destructive thing, its enormous tail sweeps everything away, and when it explodes it sets fire to houses left and right, and kills for yards round. Some long shots were thrown into, and near, the camp but they had no effect except to scatter some ladies who had come from Agra to see the battle, but who never rested until they were back in their houses, thirty miles off. Only one of them stayed, and even she kept a respectful distance.

A reward, differing according to size, was offered for all kinds of cannon balls brought into camp. The Natives who flocked around us would risk anything for money. I was riding out toward one of the picquets one morning, and passing a spot where the balls were falling pretty thick, saw a Native run to stop one as it lobbed along, but it broke his leg so badly that the limb had to be amputated. Had he got the ball into camp it might have fetched fourpence. In two days the breaches began to look practicable, and the storming parties were ordered to be ready by two o'clock in the afternoon. The day was calm, the sky serene and cloudless. The left column was to be led by the 87th, the Prince's Own, and all of us were as merry as crickets. The 14th Regiment, a beautiful corps, was to lead the right. At about half past three we moved off towards the town in silence, but were halted under cover of the village and there was an unexplainable delay. While we sat chatting, one of us noticed that a young officer had taken off his epaulets, and the plate and feather from his cap, and looked for all the world like a discharged pensioner. Whatever his motive may have been it was very unwise, for it would be certain to be commented on both by the men and the officers. The officers to be sure joked about it, and no doubt drew their own conclusions. One of them asked the young man why he had done so, and was told that it was in order to look as much like a private soldier as possible, and avoid being singled out by the enemy. How far such a thing is open to censure I do not know, but I warn young officers never to do it, for it is bound to lay them open to ridicule and criticism. This young man's intentions were no doubt right enough, but he never recovered his character in the regiment and left it some time afterwards.

The head-engineer had the attack postponed until the next day, which accounted for the delay. He did not know the depth, and width, of the breach, and wished to find out before allowing us to proceed. He stole down to it that night undiscovered, and came back very glad that he had stopped us going on, for the ditch was so wide and deep that we could never have reached the breach. A bastion had been knocked down it is true, but the debris had not filled up any part of the moat, but merely lodged on the side of it. The next morning we found that the enemy had withdrawn under cover of the dark, for seeing us march down they were sure we were about to attack that night. A strong party was sent off instantly to occupy the town. We had some difficulty in getting in, for the enemy had barricaded the gates with large stones, and great bales of cotton, but we brought ladders and scaled the walls. Not a living soul was to be seen in the place, save a few poor old people; but there were a good many dead, both of men and animals. We strolled through the town to take a look at the other side, and found the fort to be quite close. The moment the enemy saw us they began a furious outburst of cannon and musketry, but they need not have been anxious, for we could not stay long. The prize agents arrived and turned us all out, thinking no doubt that we were not to be trusted with gold mohurs[3] and rupees lying around in the banking houses.

On the following day, after a careful reconnaissance of the fort and its surroundings, the breaching and shelling batteries were re-sited, and the bombardment started afresh. The peak of its intensity was reached at about ten o'clock at night, and never before in my life had I seen fire so accurately directed. Some of the shell bursts were not above five or six inches above the walls of the fort. In a place so packed with houses, and people, every missile found its way into some poor wretch's home. No one can estimate the damage caused by shellfire, except those who have seen it on an occasion such as this. Our shells were very many, and very large, some of them being thirteen and a half inches calibre. It was twelve years since the siege of Bhurtpore, and in that time the system of shelling had improved so enormously, that whereas we had been satisfied then with about one shell every four minutes, from a single battery, it was not unusual at Huttras to see twenty a minute from as many batteries. The darkness grew profound, partly from the smoke of battle, partly because the moon was hidden behind a dense black cloud. All the usual sounds of nature on a summer night were silenced. The air was lurid with carcasses[4] which resemble a fiery man flying through the air; so that the natives call them devils of the night, or fiends of the clouds. They are used to burn down houses, or blow up magazines. To complete the hideous scene Congreve-rockets roared along the top of the bastion, breaking arms and legs, and spreading devastation on all sides. The destruction was appalling, the misery which the civilian population had to suffer was heart-rending. There was one case which I saw myself. A young woman was lying on a bed of green silk with her arms round her baby. A large shell had gone through the tiled roof, penetrated through three floors, and then exploded at the foot of her bed, wrecking some part of the fourth floor. Half the woman's head was blown off, and so was the lower part of the child's body; but the mother's nipple was still in the baby's mouth, and his hand clutching her clothes. Her husband was one of the officers of the fort, and had been killed some hours earlier. Our General had urged the garrison to send their families away to their homes, and promised them the fullest protection on the journey, but his offer had been refused with contempt. The Company's army has always acted with humanity in this way, and yet I have only known one case in which such an offer was accepted.

Everybody believed that there was an immense treasure in the fort, which was a shining prospect for most of us. To tell the truth I do not know any class of people who deserve money more than soldiers, or who spend it in a more gentleman-like way when they get it. After my marriage, and the gaieties of life in Cawnpore, my purse was as empty as a spent cartridge, and I was overdrawn with the paymaster, so that I could never find him when I wanted him. A confounded bore this, for a man always to be out when you seek a little sterling conversation with him. Many others were in pretty much the same case as myself, so that it was no wonder that we were all hoping to reap a golden harvest by the siege. With this to encourage us we pushed the operations on, most vigorously. Thinking that it would be impossible to cross the ditch, we extended our mine to within thirty yards of the glacis, and had begun to descend into the bowels of the earth. I was on a working party that day, with a hundred men, and had just arrived in the toolyard which was away to the left of the trenches; when I was thrown flat on my face by a most violent shock, which was preceded by a dreadful tremor of the earth. The wall surrounding the tool yard was thrown forward, away from the fort, and laid flat. The air was full of stones, bricks, pieces of wood, and nearer to the enemy, of bodies and parts of bodies. I got up, fearfully frightened, for the earth beneath me still seemed to move, and in an odd way I thought that something had happened to me alone. But when I glanced round I saw that everybody else was in the same case; either flat on the ground or kneeling saying their prayers, appalled at what had happened. When I got my senses back a little, and looked at the fort, I saw that it was enveloped in a vast cloud of dense smoke and dust, with streaks of fire flashing now and then from the battlements. A buzz spread through the men that the enemy's grand magazine had been blown up, and I ran, or rather rolled, along the trenches until I found somebody who told me that it was true. Looking again at the fort I saw the most tremendous thing that I have ever witnessed. The cloud which was rising from the ruins seemed to be solid, gradually and majestically ascending to the skies; carrying with it masses of many coloured vapours, which seemed to ride upon its summit. Great flashes of vivid fire shot out from the body of the cloud, and showers of glittering sand were sprayed from it on all sides. It looked solid, and yet in parts the setting sun shone through it, with inconceivable beauty. This great mass of vapours rose almost perpendicularly, veering ever so slightly now and then, as it was caught by the light wind. When it had risen so high that the sun shone clear under it, the cloud above glowed with as many colours as the rainbow; and this continued until it broke up, and strayed away into

Gen. Sir David Ochterlony, Bt.

the distance. When we could tear our eyes away from this marvel in the sky, to look at the devastation below, we saw a hideous sight. Heads, bodies, and shattered pieces of bodies, lay scattered indiscriminately among guns, swords, spears, colours, and all the debris of the ruined fort. There were three hundred and twenty thousand tons of gunpowder in the magazine, which had taken them years to accumulate. It was stored in stone-built chambers, some hundreds of feet beneath the earth. We supposed that a large part of the garrison had taken shelter there, out of the way of our shells, and were buried in the explosion. Everywhere you could hear the cries of wounded men, women, and children, and the groans of injured horses.

Our guns had ceased firing, no one knew why. Certainly none of us was inclined to exult at the huge disaster which had overtaken the enemy, but rather to pity them for the magnitude of their ruin. It was an extraordinary fact that a new temple, which stood on the edge of the crater, was untouched but only shorn of its scaffolding. This convinced some of the defenders that the gods were on their side, and heartened them to continue the fight. A bitterly cold night closed in, and as soon as the moon rose over Rumna—the wood which was the Rajah's game preserve—our guns began again, in order to complete the work of destruction. We would gladly have had peace with them rather than add to their misery, but we were responsible to our country, and were in honour bound to push on with the siege. It is not true that a soldier is without pity, but his duty must come first. So the shells again roared through the streets, and tore up the little houses by the roots. About midnight there was a bustle, and a clash of arms among the people in the fort, which made me think that they might try to break out, so I kept a special watch. Anxious to learn more if I could I crept up close to the edge of the ditch, but I was seen by the enemy, and nearly paid for my curiosity with my life. One of their shots came closer to my head than I liked, so I moved off to a safer place. I could now hear the neighing of horses, which were evidently on the bit, but it was not for me to pass on news until I was sure. A few minutes later I saw some people outside the fort, mounted and waiting for others to assemble, before attempting a dash through our mounted cavalry; a thing believed to be impossible, for our men were in a chain of posts on that side.

I told the Commanding Officer of our protecting party what I had seen. He had a hundred Native soldiers under him, and could no doubt have stopped the enemy breaking out, for they were not likely to go empty handed, but would probably be heavy with gold. When I first warned him he said, politely, that it was only my fancy for they were no flinchers. When I still insisted that I could see them coming out, he said sarcastically, "Then why don't you go and stop them. I'll tell you what it is, Shipp, you are never satisfied unless your head is in the cannon's mouth." I was considerably nettled at this kind of talk and said, "If I had half your means, Captain Brewer, I would stop them, but my men have only got picks and shovels. Even if it does seem mad, I'm not sure we could not stop them just the same." He instantly flew into a rage and said, "Pray, Sir, what do you mean by that innuendo?" "My dear Brewer," I answered, "you know that I am as poor as the inside of a sentry box. It really is provoking to see those fellows walking off with the coin under our very noses." He smiled and said, "That is true, and I'll prevent it if I can." So off we marched at double-quick pace; my men, do or say what I would, following me with their picks and shovels, though I threatened to cut down the first man that left his post. They took not the slightest notice, but as soon as I had started off myself they were at my heels. One fellow came running up to me, and pointing to a small group of houses close by the bridge said, "By the powers, Your Honour, there's a whole generation of cavalry, mounted on horses, over there and some of them look as if they are coming this way." "What the devil has brought you here?" I said angrily. "Does Your Honour think I would leave you in a blusteration like this?" answered Paddy. He was close at my elbow, with his pickaxe on his shoulder, but I had no more time for him as we were getting close to the enemy.

On seeing us they rode off to the left at full speed, and one of them came straight at me as I tried to stop him. I did my best to pull him from the saddle, but his horse's hoof unfortunately caught me on the inside of the thigh, and down I went; while he had the bad manners to fire his matchlock at me, but luckily missed. He rode on, and I got back to my station at the head of the party. We reached the end of the bridge, where there was a kind of half-moon breastwork; at least there had been, but now nothing but the parapet and the embrasures remained. Behind this the men who had followed me took refuge, until the enemy had been pushed back into the fort. There was a desperate struggle at the centre of the bridge; the enemy trying to force a way out, and our men trying to force a way in; they would not let us have our way, and we would not let them have theirs. But after some hard fighting we put an end to their journey, and to many of their lives. They disputed every inch of the way, but Brewer's Sepoys were not to be beaten, and after a hard struggle gained not only the bridge but the inner gate. They had the advantage of us here for a time, as the gate was fastened, but we burst it open in the end. Just as it was giving way I received a tremendous blow on the head, from a huge piece of wood that was thrown down from the ramparts, which knocked me over and stunned me for a moment. Seeing me fall the Sergeant cried out, "By the powers he's killed outright at last." "Not quite Sergeant," I replied, getting up, "but it was a devil of a blow." "Och! never mind that, Your Honour, it's all in the army." "No," I said, "all on the head." I had not been on my legs a second when there was a tremendous explosion, which nearly threw me down again. Just at that moment I was giving some orders and pointing at what I wanted done, when some fellow on the ramparts let fly at me with his matchlock, and shot me through the very finger I was pointing with. The ball carried away nearly all the bone of the first two joints, grazed the palm of my hand, and went on through the lapel of my coat. But the inner gate gave way at last, and we rushed into the body of the fort. Women were fleeing from us along the narrow streets, some dropping their children, or leaving them in their haste, others turning and begging for mercy. Putrid bodies of men and beasts lay about in all directions, in some cases three and four deep, so that the smell was suffocating. Some of the garrison tried to escape across the other bridge, but they were all taken prisoner and the fighting ceased.

As soon as the fort was secured, and the prisoners handed over, I had a look at the wound on my finger. It was an hour since it had been inflicted, and the whole arm ached most dreadfully. I could do nothing except harm to myself by staying where I was, so I went off to get it dressed. I may as well confess that I did not walk back, but rode one of the finest Persian horses I have ever seen, which I found loose in the fort. The good-natured prize agent afterwards let me keep him, and I sold him eventually at Lucknow to the King of Oude for two thousand rupees, which is about two hundred pound in sterling. First I reported the capture of the fort to the Major-General, who was much pleased, and then I got my wound dressed. The doctor told me that if I escaped with the loss of the finger only I should be lucky, but he feared that, because of the extensive damage, I should have to lose my hand. The wound was obviously from a rough, iron ball; and that kind of injury generally turns rusty, or more properly a nasty yellow, and is bad to heal. But in the morning another medical friend of mine gave it a dressing, and the next day it was so much better that I got into a palanquin, and went down to the fort to see what was happening there. It would be too ghastly to describe the horrors I encountered, it is enough to say that the most savage and cruel wretch alive would have turned in pity from the sight. One story perhaps may be told. A beautiful young woman, about sixteen years of age, was found wandering near the little village I have spoken of. Her husband was one of the many buried alive when the magazine blew up. Nothing could restrain, or soothe, her grief. She would run wildly about, and then pause, and hold up a finger, and say, "Listen! That was him. He spoke then. Now he is gone." Then she would tear her hair, and shriek, until she fell exhausted to the ground. Some of her relatives had been taken prisoner and she was handed over to them, but she died a few days after.

16

A Welcome Appointment

A STRICT search was made among the prisoners for the Keeledar and his friend the Envoy who had been so often in our camp, but neither of them could be found. They had probably escaped, with the large body of cavalry which had somehow managed to get away, but how they had done so was a mystery. The Europeans blamed the Native Horse and they in turn accused the European Cavalry. I have no doubt myself that they slipped between Captain Bradley's Horse, and the 8th Light Dragoons, some of whom were wounded in trying to stop them. Some Native Infantry had been set to watch that particular road and yet contrived to miss them. The enemy left behind a number of beautiful horses, and many suits of chain mail, which suggests that their cavalry wore that sort of thing. If so, it would have been very difficult for our men to make much impression on them. We wanted the Governor particularly, as he was answerable for the rebellion, and the fact that he got away was disappointing. It was a mystery how anybody could have survived the bombardment, for whole houses, and large ones too, had been literally torn up by the roots. They had thrown many of their dead into a deep well, but great numbers still lay neglected in the ditch, and rapidly decaying in the sun. They were a melancholy sight. Deputies from the other forts and dependencies of the Rajah of Huttras had been in our camp incognito, and seeing what had happened they very readily made their peace with our government. We could not find out what had happened to the Rajah, but he was a dangerous man to have loose in a country like India. If he joined the Pindarees, who were prowling about in force along our borders, he could do a good deal of mischief. In the end he was found to be with an independent chief named Nawaub Ameer Khan; and the Company, instead of trying to punish him, offered him a pension both for himself and his family if he would take up his abode in our provinces. He accepted the offer, and now lives in wealth and peace under the Company's protection. We have heard since that there were more than fifteen hundred dead in the fort of Huttras alone, besides those who were killed in the town. Two of the Rajah's nephews were among this number, and he himself was scarcely ever off the ramparts during the siege.

My shattered finger was now beginning to look dangerous. The wound had been disturbed by the extraction of several pieces of broken bone, and as the weather was now very hot, my doctor was afraid that if I travelled in the ordinary way, with the army, it might bring on an inflammation. I therefore set out for Cawnpore alone, the next afternoon, travelling by dawk, and covered the hundred miles of the journey by the following afternoon. This is one of the most convenient ways of making a journey in India. The traveller is carried in a palanquin, by eight bearers, who are relieved every ten miles, and in this way they get over a journey of a hundred miles in twenty-four hours with the greatest regularity. When I arrived my arm, and indeed my whole left side, was much inflamed and very painful, but good nursing from my wife and her family soon made me forget my aches and pains. With care my wound began to mend apace; though there were still pieces of bone working out, which had to be pulled away from time to time. On the very first night of my injury, as soon as I had got it dressed, I wrote to tell my wife about it. As often as not a soldier's wife is told, very bluntly, something which is as likely as not to be untrue. In a month, or six weeks, I was back on parade with my regiment again, for they had returned to their cantonments, little the worse for wear except for an ugly and troublesome finger which is always in the way. Though I have never been able to use it since, it is a very good weather glass, for its aches and pains generally foretell any change.

When I went down to look at the fort that morning, after its fall, I found the prize agent hard at work trying to keep our lads from picking and stealing; but if there had been a thousand of them, all as lynx-eyed as could be, it would have been just as hopeless. I have heard of a private in the Company's foot artillery, who got away with five hundred gold mohurs, worth £1,000, under the very eyes of the agent, by hiding them in his hat; and later on many other men boasted of what they had picked up. Indeed, considering the dreadful shrinkage which prize money undergoes, and the length of time before the little that is left is paid out, it is no wonder that the men help themselves if they can. At Huttras, for instance, the treasure melted to such an extent that only £20,000 was left for distribution, of which I got eighty-six rupees; but as I had previously sold my share for two hundred I got off tolerably well. No doubt the Rajah had managed to remove a vast amount of his wealth before the siege. He had persuaded the authorities at Agra, who were allies of his, to let his women pass through their territory on the way to a religious festival at some distance, and with them went twenty to twenty-four carts, undoubtedly carrying treasure.

Our station slipped back into its usual gay manner of life when there was no fighting to be done. There was nothing but parties, dinners, balls, and suppers, and such like until many were bored, and most in debt. We heard that the Governor-General, the Marquis of Hastings, was on his way up the river to join us, though why he was coming was a profound secret. There were plenty of guesses, some of them ridiculous enough. It was rumoured that Scindia[1] was to be attacked, then it was said to be Bhurtpore. All that we knew was that his Lordship was very particular in his inspection of the troops. The 87th was in first-class condition, and I was anxious to see them in action again. When the Marquis arrived hospitality overflowed. He was quite without pride, and very winning in his ways. At his parties he generally invited the greatest strangers to sit next to him at dinner, and was affable to all. And so the time passed, until August, when it was at last made known that there was a scheme afoot to annihilate the Pindarees, and everybody, except the wives, was happy. We all became as busy as trunk-makers, getting ready for the campaign. There were farewell dinners in all directions, and to end the festivities we produced an amateur dramatic entertainment. I played Lord Dubberley in *The Heir at Law*, and Lord Minikin in *Bon Ton*.[2] His Lordship seemed highly amused, and complimented me on my Lord Dubberley particularly. When the play was over, a gentleman came into the dressing room and said, "Shipp, if you play Baggage-Master as well as you play Lord Dubberley you will do well." "Baggage-Master?" I replied, "I don't understand you." "Why," said he, "you are appointed Baggage-Master[3] to the left division of the Grand Army." "My dear Sir," I said, "you must be mistaken. I have not heard a syllable of the matter." "No I am not," he said, "you can be sure about it, because as a matter of fact I went and asked for the appointment myself, but his Lordship said that he had given it to you, at the particular request of Major-General Marshall because of your conduct at Huttras, and because you were the only officer wounded there." Had I known before, the whole life and soul of a Baggage-Master would have gone into the part of Lord Dubberley. As it was no news could have been more welcome. I wrote the next morning to the Brigade-Major, to find out if the information was correct, and he replied that it was, apologizing for not telling me sooner but saying that he was overwhelmed with work. I was to join the left wing of the Grand Army at once. It had left Cawnpore two days earlier.

Now that I was sure of the news I told my wife, and arranged to set out the next day. I then waited on the Marquis, to thank him for the appointment. He received me with the greatest kindness, saying, "Mr Shipp, you have no occasion to thank me. Your own merit, and the kindness of Major-General Marshall who asked for it as a favour to himself, have got you this appointment." He went on, "I will not ask you to dine with me today, as you will probably prefer to spend all the time before you leave with your family." I expressed my most grateful thanks for so much kindness, and went home to pass the rest of the day with my wife. Parting from pleasant acquaintances is always a sad business, but leaving those whom we love is harder still. Now, when the time came to go, my heart was grieved at leaving the wife I loved to take part in new wars, from which I might never come back. The sight of her distress at my going brought tears to my eyes, and her two small sisters were as upset as she was. But I said goodbye to them and to my fellow officers, and next morning ate a good breakfast and was off before sunrise.

17

The Sagacity of Elephants

THE whole combined power of the three Presidencies was now in motion to put an end to the Pindarees.[1] They were a set of marauders and barbarians, who were prowling about the country in immense numbers, battening on the poor peasantry whom they robbed and murdered year after year. They were the remains of the old warrior sect of the Mahrattas who, driven from their homes by civil war, were now existing by plunder. They rode the best of horses, which were their own individual property, as were their arms and equipment. The leaders were those who happened to be the most successful thieves, though they called themselves after the various ranks in our Native armies. Their families went with them. Should a woman die on the road she was easily replaced at the next village, either with or without the consent of the new one. As soon as they had drained one town they moved on to the next, and lived entirely by rapine. They had long been uncontrollable, spreading devastation wherever they went, but the Marquis of Hastings was now determined to put an end to them once and for all. To do this he called every soldier he could find into the field; commanding the centre division of the army himself and personally directing the whole war.[2]

In four days I reached my division, which was then lying under the fort at Callenger, and reported myself to Major-General Marshall who was in command. He asked me to stay to breakfast, and treated me with the very greatest kindness. I cannot say that I was ever very bashful, but I was none-the-less always properly respectful to my superiors. On this occasion I thanked the General, very warmly, for all that he had done for me. He replied, "Shipp, you deserve everything that you have been appointed to. I have not forgotten your bravery at Huttras, though I was very ill before that place, and the confounded gout nearly made me overlook your merit. I wish you joy. There will always be a knife and fork for you at my table." And he shook me most warmly by the hand. I had now been told both by my own General, and the Marquis of Hastings, that I had done my duty as a soldier, and nothing can be more gratifying to the feelings. I next paid my respects to Brigadier-General Watson, Colonel of His Majesty's 14th Regiment, who was second in command of the division; who received me most kindly, pressing me to take a seat at his table for the rest of the campaign as I was the only King's Officer in the camp, besides himself and his staff. When I explained that I had already been invited by General Marshall, the Brigadier replied that he would put that right, and so I lived with him until the following May, faring most sumptuously at his hospitable board. He was a good soldier, and a kind and generous man. Because of the extreme indisposition of the Major-General, he undertook all the active part in the storms, and sieges, which occupied the left division during that campaign.

The next day I visited the strong hill fort of Callenger. It was on top of an immense mountain, with the town straggling up the slopes towards it. The fort itself capped a pile of almost perpendicular rock, in places fifty to sixty feet high, heavily defended, and impossible of attack. On this high plateau was a lake of clear water, fed by a spring, with gardens, fields, woods, and two or three temples beside. From there we could see a wide expanse of country, with the lowlands of Banda, and that most beautiful river of Hindoostan the Cane, as it flows to empty itself in the Jumna about sixteen miles away. The high hills between us and Banda were crowned with temples, approached by winding steps, cut out of the living rock. Seen from below they looked like little white spots on the sky. This climb to the fort was an experience that I can never forget. At first, the morning clouds lay lightly on the tops of the hills. Usually they clear when the sun is up, but sometimes they linger until midday; shrouding the scene so that the buildings, and the people who inhabit them, seem to belong to another world. These people are Brahmins, who go down in the morning to beg all day, and then return at night to mumble their invocations to stocks and stones. The breeze among these hills is pure, renovating, and salubrious. There are pea hens about in great abundance, which are both fed and worshipped by the priests, who are extremely angry if they are disturbed, or killed; but Europeans still manage to shoot a few, for they are as delicious as young turkeys. The government used to forbid this for fear of disturbances, but that has long since been altered. The birds have a very lovely plumage. These priests trade a good deal on the superstitious fears of the villagers, who will pay anything for a favourable prediction of the future. Should it not turn out to be quite what was promised, the priests always get out of it by saying, either that the dupe did not pay enough in the first place, or that he must do such and such a penance, or make such and such a gift to the priest in order to influence the gods in the suppliant's favour, and so the delusion is kept up from one piece of robbery to another.

We remained in the district three or four days, often visiting the fort, and growing more and more amazed that any troops could ever have taken it. Those who did so were His Majesty's 53rd Regiment of Foot, and they suffered severely in the operation. To us, who merely went up for the amusement, the climb was so exhausting that we had to rest when we got to the top; how it could be taken by assault passed our understanding. Once before, when the Natives were fighting among themselves, it had been taken by a trick. A Rajah who was going to war, asked the Governor of this fort if he would provide safe keeping for a vast quantity of treasure, which he readily consented to do, thinking that he would get it for himself. It was sent in a hundred covered palanquins, each of which was allowed to carry one female from the Rajah's household, but took instead a soldier in women's clothes. The men had their moustaches hidden by veils, and their weapons tucked away in the palanquin. The party was received without suspicion, and ranged itself round the Governor's house. Then the soldiers emerged, the bearers snatched up arms, and between them took the fort of Callenger.

The army was now complete and ready for a long campaign, so I took up my duties as Baggage-Master, and as the post is one peculiar to India I will explain it a little. The holder is a staff officer, attached to the Commander of Division's suite as much as the Commissary-General, or the Quarter-Master-General, or any other staff officer. On the march it is his duty to see that the hordes of hangers-on, who always follow an Indian army, are on the flank that has been assigned to them; and that neither men nor baggage get in the way of the troops. In India you may safely reckon ten followers to one fighting man, so you can see that the post is no sinecure. In our case, including those belonging to the Native contingent we had no less than eighty thousand men, women, and children along with us; and of these thirty thousand, at least, were there solely for what they could pick up, by fair means or foul. To keep this vast horde in order I had twenty men, belonging to a local corps of horse, armed with long whips; for it is impossible to reason with camp followers in any other way. Thus we set out, eight thousand fighting men, eighty thousand followers, fifty elephants, six hundred camels, eleven thousand bullocks, horses, mules and tatoos (pack ponies); five hundred goats, sheep, and dogs, with two hundred and fifty palanquins, and vehicles of all sorts. For the movements of the whole of this mass, except the fighting men, I was responsible. Nobody will accuse me of cruelty, if I say that I had to use the whip in the frequent cases where orders were being disobeyed. It was not the slightest use bellowing at the culprits, but in three days I had whipped them into obedience, and that saved a world of trouble later on. If some malicious fellow, in order to annoy me, got the baggage on to the wrong flank, thinking that he would not be known, I had influence enough to find him out, and he paid dearly for his tricks. They soon found out that disobedience would not do, and so orders were obeyed and my post became an enjoyable one. My Commanding Officer frequently said that if he lived, and commanded twenty armies, he would always have me for his Baggage-Master.

In a couple of days we arrived at the town and fort of Hedjeeghur, a strong place that had recently been taken by the Company's army. The Rajah, driven from his walled fort, lived in the town below, where no doubt he thirsted for vengeance. By nature he was cruel and despotic, but fear of the Company's anger made him the greatest sycophant that ever lived. The next morning brought us to the mountains we were to climb. We could see a winding path, or road, before us, so steep that in parts it seemed to be suspended from the clouds. It was beyond comprehension how we were to get our twenty-four-pounders up, with all their apparatus; but the pioneers set to work to enlarge the road, and we were left to admire the view for a while.

When I was in Nepaul I thought that nothing could exceed the beauty of that country, but the place where we were now encamped seemed to surpass it. The particular mountain in front of us was, I should think, a good English mile from the base to the summit, and other hills as lofty stood round about. Little streams flowed through the hollows in all directions, among great trees wrapped around with fragrant woodbine. Everywhere the grass grew lush and thick, and the peasants' huts standing by the waterside, and their families unafraid, made the place seem indescribably beautiful and filled with peace. But here, as in Nepaul, superstition ruined everything.

I was delighted to learn from the orders of the day that the army would ascend the mountain the next morning; but the Baggage-Master, with a thousand men as a working-party, would remain behind. As soon as the division had gone up we were to follow, and get the private baggage up as best we could. Another working-party was left to deal with the public stores. I was up early to watch the main body go. It was a noble sight. As often happens in these high passes the cavalry, seen from below, appeared to have nothing solid beneath their feet, but to pass like spirits along the face of the rock. It is a sight I have often seen, but never without a strange feeling of wonder. The elephants managed to get up with their usual loads, but refusing to hurry, and as careful of their footing as ever. By about midday all the personal baggage had reached the top, and we had also managed to haul up a few small guns. By six o'clock nobody but myself and the working-party was below. When I made my report to the Commander of the division he was astounded that it had all been done so soon, and said that he had allowed another day for the operation. He thanked me, most warmly, for what I had done. The heavy guns gave us a good deal of difficulty. Each took four hundred men, with double and treble drag-ropes, to haul them up. In the sharpest turns of the road, there were times when some of them hung by the ropes alone. One gun broke away on the incline, but luckily it was not far from a twist in the road, which stopped it without damage. Indeed, scarcely any accident happened save one, which, strange though it was, I pledge my word is a fact. A small cart, belonging to one of the camp followers, fell down a precipice which was about eighty yards deep, the sides being dotted with large trees. The two bullocks, which drew the cart, were dashed to pieces, and the driver so badly injured that he hardly looked like a man. Yet about ten feet from where the overturned cart lay in the ravine, we found a small child of about two years old, absolutely unharmed except for a bruise on his knee. Probably the cart never overturned until it reached the bottom, and not till then was the child thrown out.

I have referred to the sagacity of the elephants, and here, perhaps, I may mention one or two of my experiences with them. In 1804, when we were in pursuit of Holkar, we had a very large elephant which used to carry tents for the Europeans. It was the season when they generally become unmanageable, so his legs were loaded with heavy chains, and he was closely watched by his keeper. By day he was fairly quiet, except when he saw another elephant; and then he would go into a frenzy, in which his driver dared not call him by any but the most endearing names. Soothing them like this, and promising them sweetmeats, will often quiet them a little when harsh measures would make them violent. By night they know well enough that their keepers are off their guard. This particular elephant broke his chain one dark night, and raged through the camp, driving before him men, women, and children, animals and anything that could move. He was trumpeting all the while in tremendous anger, but nobody wanted to argue with him over the road he wished to take. It would be impossible to tell all the mischief he did, in that wild night's ramble. He was followed by a rabble of swordsmen, spearmen, and anybody with a weapon, shouting and screaming, who wounded him in a few places which only irritated him the more; while he pulled down tents, upset everything he took a dislike to, injured a good many people, and in the end killed his keeper with one blow of his trunk. The minute he had knocked his mahout down, and found that the man did not get up again, he stopped suddenly, stood looking at the body for a minute or two, as if he was ashamed of what he had done, and then went quietly back to his picquet. In front of his place there lay an infant about two years old, the daughter of the man he had just killed. The elephant picked up the child as gently as its mother would have done, fondled her a while, as everybody who looked on felt sure that the next instant he would smash her to the ground. But instead, he quietly laid the baby down, covered her a little with some clothes, and then stood watching, while his keepers chained him up again. He was as dejected as if he knew what damage he had done. From that moment he became passive and quiet; always most pleased, apparently, when the baby was near, who could play with his trunk and take what liberties with him she pleased. But he never recovered himself, but fell away and died six months afterwards at Cawnpore, as those in charge of him said of grief at the death of his keeper.

During the Nepaul campaign of 1815 a female elephant died, leaving a young one about seven years old. I used to see him every day, and believe me his distress was piteous to watch. At last an old male elephant, whose picquet had been beside the mother's, noticed the calf, caressed it a little at first, and finally adopted it. They always travelled side by side on the line of march, the little one would take food from the old gentleman's mouth, and play tricks with him as it had done with its mother. Soon the youngster grew fat, and before the campaign was over had thrown off all moping for its parent. Its name was Pearee, love, or lovely one, in English. Colonel James Price, now Major-General in the Company's army, was in charge of the breeding station at Chittygong for some years, and knew more about elephants than any other man in India. I was having tiffin with him one day, when he said that he had a young elephant just then, who was as cunning as any he had ever known. He was willing to bet that if anybody played a trick on that animal it would be returned, even if it were months after. I took him up on that. Elephants are very fond of bread, so I got a couple of slices and loaded them in between with cayenne pepper. The elephant took them, but soon discovered the joke and I had to run for it; but I gave him some ordinary bread and he seemed satisfied, and willing to be friends again. About a month afterwards, the Colonel and I were walking round the stud before dinner. I had forgotten all about the bet, and petted that particular elephant a good deal, which seemed to please him; but as I turned away he drenched me from head to foot with dirty water, and so was revenged for the cayenne pepper.

18

In Pursuit of the Pindarees

Just as I had made my report that all the baggage and stores were safely up the mountain, a messenger arrived from the Rajah of Hadjepore, and the General asked me to escort him into camp. I therefore rode to the top of the hill, and found the Rajah himself waiting for me. He had come to make his peace with the General, who was angry that he had not sent the five hundred men asked for to help with the baggage. This tremendous potentate came in great style, with five elephants, and twenty horsemen armed with spears and guns. He tried to be affable, and was even jocular with me, but I could see the scheming that was going on in his mind. He began by asking if the General was angry with him. I could scarcely muster enough patience to be civil so I just said, "You had better ask that of the person who can best answer it. If he is, he has reason enough." He then asked what the object of our campaign might be. I told him that he had better save all his questions for the General, who might be able to satisfy him. Finding that I was not so elated at the honour of being on an elephant with him as he thought I ought to be, and that he would not get the information he wanted, he started to admire my dress; taking a particular fancy to my watch, which, however I was careful enough not to let out of my hand. He winked to a man on another elephant, and said something in Mahratta which I took to mean, "It won't do," or, "He won't do." He then began admiring my whip, which I allowed him to handle. We had just got to the edge of the camp, and somebody spoke to me, which attracted my attention, and so behind my back the whip was passed from one to another of them; each swearing that they knew nothing about it, and I was forced to give up hope of seeing it again. The General gave his visitor a very cool reception, and the Rajah mounted his elephant and rode off, vowing vengeance on all Europeans if it was ever in his power to take it. I was ordered to see him out of camp again, so when I got to the limits I demanded my whip, telling him he would go no further until it was restored to me. His people made a search, but of course it was not to be found, but I was not going to allow myself to be hoaxed in that fashion. Either the whip was to be returned, or the full value paid to me. At last the Rajah asked what it cost. I told him five gold mohurs, and after a good deal of arguing that was what he paid me, and I was completely satisfied.

Our march next day lay through wild country, where hardly a soul was to be seen, though the soil was fertile enough. The whole district had been utterly ravaged by the Pindarees. We next passed through the diamond country, which belonged to the Rajah of Punna. I was astonished that, after a sharp climb of about a mile, we should come out on to a landscape that seemed quite flat for a considerable distance, but the Pindarees had ruined it all and everything was desolate and dreary, except where small groups of adventurers were digging for diamonds. In this enterprise, as in all others, a few win but most lose. The diggers buy a certain area of ground, say ten or twelve feet square for which they pay from a hundred to a thousand rupees, depending on the situation. There they dig, sift, and wash the soil; and if they find diamonds below a certain value, I believe it is ten thousand rupees, they may keep them, above that they belong to the Rajah. Few are found of any great value, but still the speculators are closely watched during their operations. A good deal of gold, silver, copper, and iron are found in the country, and the Rajah should be a rich man even if he is not a happy one. That he can hardly be.

About three years before we were in his country, he had married a most beautiful girl as his third wife. She was the daughter of a neighbouring Rajah, and soon became the most beloved of all his women. As his Vizier he had a young man who had previously been his barber, a subtle, cunning man who soon gained such an influence that nothing could be done without him. He was so completely trusted, that when the Rajah was invited to a festival, some hundreds of miles away from home, he thought his household completely safe in the care of his Vizier, even though the Pindarees were in the country in large force. It was with complete faith in his minister's ability, and integrity, that the Rajah set out on his journey. But he had not been gone a week before the trusted servant began to make love to his mistress, but quite without success. No matter how earnestly he protested his love, and vowed that without her he could not live, she refused to listen, and in the end put a stop to his persecution by threatening to expose him to his master as soon as he returned. This was a threat the Vizier had to take seriously, for he knew that his master was of a bitter and ungovernable temper, and that if his jealousy was once roused he would be in a frenzy. So the minute that the Rajah got back home he was met by the Vizier, with a tale that the young wife, who was so much loved, had herself been unfaithful; and the lie was planned with such skill, in all its circumstances, that it was at once believed. Beside himself with rage the Rajah rushed into his zenana, sabre in hand, and slashed the unhappy girl to pieces, without a word or question. He was an independent ruler and could do as he pleased, the British could not touch him. The woman's relatives made no inquiry, such things were not uncommon, and after a while the incident died down. Some time later one of the Rajah's other wives lay dying, and asked for the whole court to be assembled round her bed, for she had something of the utmost consequence to declare. The Vizier was forced to gather them in, though he guessed that his treachery was about to be exposed. The dying woman made a full declaration of all that had happened to her friend, which she had been too frightened to tell before. The Rajah tore his hair, and ran shrieking round the palace searching for the villain that had done him so much evil; but though horsemen were sent in all directions he could never be found, and the Rajah had to make what reparation he could by building a temple to the murdered girl, in which he placed her statue, with diamonds for eyes. When I last saw him in 1819 he was quite mad.

We stayed at Punna four or five days, waiting for orders from headquarters. The left wing of the army had originally been intended to watch the frontier, in order to prevent the Pindarees getting into our districts, but they had turned in another direction, towards Candish. We were therefore ordered to join in the general pursuit, and so stood toward Bopaul and Saugar, through a wild and desolate country which had been ravaged by the Pindarees. At one time, having lost touch with them, we began to fear for the safety of the various stations where our families were waiting. At Cawnpore, which was the principal place, scarcely a soldier was to be seen, they had all been drawn off for the campaign; so that when a rumour went round the quarters there that the Pindarees had come down from the hills, the women left behind were in great alarm. They barricaded the doors with bricks, and stones, and tables and chairs, anything they could lay their hands on, and nobody dared stir out. Servants who were sent to find out what was going on brought back the wildest rumours, and increased the alarm. My wife's letters to me were full of forebodings. Many ladies hired boats to go down the river to safer places, and then something happened which confirmed their worst fears, and nearly drove them out of their wits. One of the ladies, out for an early morning ride in her chair, saw a cloud of dust on the race-course. She asked what it was, and the servant said, "Brinjaree," meaning the cattle which carry commissariat stores. She understood him to say "Pindaree," and rushed, screaming, from her palanquin back to quarters shouting, "Pindaree Pindaree," and telling everybody who asked her what the fright was about, that they were already in the cantonment. This alarm of course spread like wildfire and chaos set in. Some of the women took to their boats, others hid in go-downs, and cellars, or even under the bed. Luckily my wife had a small guard of Sepoys at the house, as there were some army stores there, so she had the doors locked and bolted, and sent out a trusted servant to see what it was all about. He came back to say that the Pindarees were at that moment plundering the great bazaar! All the hubbub was only quieted when Captain Sissmore, the Acting-Paymaster, discovered that the dust cloud was caused by nothing more dangerous than a herd of bullocks bringing in stores, escorted by a small troop of local horse.

We pushed on towards Bersiah, where we found Major Logie of the Bengal Infantry, who was carrying a good deal of treasure for Colonel Adam's division. As the Pindarees were hovering about, with longing eyes on the money, Major Logie had fortified a small hill, and he and his few men had placed themselves there very securely. The day before we got there a large body of Scindia's horse, who were nominally our allies, had arrived before the stockade and behaved most insolently to Major Logie. He told them very plainly that if they did not move he would fire on them, and I know nobody in the Company's army more likely to keep such a promise. Allies though they were, they were not to be trusted with money about. While we were here we received hourly notice of Pindarees being in the neighbourhood; but they were only in small parties, ten or twelve at most, and it was useless to go after them. We should have had no sort of success but would only have scattered them, whereas we wanted them to concentrate so that we could catch them in force, and cut them up. So we just watched their movements. The Company tried to pacify them without war, sending proclamations through their villages promising to buy their horses and arms at a fair valuation, and give them land of their own, and a free pardon. But robbery was their way of life. In quiet periods a Pindaree will sleep, and loll about, for twelve or fifteen hours a day, and spend the rest in sensual pleasure, and such rapine as chance may afford. There is no race on earth more debauched than these people.

19

A Fort in the Jungle

I HAD nothing to do during our long stay at Bersiah, and so had plenty of time for parties of pleasure with my friends. The country was fertile and beautiful, and there was a wealth of good shooting, from the wary snipe to the royal tiger, without going a mile from the camp. We lived very pleasantly in that time. At length we heard that the Pindarees had climbed another range of hills, and concentrated their forces at a place called Beechy Taull; so we went off in that direction, regulating our marches by the information received from our spies. For the moment our wild enemy was stationary, and they even allowed us to get near to them without their moving; though they kept a deep and wide river between; and held a lofty hill from which they could watch the country round for a distance of fifteen miles. We approached to within forty miles of this, and then made a forced march one morning, of some twenty-two miles, through thick, wooded country. After a halt to allow our cattle and followers to catch us up, we intended to start again when the moon rose, and take the enemy unawares at dawn. But the road lay through a dense wood, and there was a ravine about every hundred yards, which we had great difficulty in getting the guns over; so by daylight we had not covered much more than half the distance, though we could see the hill about eight or nine miles ahead. We pushed on, and in about an hour and a half crossed the river Scend about two miles from the top of the hill. Our spies, who had just come out of the enemy's camp, told us that they were no longer on the summit, owing to the lack of water up there, but had moved to a place about two miles away, near a large lake, and were apparently unaware of our approach.

The General immediately sent forward the 4th Native Cavalry, with Cunningham's corps of local horse under Lieutenant W. W. Turner, the whole force being under

Brigadier Newberry who commanded our cavalry. With them went two six-pounders, called gallopers because they can move as fast as a regiment can charge. I got permission to act on Brigadier Newberry's staff. The hill was lofty and hard to climb, for it was a mass of loose stones, on which many of the poor horses broke their knees. When we got beyond it, and reached their camp, we found a large body of the enemy drawn up, and gave them a few long shots which tumbled one or two of those proud men and their steeds. We tried to break into a gallop, but our horses were too done up. However, we managed to get out of the thick woods which surrounded the place and cut down a number of their men. To our left, about a mile away, we could see a thick cloud of dust, and as we moved towards it began to meet the enemy in considerable numbers. As we pushed them some fought bravely enough, indeed the greatest coward will do that when his life is at stake, but their struggle was useless and they soon made off. We could see women among them, often with one child on their back and another on the saddle-bow, tearing across country with tremendous speed. When they had run some five or six miles some of them formed, and seemed inclined to put up a fight, but before we could get to them their hearts failed, and they rode away, keeping up their spirits by abusing us in a style which is best not reported.

Night was coming on, and we had to make the best use of what light there was left, but we did what we could, and cut up a good many of them. Lieutenant Turner's local horse had got separated from the cavalry, and the Brigadier wished them to rejoin him before night, as the whole of the enemy's baggage appeared to be in sight. I was sent to recall them, and when I was about half way, found a good many Pindarees straggling about, some of them wounded. From the look of the ground it was obvious that neither our men, nor Lieutenant Turner's, had been idle during the day. I was galloping along, anxious to get rid of my orders, when a wandering Pin had the cheek to shoot at me from behind a large tree, but though we were almost face to face he missed me. My faithful old friend, the dragoon sabre, had been badly bent by striking at the padded coats of the enemy, but during the day I had managed to seize a large spear from one of them. I had been taught the use of this weapon by one of the finest spearmen in the country, a man who had been zemindar (head-man) of the elephants at Bhurtpore, so I was perfectly familiar with it. In a moment of irritation I threw away the sabre, and laying the spear across the first joint of my left arm, with the butt under my right arm, I drove at his neck; and, though he parried it for a while, got it into his throat in the end, and then riding round like a horse in a mill twisted him out of his saddle. But some of his friends came up just then and I rode off. I afterwards regretted that I had parted company with my old friend the dragoon sabre, which had been my salvation so often before, but ingratitude is common to man I suppose. It was some time before I came up with Lieutenant Turner, and when I did, he and his men were hotly engaged, but orders are orders, and they reluctantly broke off their fight and rejoined the 4th Cavalry. Night was closing in when we overtook the enemy's baggage, and our horses were completely done up, they had not another mile in them so we called a halt. What we had been chasing was made up mainly of animals, horses, cows, sheep, bullocks and so on, with a motley crowd of old men, women and children, with nothing but a cooking pot or two, and a few clothes between them. Except for a few Pindaree women riding ponies, they were only camp followers. The Brigadier put a strong guard round them, more to protect them from outraged villagers than to secure anything for himself. I was immediately sent back with four horsemen to the main body, which was now encamped on the top of the hill, to let them know about our skirmishing.

It was no very pleasant thing riding over a field of battle in the dark, with a knocked up horse, and only four companions; but what has to be done is best done cheerfully. We found our division occupying the same ground, which the enemy had held on the top of the hill, and I was glad to see them, for both my horse and myself were at the last gasp. We had been going for twenty-four hours, and must have covered at least eighty miles. General Marshall burst out laughing when he saw me, for sweat, dust, and gunpowder, had matted on me till I looked like a London dustman. As soon as I had made my report I went off to look after my horse. She was the picture of woe, her head down to the ground, her flanks heaving, and she had lost a shoe. I had a groom just then who prided himself on being a bit of a horse doctor, and as he was very fond of the mare, he begged that he might take care of her, so I left him to do as he wished. He asked for some warm water, a little bran, and half a bottle of brandy. Mixing all this together he gave it to her, at about the temperature of new milk. She drank every drop and wanted more. It threw her into a heavy sweat, and then the groom, with three other men, rubbed her down well, and let her lie on a good thick bed of clean straw, while the groom began thumping and shampooing her all over; an operation to which she submitted with evident pleasure. He then had her shoes taken off, her hoofs pared and washed in warm water, and dried off with straw. Finally he made her get up again, and rubbed her all over with his hands, and in an hour she was looking as well as ever. He gave her another mash, clothed her for the night, and left her sound asleep. The next morning she was as fresh as could be, and though I rested her to begin with, because I had other horses, she was so frisky that I rode her again before that day's march was over.

We moved on the next day, but the main army was not able to overtake the cavalry until the second evening, when we arrived in time to see the cattle, and other things which had been taken, sold in the bazaar. The Pindarees we were after fell into the hands of General Donkin's division, with more of their baggage, and so they were pushed about from division to division, as the Marquis of Hastings had planned; until there was nothing for them to do but break up into tens and twenties, and scatter as widely as possible. Then the country people took courage, and attacked them wherever they could find them, until at last they were glad to seek refuge in any little fort that they could get into. By this time many of the Pindarees had accepted the offer of our government, many had been killed, and others gone back to their homes. We still had numberless little skirmishes with parties of them hiding in the woods during the day, and travelling to their villages at night, but to all intents and purposes the war was over. But before I concern myself with the other operations of the division to which I was attached, I ought, perhaps, to say a little more about the Pindarees themselves, for they are a most extraordinary people.

From their very birth they are brought up to rapine and cruelty. The Pindaree child learns to ride, and rob, almost as soon as he learns to walk. If he prove to be weakly, or an incumbrance to the party's movements in any way, he is killed out of hand. By the time he is five they will begin to teach him the use of weapons, at ten to fourteen he will be expected to be proficient in them, and by sixteen he will take his full place in the robber band. These number about six or seven hundred men, under a leader with a reputation for daring, and knowing where plunder is to be had. So long as he is successful his authority will be absolute, and he will be flattered by everybody. A band will take up quarters in a certain town, or neighbourhood, and levy every kind of imposition on the wretched inhabitants, even taking their wives and daughters from them if they have a mind to do so. These pests are looked upon by the people as a kind of natural calamity, that nothing can avert. They never remain long in one place, but commit every kind of atrocity, consume every thing in sight, and quickly depart. They are well mounted, decked out with the tawdry ornaments so beloved in the East, and most of them have four or five women apiece, though they rarely marry any of them. Their weapons are generally a seventeen-foot-long spear, a matchlock, sabre, and pistols, and these the women can handle as well as the men. Their horses are good, well trained, and very manageable. Should they be surprised by British forces they will run rather than fight, and plunder one another on the road should they get half a chance. Both sexes use opium in large quantities, and from this, and their debauched manner of life generally, are rarely long lived. They were the dregs of the old Mohammedan conquerors, and came after the wars of Aurungzebe like pestilence after famine. Their annihilation as a power by the Marquis of Hastings, in 1817 and 1818, was the greatest boon ever given to the great country of India.[1]

We were now sent against the fort of Dhamoony belonging

to the Rajah of Nagpore, which we reached after a long and tedious march. That personage had succeeded to his throne only a short while before, and been recognized by the Company as an ally entitled to protection, and yet he entered into a league with the Peshwar of Poona to destroy the British, in disregard of a most solemn treaty, so that while they were protecting him he was planning their ruin. He managed this with such secrecy that before the Company had an inkling of his treachery, he had surrounded a small band of British troops with about fifty thousand horsemen. The force which was in this desperate plight consisted of one regiment of Native Infantry, and a few troops of Bengal Cavalry, in all no more than seven hundred men. For them to stand and be shot at would be madness, and there was small hope of cutting their way through such opposition and reaching safety. Captain Fitzgerald in command, or rather second in command, of the cavalry suggested charging the enemy, and selling their lives dearly; though he was in hopes that they might reach a small hill, on which their opponents had a few guns mounted, and where they might be able to defend themselves. Mr Jenkins, the British Resident at Nagpore, supported him in this, and the soldiers were all in agreement. They attacked sword in hand, forced their way through the vast masses against them, took the guns and turned them on their former owners, and thus maintained themselves until reinforcements arrived. This piece of gallantry saved the lives of the whole party, and brought them honour which time can never dim. I have frequently met Captain Fitzgerald in company, and it is difficult to offend him more than by mentioning this incident. "Damn the place," I have heard him say, "I wish I had never seen it. If I am to be pestered like this for doing my duty the devil may fight next time, I won't." It is true that a soldier must always do his duty, and I have found, as others no doubt have, that energy and courage rise with danger.

Dhamoony is a stone-built fort owing its origin, so people say, to an incident which took place when the Rajah was once hunting in the neighbourhood. The hare showed good sport for a while, and then turned and killed one of the hounds. This so impressed the ruler that he ordered a fort to be built on the spot. It is surrounded by wild and inaccessible jungle, two of its sides rising from the steep banks of a huge ravine, which is a hundred feet deep in places. To look up at these walls, themselves thirty or forty feet high, from the depths below is really terrifying. There is no ditch on the other two sides, but the entrance to the place is through five gateways; each commanded by small guns, and loopholed for matchlocks. The occupants of this fort actually began firing when we were three miles off, I suppose to let us know that they intended to fight. We camped about two miles away from a small ridge, on which we afterwards set up our breaching battery. In three days we were ready, and we made them the usual offer of terms for we did not wish for bloodshed. They spurned our overtures, so we gave them three cheers and a salvo from our twenty-four-pounders. They returned both manfully enough, and from the show of heads on the wall we thought we were in for a tough job. The Rajah boasted that the place was impregnable, and it looked as if he might be right, for our shot bounced back at us which amused the garrison hugely. But in about an hour our shrapnel stopped their fun, and turbans were seen flying about in all directions, while the women and children began a most dreadful screaming. On that first day our cannon could make no impression at all on the walls, but on the next some large stones in the middle of the bastion began to look knocked about and then fell out during the course of the morning. An Irish Sergeant, in the Company's Bengal Foot Artillery, called to the Corporal, "Come here, Joy. Sure we have knocked two of her teeth out at last, and soon we'll bother her wig for her." "Ah Paddy," the Corporal answered, "that bastion will come down like sin." "How is that, Hogan?" asked the Sergeant. "Fast enough," said the Corporal, "for when one starts they come by hundreds." Hearing the stones fall, a few of the enemy peeped out to see what was the matter, but soon popped back convinced that the bastion, like their Rajah's boast, would soon be without foundation. They were right, for it began to give way in all directions.

About one o'clock we generally stopped firing, to allow the men to get their dinners, and that gave a chance for the enemy to come out in numbers for a proper look. The tower was now so dilapidated that it showed every sign of being tired of the contest. I thought that I would like to examine it more closely, so I asked Captain Cruikshank if he would come with me down to the fort, in order to see what sort of ground we had to cross. I would advise all young soldiers going with a storming party to do this, if they possibly can, so that even on a dark night they may know where to run, and where to walk. Needless to say the Captain agreed to join me. We crept down to within a hundred yards of the bastion, so close in fact that we were seen by some of those on the wall. One of them called out, "Come on, don't be afraid. We won't fire on you," and others with them said the same. We asked them what they meant by begging us to come close, and they replied that if we would cease fire they would give up the fort. We answered that if they meant that we would go up to them, and listen to what they had to say. They swore most earnestly that both the Keeledar and the garrison were eager to surrender. I was very doubtful myself about trusting them, but Captain Cruikshank said that if I would go he would too, so we did as they asked and went up close to the bastion. There they said again that they would give up the fort if we would cease firing.

It really looked as if they were in earnest, so we reported what had happened to Brigadier-General Watson, and he himself came down to the place where we had been standing. It was then settled that all the defenders should be allowed to march out of the fort, with their families and private property, but without their arms. This satisfied them, and they promised to send the Governor out immediately, as a pledge of good faith. An occupying party was ordered to stand ready in the trenches, and General Watson with the Quarter-Master-General, and some others, with a guard of twenty soldiers, waited at the outer gate for the Keeledar. He came at last, a poor white haired old man, who had wished to give up the fort at the start, but his men, feeling belligerent at the time, bound him and locked him up instead. Now that he was free, his beard clotted with tears and filth, he looked the picture of misery, and half starved. We had warned them that if they attempted any treachery the Keeledar would be killed at once, but just at that moment a most unlucky thing happened on our side.

A new battery recently set up in the village, and unaware of what was happening, began to send over a few shots, just to try the range. Their first shell fell within five yards of General Watson, but miraculously no one was hurt. Another struck the tree under which we were standing, and another burst over our heads, but still our luck held and no one was harmed. Consternation set in everywhere. The poor old Keeledar was yelling treachery; a few people in the fort fired a shot or two, and I was sent off in a hurry to stop the battery before it did any more mischief. I had not gone ten yards before a shell burst alongside me, but I flung myself to the ground in time and escaped unhurt; for I am confident that in an explosion like that the discharge rises a little. I was on my legs again in a minute, and dashed off to meet the artillery officer, who was strolling over to see the effects of his shooting before sending off another batch of eight, which were all ready. Completely out of breath I could only gasp out, "For God's sake stop firing." "What the devil is the matter with you, Shipp?" he asked in surprise. "Matter!" I said, "why, by now you have probably killed the General, and half the officers in camp." He set off as hard as he could go to find out how much damage he had done, and I followed a little more slowly, for I was shaken up. By great good fortune none of his shells had done more than frighten the people they fell near, though he had sent over the full eight. For myself I did not at all relish the idea of being killed by my own friends.

The Sergeant of the battery, who was an inquisitive fellow, came up to me afterwards and said, "Pray, was Your Honour there when the first shell fell, for I was after laying that self-same mortar!" "Yes," I said, "and you nearly laid me in the grave with it." "I should have been mighty sorry for that, Your Honour. But is the fight all over now?" I said I hoped so, if the enemy were willing to give up the fort. "I hope not," he replied, "after all the trouble we have had building that sweet, eight-gun battery yonder." "Well, my good fellow, you can't expect more from them than they have to give." "Then it's all time thrown away for nothing. It's tantalizing to one's feelings. A fight would have been some compensation." "But if you had been killed in the fight it would have been a very poor compensation." "Faith, Your Honour, I like short reckonings, and I don't like to work for nothing." I afterwards met the Sergeant in the fort, and showed him a poor woman with her legs blown off. "I hope that satisfies you for the trouble of building your battery." I shall never forget his look, and voice, as he answered. "If I'd thought that I should see such a murderous sight I would never have come near the place. Shall I take the poor soul to hospital?" "No," I said, "you would only give her more pain." She died almost as we were talking, and we persuaded another woman near-by to take the child who was with her. I hope she looked after it.

All the outer gates of the fort were barricaded with huge stones, which we had to clear away before we could enter, and that took some time. We were on the alert for treachery, and marched in as if for a storm. They threw open the gates before us, but, not knowing Europeans, they were as much on their guard against roguery as we were, and kept their matchlocks burning ready to fight to the death if anything went wrong. It was a heart-rending scene as we went in, through crowds of terrified and decrepit old men and women, frightened children, and uneasy soldiers. Our gun-fire had done terrible execution, and the dead and the dying were everywhere. When they saw that we were only acting on the defensive, the fighting men got a little confidence, and came down from their posts. Slowly they left the fort, taking with them what little they possessed. They were all in abject misery and want; for their master, the Rajah of Nagpore, had not paid them for more than two years, and they had existed as best they could on what they were able to steal from the surrounding villages. I doubt if you could have found a hundred rupees among the whole fifteen hundred of them, but if there had been millions it would have been safe enough, for we had given them our word. They quietly laid down their weapons as they came out, but some of them parted with their arms reluctantly, for in many cases they were family heirlooms. Our General allowed every tenth man to keep his matchlock and sword, for the countryside was full of wandering Pindarees, who would not have spared even these poor wretches. They moved away in the dusk, and we took possession of the fort with next to no loss during the entire siege.

20

The Elusive Rajah

THE property in the fort of Dhamoony was almost nothing. There were a few guns, mostly of iron, and a quantity of grain and that was all. What we got by selling this was put into a common fund, with the proceeds of everything else taken in the forts during that campaign. A small detachment was left there for a while, but the place was so unhealthy that it was withdrawn, and the fort demolished. The poor old Keeledar was detained, and his punishment took the form of an allowance of eight rupees a day from the government; as much as he got in a month, I should think, when he was in charge of the fort. The extreme liberality of the East India Company is quite unappreciated by most people, though all the Native rulers with whom they have ever been concerned know it well enough; and realize that once the Company's word has been given it will be kept, to the very letter, whether it is to their disadvantage or not. It is on this basis of treaties honestly kept, and aided by Old England, that the Company can defy all that the combined powers of Europe could bring against them. The Native troops are loyal and faithful, and, if they are humoured a little, make good soldiers. They have to be allowed the free exercise of their religion, they need additional clothing at particular seasons of the year, and they must never be asked to wear, or do, anything offensive to their caste however absurd we may think their prohibitions. I am convinced that two or three million Native troops could be organized, and fit for the field in a year; and if they were led by European officers, and encouraged by British gallantry, would be the equal of any troops in the world. I say this out of my own experience, having been constantly on service with Native forces. The Company has always been careful to avoid difficulties with the caste system. They use a higher class of Hindoo for the infantry, and Mohammedans for the cavalry. Whenever men of lower castes have crept in, little rebellions have been traced to that

Lieut. J. Shipp, 87th Regt.
Leading the Troops into the Fort of Huttrass

source. I am not saying that the lower castes are not equally brave, but I do maintain that the higher the caste the more likely it is that the man will make a faithful subject, and a good soldier.

Our division was now ordered against another fort of the Rajah of Nagpore, a place called Gurrah Mundellah, lying some two hundred miles away, over wild and mountainous country. Major O'Brien, the government political agent, joined us at Jubblepore, and we went slowly on with this devious march. In some places nearly the whole day's route had to be hacked out, through dense underwood, and deep ravines. There were spots where the going was so bad, that an entire day would be consumed in cutting a passage for the next day's journey. Though the country was wild and desolate beyond belief, it was as beautiful as anything in the *Arabian Nights*. One valley stays particularly in my memory, though to describe it adequately is utterly beyond my power. I awoke about midnight. Outside my tent was a little stream, on which the moon shone with such brilliance that I could distinguish every ripple. The quiet of the place was only disturbed by a slight breeze among the pines, and the sound of a bell, which showed that one of the begging priests was at his prayers. Our encampment was clear in every detail, washed by a brilliant and yet unearthly light.

After three days more of most tedious marches, we began to get close to the enemy, and had to approach the hills with caution. The country all around the town and fort we were to attack was wild, and broken, with deep hollows and excavations of one sort and another scattered about it, so that it could only be crossed with the very greatest watchfulness. We understood that a considerable number of men, from the scattered bands of Pindarees, had been enlisted to defend the place. These were to be rigorously treated as an example to the rest, and we took great care to surround the place so that none should get away. Brigadier Watson went on ahead to do this, with the cavalry and some infantry, and I joined his party. We started in the afternoon, working our way forward through heavy jungle, over rivers and great hills. A little after dark two shots were fired at us from an eminence on our left, and a company of infantry was sent to reconnoitre the spot they came from. It turned out to be a small picquet of the enemy, their fires were still burning, and there were several cots about, but the men had fled. We were very much obliged to them for this hint that we must be on our guard. From our spies we learned that we had first to cross a great hill, on which the enemy had a strong post, and that beyond that we should find lowlands with a good deal of water about, and further on still lay the Nerbuddah, where we could expect opposition, for the river was deep and wide with a violent current. Acting on this information the General sent a party on ahead, to clear the hill without involving the whole division. We were a long time getting up, so that by the time we arrived the rest of the force had reached the bottom. The enemy got warning of them by the neighing of their horses, and the confounded clatter of the dragoon's swords which can be heard a mile off; there might just as well be bells round the horses' necks, and it would be a lot more musical. As soon as they caught the sound the enemy fired their long ginjalls, which can kill a mile away, but only wounded a poor grass-cutter of the 8th Native Cavalry in the leg. At that moment, our party was so close to them that they had no time for anything more, but fled, leaving eight or nine of their ginjalls hanging from the branches of trees. There were some native beds about, with a dozen or so fires, and rice cooking over them, but we destroyed this according to our usual custom for fear of poison. We smashed the ginjalls too, for they were too clumsy to carry. As we went down the hill that brilliant moon came out again, for which we were very thankful. Blundering about in the dark, with the chance of a pound of iron round your ears at any minute, is not very pleasant. We could see torches and fires in the distance, and some nearer at hand, which were no doubt signals of our advance.

For about an hour we halted by a small brook to rest, and quench our thirst, and then went on along a fairly good ground, but one crossed by little streams so that our feet were continually wet and cold. We were advancing through rice fields, and though the land seemed fertile enough we saw neither man nor dwelling. At last a light appeared, about a mile ahead of us, but it looked to be moving, for in spite of our advance it still kept its distance. It seemed to be a light carried by the retreating enemy, but it turned out in the end to be nothing more than an *ignis fatuus* on its midnight rambles. We halted for the rest of the night at a small village of about twenty huts, where nothing had been left but pariah dogs, and a few wandering cattle. Grog and biscuit were passed round, for those who had failed to bring any food with them. I had never carried any myself on previous occasions, and had gone hungry many a night, but this time I had a considerable quantity of biscuit with me, and a bottle of brandy which others were glad to share. It was cold in the early morning, and we had no covering, but we were tired and slept soundly in spite of that. My favourite mare had a blanket which I would not deprive her of, for though she had some of the biscuit, she would not touch the brandy. To my surprise, I woke up in the morning to find her naked and woebegone, shivering with cold, while the groom was wrapped up in her blanket and snoring like a pig. I gave him a whipping which would keep him warm for a very long time, and stopped a rupee from his pay to buy the mare sweetmeats, to which she was very partial. To emphasize the point I made him feed them to her himself, which, to give the poor fellow his due, he did very good-naturedly.

Soon after daybreak we were on our way again, but found that the enemy were further off than we supposed. We marched ready to fight in an instant, for we were certain that our opponents would not lose so good a chance to attack us. But we arrived at the Nerbuddah without a shot. It is a wide and rapid stream, roaring along over its rocky bed; and is an obstacle strong enough to stop any army, except our own, if it were at all defended. The banks on the opposite side were bold and steep, but a way had been cut down to a ford, so that wheeled vehicles could pass. If this had been held we should have paid dearly, but there was not a man about. As the enemy had ignored such a fine position, we naturally thought that he had a stronger one further back, and one which suited him better. We went cautiously on, another mile or so, and then noticed a few stragglers peeping out at us from the edge of a wood. I rode after one of them, but when I caught her found that it was only a poor old village woman, who was nearly frightened to death; but when she saw that I was not going to hurt her, she told me that all the soldiers were in the town and the fort, and that all we should meet on the way were inoffensive people who were trying to get away from the fighting. We fell in with a large party of this sort almost at once, and as they were in battle array, and appeared to be armed, we would have fired if we had not noticed women and children among them. We discovered that those who did not wish to fight in the Rajah's war had left the fort, so with commendations to these people on their loyalty to the British Government, we let them pass unhurt. From the top of a hill, a little further on, we could plainly see the town with its thick high wall, and a strongly built fort inside. With the glass it was possible to discern masses of people, moving about on the ramparts and bastions, and great guns grinning from the embrasures. They let us have a taste of these, firing off some sixty-four-pounders, which made us give them a wide berth. One of our guides said that he had been inside the fort as a begging priest, and we had no reason to think that he was lying. He produced a long sketch of the fortifications, their strength, the number of troops inside, and so on; which caused the more timid among us to make their wills, and even the bolder ones to realize that there was tough work ahead.

Muskets were now new-flinted, pistols reloaded, swords sharpened, and every kind of warlike preparation made; while scouts searched for the way up to some rising ground called the Home Doongra, which overlooked the fort about two miles from the centre bastion, and where we intended to camp. Whenever the enemy saw any of our men up there they took a long shot at them, from a gun of an enormous size. I have always found that, where there was good cannonading, the gunners had formerly been in the Company's army. Some, I daresay, deliberately join our artillery in order to learn the trade, and then depart to some Rajah. The gunners are the only people in the Native armies who are regularly paid, getting, some of them, fifty or sixty rupees a month, while the other soldiers are glad to get four. The Company allows any servant, or Sepoy, to leave whenever he wishes to go, so it is very easy for a man who has been taught all the details of a soldier's profession to transfer his services elsewhere. There were three or four men who had learned the science of gunnery in this way with the Rajah's troops, and they were very good shots. Such experts are generally in so great estimation with their men, that they will die rather than leave the gun they command. Two, I know, were killed, and another went back to his home in Allahabad.

When the Rajah of Nagpore broke his alliance with the Company the inhabitants of this fort promised to stay loyal, and to receive British troops, so one regiment of Native Infantry and some part of the 8th Regiment of Bengal Cavalry, were sent under the command of Major O'Brien. As soon as the garrison saw what a mere handful they had to deal with, they fired on them, and the little force had to withdraw. But the Rajah himself had been captured, for as soon as his treachery was known, the British Resident at Nagpore sent Captain Brown of the Bengal Native Infantry, with a party of men to seize him. On their approach the Rajah hid in his zenana and sought protection among his women. Under any other circumstances that place would have been sacred, but the Rajah had to be got at all costs, so our men went in and arrested him. This sent the women into a tremendous fury, and they flew at Captain Brown; who was lucky to get away with a badly scratched face, a good deal of hair pulled from his whiskers and the top of his head, and the loss of one wing of his military full-dress coat. The Rajah, now a prisoner, was sent off under the special charge of Captain Brown to the frontier of our provinces, but he managed to make an extraordinary escape. The Captain was anxious not to hurt his pride by putting him in fetters, or taking away his belongings, but left him at large in his tent. He seemed to be quiet, and sorry for what he had done, so perhaps vigilance was relaxed a little; but no matter how sharp a watch had been kept, he would have got away. Some of his guards, and some of our Sepoys, who had no doubt been bribed, planned to set him free under cover of night. These people managed to get themselves on guard duty, but their officer had positive orders to see the Rajah himself, personally, every hour, and I believe did so. During the previous day the Rajah pretended to be ill, and lay wrapped in his bed-clothes. Seeing him still lying like that when he went his rounds, the officer in charge thought that everything must be all right; but it turned out afterwards that what he saw was nothing but a pillow, covered with bed-clothes, and with the help of those whom he had corrupted the Rajah had got clear off. This carelessness was visited upon the Commanding Officer, who was brought to a general court martial because of it. He was acquitted however on account of the treachery in his detachment, but it should be a warning to all young officers to perform their duty with the utmost care. That Rajah was not a man to be trusted. Of the Sepoys who broke their allegiance, and were afterwards taken, all were shot. It was the only possible way of dealing with them. Some of them he had bribed with valuable jewels, others with lavish promises of future rewards. But though, when he escaped, he was in the heart of his own country, nobody would offer him refuge. He was hunted from fort to fort, and from door to door, until at last he was found dead somewhere in Scindia's country.

We camped for the night in a small clump of trees near the Home Doongra, the eminence I have spoken of before. As the night was very sultry my tent had been pitched on the banks of a small stream, which was lined with thick bushes. I had not lain down for very long, when I heard the sound of so many animals moving about in the bushes that I began to think the neighbourhood a dangerous one, and that a tiger or something like that had taken a fancy to a meal of Baggage-Master. Listening carefully I heard what seemed to be bird calls, and then knew that there were thieves about, so I cocked my pistol. A voice said distinctly, "He wakes. Squat down." Jumping from my cot I ran toward the place, but they were off, and in the dark it was impossible to catch up with them, though I would guess that there were five or six at least. I ought to have changed my quarters, but the moon came out just then, and made the place look so enchanting that I stayed where I was till morning.

As we reconnoitred the next day the sixty-four-pounder took a shot or two at us, but the rest of the division came up, and we formally invested the town, and the fort. We took up our position on the east side of the fort; with the river, a clump of trees, and a large village in front which screened us completely. It turned out that the plan, filled in with so much detail by our spy, was completely false, and that he had never been near the fort in his life; but had hung about in the woods and villages and manufactured it out of whatever information he could pick up. We trusted him completely, for he had worked for us for more than twenty years, but he had grown old and lost his nerve. Because of his past services he was given a pension, and a little hut to live in, so that he could spend the rest of his days in peace. We had, however, absolutely sure information that a lot of our old friends the Pindarees were in the fort; and that some five hundred of them intended to help with the defence. We invested the place so closely that not a man could get out, and we were determined that the garrison should pay for their treachery, and the Pindarees for their insolence. Every night we formed a complete, and close, chain of sentrics round the town and the fort, though the distance was more than three miles. In addition a strong mounted, and dismounted, picquet with their horses always on the bit, was posted at every quarter of a mile. Wishing to save bloodshed our General offered the garrison mercy if they would surrender, but in their usual way they spun out the negotiations with every possible trick, so that they could strengthen their defences the more. They thought that our guns were only there to frighten them, and they were encouraged in this delusion, first of all by their priests, and then by their own confidence that heavy guns could never have been got over the mountainous route that we had been compelled to follow; for, as they said, it would be difficult for even a hawk to find its way over such precipices. They were so certain of this that they refused all offers, even that of a safe conduct for their women and children. We soon convinced them that they were wrong about the guns, and begged them not to risk their wives and families, but they treated it all with contempt. We kept on until the very last moment and then began our cannonade. As I have noticed before on these occasions, every bird and beast within hearing fled from the noise of battle, and the world was left deserted for man to fight in. The heavy cannon balls crashed on their way. The enemy hoisted their flag and returned our fire.

But we did not start shelling immediately as the batteries were still unfinished, and the General, knowing what execution they would do, made a final effort to save the women and children in the fort. He offered them protection to any place they might wish to go to, and the chance to take their private property with them, but stressed that if they refused this then he would begin shelling, and the destruction would be dreadful. The enemy knew that he would be as good as his word, and at last decided to let their families go. It was agreed that they should leave at ten o'clock the next morning, and they were told to rendezvous in a large mango grove. When that time came we were glad to see an immense number of people arriving there, nobody wants women and children to suffer. They poured out like a great funeral procession, some were weeping, but none appeared to doubt their safety. A few men came with them but without arms, while from the walls above the soldiers, in great numbers, watched their loved ones go in peace leaving them to the battle. Some of the women were very beautiful, and wore their richest clothes. In all there were about a thousand of them. When they told us where they wanted to go they were marshalled in some order and sent off under guard. A little way off from us, they turned round for a last look at the menfolk that many of them would never see again. We gave three cheers as they passed out of sight, to let the soldiers in the fort know that we had kept our promise, and they returned the shout. Out of a feeling for the women and children, who were leaving their loved ones behind to endure the battle, we did not begin the shelling until they were too far away to know that it had started.

We opened on them about noon, but the first shell dropped about half way between us and them, and was greeted with cries of derision. The next one made them change their tune, and had them scurrying in all directions. After we had sent over about a dozen, the Rajah himself appeared in state on the King's Bastion; he was easily spotted by his ceremonial umbrella. He had twenty or thirty people with him, and they were about a mile and a half away. Seeing him appear, the Captain of artillery laid one on specially for him, and strange to say the shell landed on the very top of the bastion. Immediately, even before the smoke had well cleared, the state umbrella disappeared and every living soul with it. The shouting in our battery was terrific, but not a word came from the fort, and it looked as if they were all occupied with their own safety. "That's picking their teeth for them," said an Irish Sergeant. Even at that distance we could distinctly hear the cries of the wounded, and knew from our own experience what they must be suffering. The return fire from the fort was good and steady, some of their long shots would not have disgraced European gunners. As I have said, I was Baggage-Master, but during the siege I also acted as Aide-de-Camp to Brigadier-General Watson, who personally supervised the operations; constantly riding round the chain of posts, and in and out of the batteries, closely watching the progress of the siege. Our chief breaching-guns were on the east side of the fort, with the river between ourselves and the enemy. Many of them, stealing out to get a drink from the stream, were killed in the attempt. I have often argued heatedly with my brother officers, whether it is right for me to hide myself in a hole, or behind a wall, and in perfect safety myself, shoot at any of the enemy who happen to have to show their nose. True enough it is the people you are fighting whom you treat in this manner, but I still feel that to deal out death from a place where you are yourself in perfect safety smacks of cowardice, even if it is not murder. Give me man to man, and sword to sword. The other method cannot be just, though it is often done.

We breached a corner bastion at a place where its base ran down to the river, and where we could approach under cover and take the defenders unawares. Everybody was eager to get to work, for the breach looked fit for storming. Many were so cock-a-hoop that they vowed they could ride into the gap, or drive up it in a gig. Hearing this sort of rash opinion, from young men who were too eager to rush into danger, Captain Tickell, our engineer, smiled and said, "You can be certain that when you do storm you will not find it easy. I will take a look myself. It is better to lose one life than a hundred." So, crossing the river about a quarter of a mile lower down, he stole along the bank unobserved. He ordered all the batteries to concentrate their fire on the top of the breach, if the enemy noticed him. We watched him go, and trembled for his safety, for he was a brave officer and one of our best engineers. It looked to be a difficult climb, but he got to the top of the breach, and waved his hat to let us know that he was there. Some of the defenders rushed out at him, but he jumped down the fallen masonry and got safely away; while we opened on the enemy with everything we had, and some of those who came out to kill were killed themselves. When Captain Tickell got back he said nothing, for the silly boasts of the young men had made him angry; but he directed the fire of his battery on to a large tree which had been shot down, and now lay in the path of the assault. It completely blocked the foot of the breach, and if we had been foolish enough to storm in a hurry, there must have been heavy losses. He said afterwards that he was glad that the big talk of some had stung him into making a personal inspection, for he had thought, at one time, that the tree would have helped us instead of being the deadly hindrance that it was. The first shot landed a shell perfectly in the tangle of its torn-up roots, and blew the whole thing to pieces. Bystanders started to chaff the officer, who had laid the gun, about his good shooting. "By the powers," said an Irish Sergeant, "that is what I call a moving shot." "A remover certainly," said the officer, "but I wish you would move that big bough that hangs on the bastion." "I will have a try if Your Honour pleases," replied the Sergeant, "but I would rather see Your Honour finish what you have completed, and then I'll do the rest." We were all joking among ourselves, and laughing at Pat's drollery, when the storming party was ordered to fall in. New flints were fitted, bayonets fixed, and at about three o'clock in the afternoon we crossed the Nerbuddah, and marched along the river bank to our other breaching battery, and there waited for further orders.

At about four o'clock the party moved on with the General himself and his suite at the head, for he wished to lead the storming party in person, and I, with the rest of his staff, was anxious to share his toils and his glory. It was no easy task I assure you, for we fagged and fought hard for nearly three hours. The attacking force was made up of two companies of the 14th Bengal Native Infantry, supported by the 13th Regiment. We started slowly along the bank, as quiet as a midnight thief. When we got some ten or twenty paces from the breach, we were visible to those on a projecting bastion of the fort, who sent out a party to hold us off. This they succeeded in doing for a while, but our brave Native troops, inspired by their gallant leader, beat them from their posts. They then withdrew to some huts which had managed to escape being burnt, and fired at us from loopholes in them; until, in some way, they set fire to the places and burned themselves out. This stopped us for a while, as we could not pass the blazing huts, and we lost some few men; but seeing that if we stayed there much longer we should all be destroyed we rushed through the flames; only to find a large body of men drawn up on the other side, ready to oppose us. There was a hard struggle for a time, but when our brave little General gave the order to charge the butchery began. The enemy fought desperately, rushing on our bayonets sword in hand, but when at last they did begin to run the carnage was dreadful. I saw one grey-headed old Arab, with two bayonet wounds already, lying on his back and slashing away with his sword in a most resolute manner, until a bullet through his head put an end to him. We drove the fugitives before us, while they edged away to our left in the hope of escaping in that direction, but we had already sent strong forces of both infantry and cavalry to block the route and hem them in. Fight they must, and fight they did. I never saw men fall so fast. Bunched together as they were, every shot told; until in desperation hundreds of them flung down their arms, and took to the water. Most were drowned, and those who did get to the other side were taken prisoner. A few escaped into the fort, and the rest surrendered.

In a deep ravine were about a hundred women and children, who had been kept behind to grind corn for the garrison. They had suffered dreadfully from our shelling; but we left them a guard to protect them from any deliberate attack, while we pushed on, for we were still exposed to a smart fire from the fort. In about an hour we had managed to clear the town, and it became necessary to find some sort of shelter for the night, so that we could be out of the way of firing from the fort. This we did by taking possession of the temples, and the principal buildings at the entrances to the main streets. Things began to quiet down, save for the groans of the wounded and dying; whom we were powerless to help, though the guard protected them from robbery or insult. A town after a battle is no pleasant sight, and we were glad enough when darkness hid this one from us.

21

A Very Beautiful Girl

It was ten o'clock at night when we got possession of the town, and I was sent off to examine a distant temple, to see if it would make suitable quarters for some of our troops. It stood at the end of a long street, and I had to grope my way along, helped only by the light of blazing huts or the faint stars. There was no need to risk many men on such an errand, when one could do all that was needed. It was one of those unenviable tasks which fall in a soldier's way now and then, and which he must face if he is to do his duty. So I went cautiously along, with a pistol in each hand, keeping a good look-out around me; occasionally stumbling over a dead body, but with no time to look behind. Suddenly somebody gripped me by the leg and said, "Who are you?" I jumped away and said, "Friend." "Then give me some water," the voice replied. I had none to give, and was on a mission, so there was nothing I could do but leave him. I had hardly got over this fright, before a huge beam fell from one of the blazing buildings, and I heard voices and people running to where it had fallen. I stopped for a minute to listen, and then went slowly on until I came at last to the foot of the temple steps. There was the tinkle of a bell somewhere, and when I reached the door at the top I could hear the murmur of prayers beyond it. Stepping quickly into the room, I saw, by the light of a small lamp hanging from the ceiling, an old priest flat on his face in supplication before his idol. I gave him the usual salute and was about to speak, when he blew out the light and dashed from the temple. What he took me for I do not know; probably a ghost.

I went back along the same street again, but a little faster this time. When I was about half way along I heard voices, then the sound of horses' hooves, and finally saw the outline of men on horseback approaching. From their conversation I guessed that they were some of our ally, Scindia's, men who were out looting; and dodged them as best I could for I knew that they would think nothing of cutting my throat, just for the buttons on my uniform. Hiding there in the dark I could hear a huge dog howling, and guessed that he was watching by the body of his master, and there in fact we found him the next morning, crying piteously whenever anyone approached. We could not get him away, so he was shot to put him out of his misery. At last I got back to the General, and made my report, and then led two companies to the temple, but the old priest had not come back. That done I returned to the General, and helped him establish the rest of the troops for the night, then he and his suite, myself included, returned to camp, had a good dinner and a sound night's sleep.

When we went back to the town the next morning we learned to our astonishment that a Captain and about fifty men had been in the fort for the greater part of the night. The General could hardly believe his ears, but the news was true none-the-less. The gate was thrown open for us, and we went in to find that the death and destruction there was worse even than anything we had found in Huttras. The details would be too grim to describe, it is enough to say that during that day we threw upward of five hundred bodies into a large well, where the enemy had already flung a great number of their dead. The well was closed up, and an artillery man, with a bayonet, scratched on the stone the simple words "The Soldier's Grave." But we had scarcely gone a hundred yards that morning when we met Captain B and his men with the Keeledar and another person in custody. The General asked him, sternly, by what authority he had allowed his force to enter the fort without instructions. The Captain told a lame story, about having been offered a bribe to let the Keeledar escape; and that when he refused it he was told that he might march his men into the fort, if he liked. There was obviously some mystery behind it all, and an ill-natured world made ill-natured remarks about it. Certainly something that came out afterwards would have made a court martial necessary if the Captain had not been killed, and the affair buried with him. He was an officer of a hitherto unblemished reputation. The Keeledar was a most respectable-looking man, elegantly dressed, but I never saw anybody more dejected or careworn in my life. He made the most profound salaams to the General, saying, "Do as you like with me." I was told to inform him that he would have to face a court martial, and that his sentence would be death, unless he could prove that he had rebelled under orders. He answered, "I am as willing to meet death as I am to meet you here." He was placed in custody, and our next object was to get rid of our prisoners. There were about two thousand of them, and nearly a third were wounded. The greater part were deprived of their arms and sent home.

As I had arranged everything for the protection of the property I was appointed prize agent for headquarters, and immediately began collecting everything on one spot. My first care was to put double sentinels at the entrance to the zenana, until I, and the other two prize agents, could search the place. I took a peep later on at my two men, and found that one of them had deserted his post and gone inside. Immediately afterwards I met the rascal coming out, carrying a couple of boxes about two feet by three. I asked him what he had got, and he answered, "Nothing but a little paun," (betel).[1] I told him to give the boxes to me, and he did so. They were tremendously heavy. I opened them, and there was all the zenana jewellery inside. On the verandah there were great bales of silks, and of shawls sewn together like patchwork quilts. The Keeledar's wife and two daughters were seated inside, and seeing me they flung themselves at my feet, and begged for mercy. I would as soon have injured them, or given them insult, as I would my own mother; but this they could hardly believe, for in the Native wars women are the victims of the conqueror's every whim, but in no case has this been allowed in the Company's armies. These poor women were in a frenzy, and nothing I could do could calm them, until I swore solemnly by God that they should in no way be harmed. Their gratitude then was overwhelming, that of the eldest daughter particularly, would have moved the hardest heart. She was the most perfect beauty I have ever seen, slender and elegant, with beautifully regular features, lit up by two dark eyes under dark eyebrows. In a voice of the greatest sweetness and charm, she begged for protection; clinging to the sabre which hung by my side which such affecting importunity, until I pledged myself for her safety. I took her, and her mother and sister, to a room upstairs until they could be joined by the Keeledar, who was under arrest. Most people thought that nothing could save him from the full penalty of his rebellion.

We were the whole day in getting the prize goods properly together. There were elephants, horses, camels, bullocks, animals and merchandise of every kind. The General himself visited the Keeledar's family, and promised them safety, and everything that they needed. He particularly ordered that all their clothes, many of which were very splendid, should be given to them. He was as humane as he was brave, and the sight of those weeping women moved him deeply. "It is a sad sight, Shipp," he said. "What can we do to help them in their distress?" He ordered me to tell them that he would give them all the aid he could, and that they might see the Keeledar that very day, and every day, but that for the present he must be imprisoned by himself. They were heavily veiled when they visited him, and they all did their best to comfort him, the elder daughter especially, assuring him that he had fallen into the hands of merciful enemies. The old man sobbed and cried a good deal, but he cheered up in the end. They stayed with him about two hours on that first occasion, and then went back to their room in the zenana, relieved at having seen him.

A general court martial, composed entirely of Native officers, was set up to try the Keeledar under a warrant issued by the Governor-General in council, on a charge of treachery and rebellion against the government. The venerable Soubahdar who presided on this occasion had seen forty years' service, and was a shrewd and clever fellow. The proceedings were conducted by a European officer, and written down in English. The accused's crime was read to him by the interpreter. He seemed to understand it perfectly, and pleaded guilty in a firm, manly, voice, seeming to be quite ready to pay the penalty for his fault. The President turned to him, and said, in a most moving fashion, "Keeledar, you have put

The Hall of Audience, Delhi

The Palace at Agra

your seal to your own death warrant by that confession, but have you not got a wife and children? If you do not value your own life do you also want to murder them?"[2] So impressive an appeal made the Keeledar think. He struggled with himself for a moment in great agitation, but the President said, gently, "Take your time. Think before you pronounce the doom of your wife and children. Your time is ours." The whole court, judges and spectators alike, waited anxiously for the old man's reply. At last he said, "What you say about my wife and children is very just. I will not make them suffer, but what will the Rajah think, if I should deceive him?" He was told of the Rajah's own treachery, and how he had run away, and was now probably dead. This news upset him greatly, but after a pause he drew out of his bosom a long roll of paper; which contained the most peremptory instructions to fight the English "as long as one stone of Gurrah Mundellah stood upon another, or one drop of water remained in the Nerbuddah to wash away their blood." He received this letter, on the very day when he promised to give up the fort to Major O'Brien. Other documents also showed that his resistance to the government was due to the positive orders he had been given by the Rajah, so he was fully acquitted, but kept a prisoner for a while, and then pensioned by the Company. He afterwards told me that his difficulty had been whether to sacrifice his life, or make a bitter enemy of the Rajah. He was very grateful for the merciful treatment he had received, but it would certainly have been a blot on our victory if he had been executed. When I told his family of their father's acquittal they were overcome with joy, prostrating themselves to the ground, and crying, "Bless the humane English! May they flourish in the land!" When he was allowed home his family welcomed him with extravagant delight, but from that day none of us was allowed to see the beautiful daughter again. When the country had quieted down a little, they were all allowed to go home.

We sold our prize goods by public auction, and the sale lasted a whole day, bringing us in a good deal of money. After leaving a regiment for the protection of the fort of Huttras, we went on our way towards Saugar, taking a number of small forts on the route, but none of them offered any trouble, for the garrisons gave them up easily enough. But we had scarcely settled down in cantonments before we set off against the strong stone fort of Gurrah Khootah, some time in March 1819. We were not sorry to be going, as we had a grudge of some months' standing against the Governor of this place, because of his insolence and it was time to bring him to his senses.

This fort of Gurrah Khootah had an odd history. It belonged at one time to Scindia, an ally of ours, but the garrison sold it to another Rajah for ten months' arrears of pay. Some years before that it had belonged to another Rajah still, who had been besieged by a considerable force from the Deccan, which persisted in its attack for eighteen months but could not take the place. The then owner, knowing that he could never free the place by himself, begged a bastard Frenchman named Jean Baptiste,[3] who was in Scindia's service, to rid him of the invaders, promising him lands in the neighbourhood for his reward. He accepted the offer, drove the besiegers away, and occupied the ground they had camped on with his own forces. On the day when he was to be given his reward, he marched into the fort in full military splendour, with colours flying, trumpets sounding, and drums beating, and was received as a deliverer, for there was no suspicion of treachery. While he and his men were being given the usual oriental welcome, shoulder to shoulder, breast to breast; suddenly, at a prearranged signal, the Frenchman's forces pounced on the unarmed garrison; drove them out, took their wives and daughters for their own, and possessed the fort. Jean Baptiste then either gave it, or sold it, to Scindia, who placed it in the charge of an Armenian named Harratoone. It was this man's forces who sold the fort for arrears of pay, and the one who bought it was the grandson of the Rajah Jean Baptiste had cheated. It was his, of course, without paying for it but he handed over the money, eighty thousand rupees; the old garrison walked out and he walked in, but the Armenian was left in command.

Scindia however still considered the fort to be his, and as he could not take it back himself he asked us to do it for him.

We would rather have fought against the old garrison, but orders are orders. The fort stands on the river Scend, which protects two sides of it, for the river is very deep. The other two sides are guarded by a strong stone wall, which runs along the edge of a branch stream. We had to take this outwork, therefore, before attacking the fort. A corner bastion was selected for our first attempt, at a spot where the branch stream was little more than three feet deep. We had a breach in a few hours, and were due to storm at moonrise. The ascent above the stream was steep, and difficult. Our General was in the battery when the attacking party moved out, and I was a little surprised to see him go with them, but I stuck close to his elbow. The enemy soon noticed us, and opened a heavy fire but their shots were high. Our brave Sepoys went in like heroes, and at one time there was desperate fighting at the top of the breach, so that it even looked as if our men might give way. As soon as he saw this, our courageous little General dashed through the water, and in an instant was up on the breach among the men, cheering them on to still fiercer efforts. With this new impetus the enemy were driven back into the fort and we gained possession of the outwork.

We left the men comfortably settled in a large house, about two hundred paces from this corner, where they were to spend the night, while we went back to camp considerably pleased with the day's exploits, which had certainly not disgraced our arms. The next morning, the chief engineer chose a spot for a battery on the other side of the river, opposite to an enormous bastion which ran down to the water's edge, like that at Mundella. In four and twenty hours the heavy guns had been placed ready for their work, and their magazines established in a village behind them, to which a sunken road had been dug, so as to have safe communication between the guns and their supplies. The General gave the most positive orders that no ammunition was to be kept in the battery, but everything was to be brought from the village as it was needed. When we returned from making these arrangements, and had settled down to breakfast, I had scarcely swallowed a mouthful before the General grew worried and said, "Shipp, saddle your horse immediately, and go as hard as you can to the grand battery,

I have a feeling that something is very wrong there." I was away in a minute, but when I got to the place I really thought that I should have fallen off my horse with the shock, for there were all the tumbrils, with shot and shell, and thousands of rounds of gunpowder, drawn up in the battery itself so that a single ball from the fort would have sent the whole lot sky high. I ordered it all to be taken back to a point behind the village, and luckily we got it there without any firing from the fort. It turned out afterwards that the Captain who had received the orders from the General, had passed them on to a Subaltern, who had passed them on to a Sergeant, who had passed them on to a Corporal, who ordered a poor stupid bullock-driver to see to it. I would strongly urge all young soldiers to remember that rank cannot excuse them from the duty of attending to things personally. If, through that neglect, the tumbrils had been blown up, many lives would have been lost, and our power to continue the siege destroyed, while the enemy would have had a further opportunity to strengthen their fort. It would have meant that crimes without number could have been charged against the officer—utter contempt of orders, pointed neglect of duty, wantonly destroying the lives of his men, and the property of the government which had been entrusted to him. Nothing could have saved his commission. As it was he had a narrow escape, for the last tumbril had hardly got back to the village, before the enemy opened a heavy fire on the spot where it had stood not five minutes earlier. On my way back I met the General himself, coming out for he was still worried about what might be happening. He admonished the Captain in the most severe terms, but he was as good-natured as he was brave and soon forgot about the incident.

We went round the other works, to make sure beyond doubt that orders were being obeyed. In the mortar-battery the General thought that the magazine was too close to the guns, but the officer in charge explained its special construction, and assured him that it was safe, so we let it pass and rode home again. The next morning we went down to watch our breaching-guns begin their work. Shelling had been started the day before, and had done great execution. The heavy guns were loaded, the match lit, and ready for the touch-hole, when a terrific explosion in the mortar-battery sent shells rocketing up all over the place; and exploding just over the heads of us in the breaching-battery. I was sent off at once to find out what had happened, and in my eagerness took a short cut, which brought me within a couple of hundred yards of the fort without realizing it, until their fire reminded me. Explosions were still taking place in our shelling battery, and I had no time to go further round so I kept on, and began to cross the river at a place which was completely commanded by three guns from the fort. The water was about four feet deep, so the going was slow, and as soon as I got to the middle they opened on me. Their first shot went about twenty yards behind me, the next fell short, but the third dropped so close that my horse and I were drenched with the spray. Slipping out of the saddle on the side furthest from the fort I pushed on, but the worst place lay ahead. However, the enemy seeing me fall from the saddle thought that I was dead, and set up a great shout of triumph, which angered me so much that I got back on my horse, gave them a wave of my cocked hat and dashed on. They fired three times more, but missed me, and were so fully occupied taking advantage of the general consternation caused by our mortar magazine blowing up, that I was allowed to complete my journey.

The first thing that I saw, when I got near the battery, was a Native gunner literally skinned from head to foot, and crying piteously for water. More Native soldiers and Europeans lay dead further on, and there was confusion and dismay everywhere. The cause of this great disaster I found had been a chain reaction, running through all the ammunition in the battery. Hundreds of shells, loaded and fused, and ready for use, had been piled behind the mortars; then, as it was being fired, one of the shells burst in the muzzle of its gun, and the fuse flew out and landed among the waiting heaps, their fuses caught and off they went. Just at that moment a soldier entered the magazine for something, and left the door open; the exploding ammunition got into the magazine and the whole lot went up. The soldier was the poor fellow I had seen lying skinned outside the battery; he had been blown at least twenty yards, and was so terribly injured that he died two days later. Sixteen men, four of them Europeans, lost their lives in this catastrophe. The explosion was very freakish in its effects. Three of the victims were lying dead in the battery, without their bodies showing the slightest signs of gunpowder. They had died simply from the results of concussion. One, a European, was blown some yards into the river but not hurt at all. Conductor Glossop of the Bengal Foot Artillery, a man weighing upward of twenty stone, was standing right among the shells when they started to explode, and escaped without a scratch. Truly the ways of Providence are inscrutable. The General himself arrived very soon, and having learned the cause of the disaster could do nothing more than sympathize as we had done. No one was to blame, for the accident could neither have been foreseen nor prevented.

The enemy of course took full advantage of our trouble, and rushed every man, and every weapon, into positions where they could damage us most. But as soon as we had got the dead and wounded back to camp, all the mortars and howitzers in the two batteries were reloaded, and let fly in such style at the crowd which had gathered in the fort to watch us that none remained, save a few bearers who were carrying away the dead and injured. We gave them three cheers, but they were in no mood to reply. Our great breaching-battery then opened fire, and we sent that lot off with three cheers as well, and this time the enemy shouted back. After that the firing went on, coolly and systematically, while we returned to camp and that evening buried our dead.

I had an odd escape the next morning. Captain Daggalier of the 13th Bengal Native Infantry invited me to breakfast with him, in a large house where he was staying, about five hundred yards from the fort. We were seated at table in an upstairs room, enjoying our meal and facing each other over the repast, when a three-pound shot came through the window, and flew under the table between me and Captain Daggalier. Never did I feel so glad that I had got long legs; mine were, in fact, so lanky that I had only been able to screw them just under the edge of the table; if they had been of normal size, and stretched out well underneath, they would have been carried away to a certainty. Needless to say everything in front of us was smashed, and thrown about the place, but I managed to find another party, and breakfast with them before going off to meet the General, who wanted to examine our approaches from this side.

22

Digging for Buried Treasure

THE particular bastion which we were battering at was a tough piece of masonry, extremely thick and well put together, so we pegged away at the foundations. At last they gave way, and the rest of the structure showed signs of following, so that by the next morning the breach looked practicable. I said to my old friend the Irish Sergeant, "What do think of that for a breach?" "The devil a better within a day's march," he replied. "But do you think we shall get in, Sergeant?" "Never a fear of that, for there is not a living soul but what our shells have kilt, and destroyed, and you have nothing to do but shoot the remainder and the place is yours." Pat was always good for a laugh, but he was angry this time and said, "Faith you may laugh, but how would you like to be kilt yourself? Answer me that."

The assault was ordered for the following morning, allowing all possible places from which the defenders might harass our men to be knocked off in the meantime. Already a splendid palace, just behind the breach, was in flames. The Keeledar was beginning to think of giving up the place, for his defences were crumbling, many of his men were dead, and the garrison had suffered from a number of explosions. So he sent an envoy to our General, promising to surrender the fort if his troops were allowed to march out with their arms, and private property. There could be no difficulty in agreeing to that, for their arms were not worth ten pounds, and the whole of their private property was the clothes they stood up in. It would be a most difficult breach to storm, and even if we were successful it would cost us at least fifty men, so the General accepted the Keeledar's offer, much against the wishes of some of the Company's officers, who blamed him for letting the enemy carry off their arms. He did so with the advice of his staff officers, who had been with the Company's army, some of them for many years; and who were not impressed by the hotheads, whose eyes were over-much on the chances for promotion. Next morning the garrison marched out, fifteen hundred men, well armed and equipped, better in fact than we supposed, so we had no reason to regret that we had not thrown away men's lives. Originally they had been two thousand strong, but were now reduced by death and wounds to three-quarters of that number. When we marched down, the gates of the fort were still closed, and the men at their station on the ramparts. I was ordered to tell them that the time had come for them to go; if they did not, we would storm at once for our men were drawn up ready at the foot of the breach. At last the gates were thrown open, and the Keeledar marched out at the head of his men, with a firm, steady, pace. He was a fine-looking man, as indeed were all his soldiers. They brought their wounded with them in cots, and begged that we would look after them. As he passed our General the Keeledar gave a salute, which was coolly returned, so they marched out and we marched in.

There was the same kind of devastation inside the fort as we had seen so often before. Houses were torn up by the roots, the dead bodies of men and animals were scattered about, particularly by the gate, and over all that appalling smell. The Rajah's palace had been literally blown to pieces, its fallen pillars crushing men, women and children beneath their weight. We found the old Armenian Governor in the centre of the fort, such a picture of woe as one may rarely see. He had been imprisoned in a small cell, and nearly starved to death throughout the siege. An old man, for he was over sixty, with white hair and a light complexion which made him look perfectly cadaverous. You could have laid your finger in the deep furrows that lined his face, and his beady dark eyes were sunk deep in his head. His father had been an Armenian, and his mother a Native woman. We let the poor old wretch go to his family, which had been sent to a near-by village during the fighting. The fort was nothing but a mass of desolation, and poverty, for the first garrison had taken away everything of value when they sold it. But there was a rumour that Jean Baptiste had hidden thirty lacs of rupees[1] somewhere about the place, and we were determined to find it. We dug up large pigs of lead, bars of iron, and sheets of copper, pits of grain, and vats of ghee, and would have found the money too no doubt if it had been there, but it was not. After we had dug down about twenty feet, and worked our way under the palace, we opened up a kind of dungeon which we entered at the risk of treading upon dangerous reptiles. From this several cells led off, which had been used, most probably, as prisons for those who could not see eye to eye with the Rajah. After searching in every hole, and digging in every corner, we came at last to a newly built wall, and knocking a hole in the top we saw a door. After we had forced our way through, we entered a large room, which had been recently cleaned and whitewashed, in the centre of which was a trap-door with a huge lock. Our hearts beat high with expectation, we had found the treasure at last; but we were disappointed for the door led to nothing but a tomb, in which lay the body of some poor murdered person. We gave up the search, and the whole of the property we had captured sold for no more than fifteen hundred rupees, and even that we were obliged to hand over to Scindia some time later.

The melancholy task of burying the dead was our next concern, and in the course of it I had the solemn duty of following one of the Company's artillery men to his last rest. One of the funeral party kept lagging behind, and I asked him sharply why he did not keep up. He answered that just before he was killed he had been fighting with the man whose body we were following, and he did not think that the dead man had forgiven him yet. "Phoo," I said, "the man can't hurt you now, he is dead." "Begging Your Honour's pardon, I once knew a dead man who came to life again, and this one said that dead or alive he would give me a beating, and I wouldn't like to provoke him." "Don't talk nonsense," I said. "Nonsense, Your Honour," he replied, "it's no such thing. He was a mighty cunning man when he was alive, and who knows what he has learned now he is dead." Nothing would induce him to come nearer, until the corpse was lowered into the grave, and the earth half filled in, then he looked down and said with some satisfaction, "Faith you are snug enough now Joy," and he went off, still no doubt expecting a visit from his dead comrade some day, so great is the power of superstition. When all was finished we moved out, leaving behind a regiment of Native Infantry to look after the place, until Scindia could send a garrison of his own that he could rely on. We learned afterwards, that he was by no means pleased with the way we had knocked his fort about.

Now that things looked quieter I got leave to visit my wife in Cawnpore, which is four hundred miles from our station at Saugar. I covered the distance in fourteen days, and it was delightful to be with my wife again, and forget war for a time. Cawnpore was a gay place just then, and I was so occupied with festivities of one kind and another, during the whole of my eight or ten days' leave, that I was quite worn out when the time came for me to return. My wife accompanied me for some miles along the road. She loved me so that she would willingly have followed me to the field, but things happen on a line of march that no decent woman should be allowed to see. Even so, some will insist on being with their husbands, and stay with them even in dishonour and a shameful death. It is a pity either that women love so much, or that men deserve their love so little. I would rather endure the hardships of a campaign than go through the misery of parting with my family, but that is no reason for exposing them to some of the things to be seen in an Indian encampment. In thirteen days I reached Saugar, but met with such torrential rain and scorching sun, that the foundations were laid of a disease which nearly cost me my life, though it was some time before it showed itself.

It was intended that my division should stay in its present quarters for some time, to keep an eye on the recently conquered provinces of Saugar and Candish, so we began to build huts against the winter and to think of sending for our wives. Mine was the first to come, and though the journey was dangerous she reached me at the fort of Huttras, where I had gone to meet her, in four days. Within a month ten ladies arrived, and our little station was the gayest of the gay. I mentioned earlier the trouble we had with baboons in Africa; the monkeys here were just as bad, one old male being a perfect nuisance. He would run off with silks, satins, shawls, or even gold and silver, anything in fact that he could lay his hands on. He took a fancy to a shawl which he saw in a shop one day, but it was rather long, and hindered his escape. The shopkeeper caught him by the tail and held on while he shouted for help and kicked at the beast. The monkey screamed and bit the man, the shopman bit too, and took off an inch or so of his adversary's tail, which none the less got away with its prize. Bloodstains led the pursuers to a dilapidated mosque, where the monkey was shot, and a hoard of things found which many an honest neighbour had been accused of stealing. These animals are spoiled by the Hindoos, who pet and feed them; this one was so large that he would have been too much for any one man. These artful, and mischievous creatures are best let alone.

Our festivities at Saugar were brought to an end by orders to proceed against the strong hill fort of Asseerghur,[2] some three hundred miles away. The rainy season had begun, which made our wives even more anxious than they usually were at the start of a campaign, but none of their husbands shammed sick, in order to stay behind. The heat was so intense, that in a large double tent, with grass mats hung around and continually wetted, the glass stood at 120 or 130 at midday. After a shower, the earth steamed like a hot-bed. In spite of this we were obliged to push on, by forced marches, to reach Asseerghur as soon as possible. There was not many of us, but we had a considerable battering-train. The country all round the fort was barren and desolate; infested with wild beasts, which carried off many of our small cattle each night. The forces from the Presidencies of Madras, and Bombay, had got there before us, leaving a space, and a dreary barren one it was, for our Bengal troops when they arrived. The earth around us was so bare, that there was nothing but a few prickly bushes to be seen. We were about a mile and a half from the fort, whose gigantic sides, even at this distance, seemed to hang over us. How we were to get up such a terrific precipice would certainly have puzzled a wiser head than mine. Major-General Doveton, in command of the whole force before Asseerghur, very courteously invited us to breakfast, but we could not take to their insipid dried fish, and dried meat; we missed our Bengal luxuries, so we made a second breakfast when we got back.

The fort had been the property of Scindia, who had ceded it to the Company for some equivalent, but the Governor had the impudence to disobey both his master and us, and fired on the troops of both when they passed. He thought, I suppose, that the place was impregnable and decided to keep it for himself. It certainly occupied an enormously strong position, which had been further strengthened with great skill. The idea of climbing up to such a place, or breaching its walls, seemed absurd. The hill on which it stood must have been at least a couple of miles from the top to the bottom; and one perpendicular rock, about two hundred feet high, was heavily defended with great cannon and ginjalls. There was a splendid mosque in the centre of the town, whose two minarets seemed to pierce the clouds. Some way away from this temple was a large sheet of water, fed by a spring, and the enemy's troops could take shelter from our shells in excavations among the rocks. The fort itself was about two miles long, by a quarter broad. There was a walled town on the south side, in which was the principal entrance to the fortifications, and this was very strongly defended with numberless underworks and bastions. It was a beautiful enough place to look at, but promised to be desperately hard to take.

The morning after our arrival I went with the General to examine the sites allotted to our batteries. At first the summit of the mountain was covered with clouds, but they soon cleared away, and we found that the place assigned to us was about two-thirds of the way up, towards the perpendicular rock; where our guns had to be elevated so much that we were forced to sink their trails in the earth, which hindered the recoil and damaged them considerably. It looked as if the most we could do would be to knock off a few defence points, and that we should have to depend on shelling for the main effect, so to it we went as hard as we could. One night, about this time, I dined with an officer of the Madras Army and took a little too much wine. I started home on my favourite mare, but missed the way, After riding a good deal further than the proper distance between our two camps, I began to be anxious, and as I was in thick jungle I stopped to consider what I ought to do. That moment might have been my last. I had laid the reins loose on the mare's back, when she suddenly bunched herself together, swung round and snorted. Luckily I managed to grab her mane, and in turning saw a huge tiger squatting in the road we were following. It would have been death to run from him, so I pulled the mare round again, and urged her towards the beast; but not a step would she take. I had a pair of loaded pistols in my holster, but did not wish to throw away my fire; though I drew one out, and went on struggling with the mare, and making a great noise about it. The tiger watched us a moment, and then slunk away, to the great joy of man and horse. It was not long before I was back in my tent. I had a pretty fair idea of the spot where this adventure had taken place, for I always like to study the ground we are to fight over, so I returned to it the next morning, and found that the tiger had been devouring a small cow when we ran into him. It is always wise when meeting a ravening animal of that kind, not to run away. A Captain in the Company's service told me once that he had been out shooting alone, and had discharged his piece, when a large tiger made his appearance. He stood his ground, and man and beast stared at each other for a while, until the Captain, who was a funny fellow, bent down and looked at the animal through his legs; and in that posture moved away, which so surprised the tiger that he made off at once. I cannot absolutely vouch for the truth of this story, for he told another that was even stranger. Some of us were discussing once how long a man could go without food, and live. I said that in my opinion seven days was about the limit. The Captain however thought otherwise, and begging my pardon most politely vowed that, when in the West Indies, he himself had often gone without food for weeks, and that once for six months he had eaten nothing but Cayenne pepper. If he relished a diet of that sort he was obviously a hot man, so none of us cared to contradict him, but this last tale might indicate that his stories were not always to be trusted.

A few days after we had begun the siege against this very strong fort, General Watson, who commanded the Bengal

Division, came into my tent obviously very well pleased with himself. "Shipp," he said, "I have got some good news for you. I am sure you will be pleased." "Well, General," I said, "good news is always acceptable, what is it?" "I have at last got permission to lead our storming column in person when it attacks the fort. I am sure you and Knolles will support me." "I am always ready to do my duty, Sir," I replied. "I know that," said the General, "and before a week is over we will plant Old England's banner in glory, on the top of the highest tower it has ever reached. That fort must be the loftiest in the world. Fifteen hundred feet, at least, above the level of the plain." Such gallantry however was not needed, for the fort surrendered some little time after this, and the General still lives in the bosom of his family, happy in his native land. He had a long and most distinguished career in the 14th Regiment, first as a Subaltern, and ultimately as Commander, and during the whole thirty-three or four years was never absent from duty for one day. He was greatly beloved for his kindness to all about him. I myself would be guilty of base ingratitude if I did not say how much I owe to his disinterested friendship and generosity, on numberless occasions.

Our incessant shelling killed so many of the enemy, as they went to the pool for water, that the stench of their dead bodies became intolerably offensive. Unable to endure it any longer, the garrison persuaded the Keeledar to surrender and as he was a great coward he most readily consented. He sent us a messenger, saying that if we would cease shelling he would come out and make some arrangement. Our officers agreed to silence the guns for a few hours, for it was plain that we stood little chance of taking the place; but we added that if our terms were not accepted we would start again with redoubled force. So it was agreed that one more parley would be granted. The Natives, in their high-flown way, say of this fort that none but the crafty hawk high-lingering over his prey, or the morning lark soaring and sweetly singing over its young, could ever see the inside of Asseerghur.

The little town outside had been taken, some days before our arrival, by a division of the Bombay Army under Colonel Frazer, of the Royal Scots, but they found holding it warm work, for it was so completely dominated by the fort that every street could be raked by heavy fire from a distance of no more than three hundred yards. Our soldiers had to seek shelter in the temples and huts; without this cover the town would have been untenable. If, in the course of their duty, they had to run from one spot to another, they drew a hundred shots at once. The enemy had a strong party constantly on the look-out; for they thought, with some reason, that our capture of the town was but a first step to an attack upon the fort, and this they were determined to prevent. Nothing will stop soldiers looking about, and in spite of risk they will go off after plunder; but some of our men paid dearly for this violation of military law. Our principal post was in a large temple, which the officers occupied on one side, and the men on the other. One by one, the rank and file stole off in search of plunder. As soon as the enemy noticed this, they made a sudden attack on the remaining few, and the Colonel was killed while defending himself against unequal numbers. When the rest came back they were overwhelmed to see their Colonel dead, and comrades who had shared with them in the glory of capturing the town, either killed or wounded. This is but one instance out of many in my experience, of the fatal effects of indiscipline. No prospects of gain can justify a soldier in leaving his post; if he does he can be sentenced to death on any of three counts—for leaving his post in front of the enemy, for abandoning his officer, and for plundering. A crime of this sort breaks almost every section of the articles of war.

23

The Surrender of Asseerghur

TEN o'clock came, and no messenger from the fort. A little more time was allowed, and then the shelling began again, and the hilltop became once more a mass of fire and smoke. This went on until the afternoon, when word came down that the Keeledar would arrive immediately, to ratify a treaty and give up the fort. Again the shelling stopped, and at about two o'clock the great man started down in his palanquin with three or four followers. All the general and staff officers were ordered to gather at General Doveton's tent to meet him. On his way to us, our people led the Keeledar through the park of artillery, so that he could see for himself that we had at least fifty more guns in reserve, above those we were using. This Keeledar was an ugly-looking fellow, a great, fat, buffalo of a man, with enormous rolls of flesh about him. He was so dirty and greasy that he might that moment have been turned out of an oil shop, but he swaggered into the General's tent, chewing paun with all the arrogance of a Nabob, and apparently expecting a welcome. He was disappointed, however, and though he was asked to be seated his reception was cool. Major-General Sir John Malcolm,[1] the government's political agent, showed by his attitude that this was no meeting of friends. When everybody was sat down Sir John said, bluntly, that the British Army had no time to spend in unnecessary talk, so there was no need for the Keeledar to waste words. Nothing would do but the surrender of the fort, and for the Keeledar himself to answer to his master Scindia for his rebellion, and disloyalty. The fat Keeledar gathered himself up into something like speaking order, and at last mumbled out that he was surprised a person so familiar with Eastern customs and usages of war should propose such a thing as their laying down their arms. Sir John must know that a Rajput would die a thousand deaths rather than do such a thing. Sir John replied that he did indeed know the customs of the country, and the character of Rajput soldiers; but these were terms offered to rebels, whose lives were already forfeit, and if they persisted in their obstinacy he would have to advise the government to exact the full penalty. He said this with so much displeasure that the fat Keeledar was in no doubt that he was among those to be hanged, and quaked for fear. He sat and stared at Sir John for a while, unencouraged by what he saw; and then, at last, said that he could not propose such terms to his men; but, he went on, letting his villainy blossom out to its fullest evil, "could you not promise them their arms and property, and then when they are safely out pounce on them and take both away?"

General Doveton, Sir John Malcolm, and half a dozen Brigadiers jumped up at once, and I really thought Sir John would have cut the fellow to pieces there and then. "You rebel!" he shouted, "how dare you make such a suggestion to these gentlemen? You deserve to be cut down on the spot for such an insult. Go back immediately. Go and fight for your fort, and we will force you to do what we now offer out of pity. Go back to your fort." The fat man was tremendously upset at Sir John's anger, but he managed to stammer out that he was then out of danger, and intended to stay so; "I will not go back to the fort to be killed." Sir John cried, "But you shall, even if I have to carry you on my back." One of the officers, I think it was General Watson, remarked, "What a load of infamy you would have if you did, Sir John." The Keeledar now found that he had gone his length, and began to smooth things over a little. He said that he would do his best to persuade his men to give up their arms, but he dreaded the result. I happened to catch his eye, and it was easy to see the hatred and desire for revenge which was burning in his soul. At last he said that he would guarantee to give up the fort by ten o'clock the next day, unconditionally; and to this he pledged his word, such as it was, offering to confirm it with his hand and seal if need be. After a good deal of consultation, and apparent reluctance on our part, we agreed to accept his surrender, but with the proviso that if they did not march out at the time agreed upon all negotiation would be at an end, and no further talk would be listened to. The Keeledar then

Lord Lake, 1744–1808. C-in-C India 1800

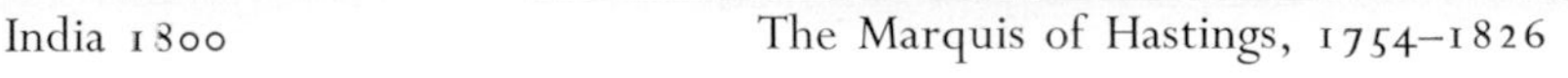

The Marquis of Hastings, 1754–1826

left the tent, and rolled into his palanquin, leaving everybody thoroughly disgusted with him. Sir John Malcolm was as good as his word, and saw him to the very gate of the fort. Multitudes of people were gathered there to meet their infamous Governor. What could they expect from such a man? This fellow had the audacity to tell his men that he had frightened the English into accepting all his demands. They were to march out with their arms, their property, and everything they wished.

Under this impression the whole garrison came out, and made their rendezvous under a hill, where a strong party of our men were waiting to march in. There were about seven or eight hundred of the poor, half-starved wretches, some of them almost naked. Sir John, having severely admonished them for their rebellion, ordered them to lay down their arms and property. The infamy of the Keeledar then came out, and his men would have torn him to pieces if we had not interfered. When he was asked if he had indeed made such a promise he laughed, and said, "There was no other way of getting them out, and I was not fool enough to stay in the fort and get my brains blown out. You have them now, do as you like with them. I have finished." The Keeledar was imprisoned, and Sir John addressed the wretched-looking creatures of the garrison. "I have every reason to think that you came out under the impression that the English would allow you to keep your arms and property; but no such thing was ever promised by us, nor could such terms be expected by a rebellious garrison. But you have been deceived by your Keeledar; however, since you surrendered under the impression that you could keep your arms and property, we will allow you to do so. You may go. I advise you to return to your homes, and make your peace with your greatly offended master, Scindia." They were escorted for some miles from the camp, while the Keeledar was sent as a prisoner to Scindia. I never heard what became of him, but there is little doubt that he was acting under Scindia's orders all along. That personage had been in league with the Pindarees during the campaign, but the presence of the Marquis of Hastings, with the central division of the Grand Army under the very walls of his capital, had prevented him becoming active.

Thus ended the campaign of 1818–19. We had no reason to complain of not being given the honour of storming Asseerghur, for all the guns in the world could not have breached the place. Our twenty-four-pound cannon balls had only managed to knock off little pieces of projecting rock, and so made the ascent more difficult by removing what little hold there was. The place where we tried to make a breach was a kind of little nook, which looked as if it might have been a waterfall at one time. If we had battered at it until doomsday we should never have got up; and if we had, a dozen old women could have killed us all by rolling down stones from above. It was very fortunate for us that this fort was given up. I speak feelingly, for if my General, who was the oldest Colonel in the army, had led the storm as he proposed, I should have been with him. Often as I looked at the spot during the siege I thought, "This is where my career ends." I began to arrange my papers, and even to look for some romantic little place where my body might be laid. But I had a wife, and a fond wife too, which embittered the prospect. I am far from pretending that I ever had any wish to die, but when I have to go, I would far rather make my exit in battle than in bed.

In the afternoon of the capitulation we went up to examine the fort. Every step I took convinced me that we could never have stormed the place. Going up, quite at my leisure, I had to rest half a dozen times before reaching the grand entrance. It took me ten minutes to get to the gate, and I was quite exhausted. Beyond question it would have been the grave of hundreds if we had tried to storm. They had huge stones piled up on the walls waiting for us, so nicely balanced that a child could have pushed them over. The town stood on a considerable table-land, on which were fields, woods, and gardens, with the large pool in the centre that I have spoken of, clear and cool, but all the margin thick with dead bodies and congealed blood. The men had been shot in the act of drinking. In all these places the scenes after they have been taken are heart-rending beyond words, and it is useless to detail them over again. The blood seen all the way between the great temple and the pool, showed how heavy the loss of life must have been; but many of the bodies had been thrown over the walls, to find their way into some hollow, or perhaps a tiger's den. The fort as a whole showed nothing but poverty and distress; after the loss of the town they must literally have starved. There was a wide and beautiful prospect from the top, even the city of Borhanpore, fourteen miles away, could be plainly seen, and so lofty was our eyre that we seemed to overhang it. Our men in the camp below looked like babes. When evening closed in, it became very chilly, and soon sent us down below where, even when the sun was down, the glass often stood at eighty-five or ninety, due no doubt to the great heat of the earth for the breeze was cool. The soil here is a glittering red sand, with rocks breaking through in places. We were all glad to leave it.[2]

24

Happiness and then Disaster

THE combined army moved away from Asseerghur. Our division was to go eventually to cantonments, but on the way we were to escort Sir John Malcolm to his new station of Mhow, taking in on our route the celebrated cities of Indore and Ougein. These lay some miles out of our direct road; but no traveller ought to pass such places without viewing their splendour, and the magnificent architecture for which they are famous. They will fully compensate the visitor for any extra trouble he may take to reach them, and give him wonders to meditate over for the rest of his life; as well as convincing him that, in comparison with the East, the architecture of Europe is only in its infancy. The approach to Mhow is very difficult and tiring. One mountain which we had to ascend had what road there was cut along the face of a precipice, and so narrow that it was invisible from below. Here again, there was that astonishing sight which I have mentioned before, of a great army passing apparently unsupported along the sheer surface of the rock. This particular pass was the entrance to Holkar's territory, and was protected by a strongly built fort, well filled with men and arms; there was also a gateway supported by two large bastions, about two hundred yards from the top. Along this road there are a number of wells cut out of the living rock, for the refreshment of travellers. It was a hard day's march from the bottom to the top; how the pack animals, with their enormous loads, managed it was a mystery. But nobody suffered any greater harm than broken knees, or bruised shins, though I myself was so stiff after the climb that it took me three days to recover.

We encamped at the top of the pass, and though the atmosphere at the bottom was very hot, up there it was cool, clear, and salubrious, so that we seemed to be in another country. For about a hundred miles more the road continued at this height, and the whole district was in general flat; then when we got near Callenger we dropped down again, almost to the level from which we had climbed. In two days more we reached the new station of Mhow, which was to be Sir John Malcolm's residence, and there we spent a very pleasant couple of days. Sir John was most hospitable, offering us every luxury that could be procured. He is also a man of great wit and humour, so that there is bound to be plenty of fun whenever he is about. No matter how liverish a man might be, Sir John would laugh him out of his complaint in no time. I was stiff and sore all over just then, and anything like laughing gave me terrible pain, but Sir John would make a dead man laugh. He shook me up so that I actually got rid of my sufferings. He said to me one morning, "Shipp, did I ever tell you the story of how I was once invited to breakfast with a man who never spoke a word to me all the time I was there?" I answered, "No, Sir John, and I am in no state to hear it." "Oh," he said, "I must tell you. It is rather a serious story than otherwise." Finding that there was no way out of it I held my sides, to minimize the damage as much as possible, and listened. He had a peculiar way of his own in telling stories, which added greatly to their effect. He liked to stand close up to the person he was talking to; and the high, squeaky, voice he used, especially when he was pleased, increased the drollery. "I was once invited to breakfast," he went on, "with a queer old Colonel of Bombay Artillery. He was famous for giving good breakfasts, so I accepted readily enough, and went along rather early, walking straight into the breakfast-room without any ceremony. It is the custom, as you know, when the table has been laid to cover the things with a cloth to keep the flies away, and this had been done. I thought it odd that there wasn't a single servant about, but I walked up and down the room, very contentedly, for a quarter of an hour, waiting for somebody to come. At last I got quite hungry, and thought that there would be no harm in helping myself to a biscuit or two. I turned back the corner of the cloth; and there, staring up at me, was the face of the Colonel, laid out dead on his own breakfast table." He emphasized the point of his story with a tremendous thump between my shoulders, which startled me so that I thought the dead Colonel himself had jumped out at me. However it must have done me good, for I lost all symptoms of my complaint.

Sir John good-naturedly went on with us to Indore, where the British Resident, Mr Wellesley, gave us an equally hospitable welcome. With him we went to visit the court of Holkar, who had rebelled against the government a short time before, and had his troops dreadfully cut up at Maidpore, so we could hardly expect any very great cordiality. However we went, mounted on elephants, and were received at the outer gate by some of his junior officers, who showed no enthusiasm at our coming. We dismounted, and were met in the inner court by people of a rather higher rank, and were led into a long room, where the floor was spread with a white cloth and which had a large quantity of pillows and cushions lying about on which to recline. Young Holkar[1] rose as the Resident entered, and we all had a hug at him. He was a dirty-looking boy, about thirteen years old, rather shabbily dressed and obviously sulky. It was said that he had never been known to laugh out loud. There were the usual greetings, sprinkling of scents, and so on, but we could see that the Rajah was not pleased. It was Sir John Malcolm who had given his troops such a drubbing, and this the young man could neither forget nor forgive. Only with difficulty, and from fear of offending the British Resident, could he be got to behave with ordinary civility. Sir John however quickly upset their ceremonious gravity, and soon the place resounded with fun. The once frowning Rajah, who was said to be unable to laugh, threw himself back on his cushions and fairly shook with merriment. It was some time before order could be established, and then there was an interesting conversation, after which a distribution of presents took place, the young ruler being quite liberal, and we broke up in a much more friendly spirit than we met.

The next morning we said farewell to Sir John Malcolm and Mr Wellesley, going towards Ougein by forced marches to make up for the time we had spent at Mhow, and Indore. The Bengal Division, which had been with us until now, took the direct route to Saugar, which they reached some days before us. At Ougein[2] we encamped in a small clump of trees, about a mile from the city. That place is situated on the river Scend, opposite to some large and beautiful gardens, which had been the favourite resort of Scindia at one time, but he had not visited them recently. The once splendid palace of this ancient city had been allowed to fall into ruin, and all that remained of it was occupied by a few priests in the former zenana; while the rest was given over to snakes, scorpions, and every kind of reptile. The beautiful pleasure grounds are still kept in some order, and are the resort of the religious mendicants who are glad to live in what is considered to be a place of special sanctity. In the morning you may see them standing in the stream, and pouring its clear water over their heads in an act of purification and worship. In the course of the afternoon we visited the old city, which had been buried by an earthquake. We could still see the tops of temples, trees and houses; in places there were still deep chasms in the earth. We bathed in the river, to the great annoyance of the priests, who did not hesitate to tell us that we defiled their sacred stream.

There is a subterranean passage which is said to run from Ougein to Benares, some two thousand miles, and this we decided to explore. Over the entrance to it was an ancient gateway, its crumbling towers covered with sculpture, illustrating the old Hindoo tales which are no doubt as false as they are wonderful. Just inside were three or four steps, leading down to a square room, which was perfectly green from the continual damp of the place. It was about six feet square, and in one corner of it was a wrinkled old man, lying on a bed of ashes; both his hair and beard were perfectly white. He looked at us sharply as we entered, and after we had exchanged greetings, he sat up and demanded, with an air of considerable authority, where we had come from, and what we intended to do. I was appointed interpreter, and told him that we wished to see the wonderful underground passage. "Yes," he replied, "wonderful indeed. Two thousand miles, dug out of the earth by the hand of man, and which cost as much money as would purchase another world." "But," he went on, "where are your provisions, your oil, your sacred writings? If you wish to explore this great wonder of man's power, you will surely not begin without invoking the aid of God. The journey is long, dangerous, and tedious." "How far does it go, then?" I asked, "if so many precautions are required." "To the famous city of Benares," he replied. "The other entrance is at that place, though scarcely known to mortal man. This is as true as it appears wonderful to you, who are unacquainted with hidden mysteries. But if you doubt me go, and let your own eyes convince you of the truth of what I have said."

We lit candles and went in. At about every ten yards the passage dropped into square rooms, like that we had left, but these became so damp and chilly that we soon turned back. But even in this short distance, it was easy to see that it was a secret passage leading from the zenana to the palace, which was about a quarter of a mile away. It had been built for some nefarious purpose no doubt, and those chilly cells, if they could have spoken, would have told many a woeful tale. Not wishing to offend the old man by seeming, just then, to disbelieve what he had told us, we gave him a few rupees, which he took with the eagerness of a miser. His eyes sparkled as he held the money in his hand, and bowed to the ground before us in his thankfulness. He told us some wonderful stories; among others, that some Brahmins had set out a short time before to explore the passage; but when they got about half way some died, and the others thought that it would be wiser to turn back, while they still had oil and provisions enough to last them during their return. When they once more reached the spot they had started from, they found that their journey had taken several months. The hoary-headed old mendicant told us this lie with all the straight-faced gravity of truth, and even called upon his Maker to witness to it as a fact. We did not think it worth while arguing with him, though I did say, as we left, that the passage ran no further than the palace, and that his tale was a trick to get money from Englishmen.

This old man also told us the story of the earthquake, which had destroyed Ougein. He said that, once upon a time, a white man had lived there for some three or four years, subsisting on the gifts of the benevolent. When he had got together a little money he bought a small temple, and drew in a number of converts to his religion; he became, in fact, so powerful in argument and persuasive in his discourses that the

Brahmins grew alarmed, and consulted together about what they should do. But what their plans were was never revealed, for on a long remembered day the great earthquake came, and swallowed up the whole city with all its myriad inhabitants. By it, the gods had shown their strong displeasure that a Christian temple had been allowed in that sacred place. The temple itself had disappeared, with all the rest; but just before the catastrophe happened the white man, strange to say, had gone to visit a school of his in a distant village, and so escaped, but nothing was ever heard of him again. We visited every place in Ougein worth seeing in that day's ramble, before returning to our tents and our General's hospitable table.

Our route to Saugar was by way of Bopaul and Belsah, old Pindaree haunts; but nothing of any importance occurred on the road, except that some of our servants lost their way one night, and we never saw them again. There was no doubt that they had fallen a prey to the bandits, which infest this part of the country. We were all glad to be in Saugar, with our wives and families once more. I was particularly happy, for I was blessed with a loving wife, who was to me all that a wife could be to her husband. After about a month, the division to which I belonged was broken up, and I was sent to rejoin my own corps at Cawnpore. This was in July 1819, and from then until the early months of 1821, there was nothing but the normal routine of station life, and the great delight of being with my family. During that time I was raised to the rank of Lieutenant, and on the 22nd of March, 1821, my happiness was crowned by the birth of a son, and yet at that very time I was on the brink of utter disaster.

I will not dwell upon it. It is enough to say that I had entered into an agreement with the late Lieutenant-Colonel, then Major, Browne to run some horses in partnership with him at the next Cawnpore races.[3] My father-in-law was in a bad state of health just then, and about to return to England; so I got six months leave in order to accompany him to Calcutta, and while there to buy horses. The circumstances of this most unfortunate transaction ended my career in the army. I was brought before a court martial, and sentenced to be discharged from His Majesty's Army. The Commander-in-Chief, in an order of the day which was read at the head of every regiment in His Majesty's Army then in India, softened the sentence somewhat, but confirmed its main effect which was that I had been dismissed the service. "Lieutenant Shipp," he wrote, "by his persevering resistance to the advice of his late most respected Commanding Officer, of the General of his Division, and of the Commander-in-Chief, brought upon himself the heavy penalty of the forfeiture of his commission. Although there are circumstances calculated greatly to aggravate the offences of this officer, still, the Commander-in-Chief is willing to hope that in yielding, as far as he feels it consistent with his duty, to the earnest intercession of the court, he runs no risk of shaking the foundations of discipline, and subordination. The sentence of the court is accordingly remitted; but as, under all the circumstances of the case, the Commander-in-Chief deems it quite impossible that Lieutenant Shipp should continue to do duty with the 87th Regiment, he grants him leave of absence from it, and shall recommend that he be removed to the half-pay list." For what satisfaction it was Major Browne himself, in the course of the court martial, had declared, "I always considered him, and indeed know him to be, up to the present moment, one of the best officers in His Majesty's service."

25

The Last Parade

WHEN a soldier has been tried by an honourable military tribunal, composed of fifteen British officers, and the sentence of the court martial approved by a merciful and gracious Sovereign, it is both fruitless and improper for the one who has been sentenced to urge anything more in his own defence. I therefore bow to my fate, but I love my country as truly as ever I did, and would risk my life to support her freedom and her laws as willingly as ever. The trial lasted thirteen days, and during that time I was exceedingly harassed and in a state bordering on frenzy. There was a host against me, but none to advise me. I stood alone and unaided, with only a limited education, to rebut the whole mass of evidence which was brought against me. During the long wait which necessarily occurred while the proceedings of the court martial were sent to England, examined there, and sent back again, my greatest comfort lay with my family. At times the thought of my recent fall would send me down to the depths of despair, but my wife was always there, to comfort me with hopes of better days to come. I removed to a place some miles from the regiment, for I could not bear the commiseration of the soldiers whenever we met, for it only served to increase my despondency. It seemed better to leave the station, where my profession had been my pride and glory, and be where I would not meet the pity of the brave fellows who had shared so many dangers with me. As I passed down the Ganges, floating by the houses of the officers which overlook that stream, my feelings were such as I never can describe. I was as near the bottom now as on that day when I first set out in life, and looked back to the spire of Saxmundham church, and my mother's grave beneath the poplars. Yet I was not so totally alone now, for I had a wife to share my sorrows. Many of the men whom I had befriended, or helped to promotion, followed my boat along the banks of the river until distance compelled them to return to their lines. Their friendship had some comfort in it, and yet emphasized again the depths of my fall.

I had scarcely begun to face my difficulties with some degree of hope, when a second blow fell; so utterly unexpected, so bitter, and overwhelming that nothing in life could have been a heavier affliction. During all the worry of my trial, and its preliminaries, my wife had been so weighed down with anxiety that she was brought to bed of a premature child, and nearly died; but with good nursing she recovered, and regained all the health and beauty of early womanhood. She was expecting another pledge of our mutual love, and by a strange coincidence her mother, brother and sister all arrived at my house at that same time. They were there when, after protracted labour lasting twelve hours, she gave birth to another boy, and died having that morning completed her two and twentieth year. All my other misfortunes were doubled, and trebled, by this last blow. There seemed nothing left on earth for me to trust in or love. My poor child, still kissing and fondling the dead face of his mother, tore my heart asunder. Nothing could drag him from her, so terrible was his grief that we thought his mind must be permanently unhinged by the shock. He would kiss and hug any little thing that she had touched, such as a rag, or a piece of paper. My mother-in-law was so prostrate with sorrow that for six months she hardly recognized those who were about her.

Just in the moment of this crisis I learned that the sentence of the court martial had been confirmed in England, and I was ordered to proceed to Fort William, and from thence to be sent home and placed upon half-pay. My poor wife was at least spared this last bitterness. When the letter containing the news was brought to me, I was sitting on a couch with my two motherless babes in my arms; one four years old, the other but a few days. As my eyes scanned the writing, and caught the words "dismissed the service," I broke into a passion of tears. To wind up a military career like mine in this way was heartbreaking. I had been in the army from the age of nine to forty-one—thirty-two years. I had received six wounds from matchlock balls. One of these was just above my eye, and has so impaired my sight that I have been forced to use glasses for some years past. There are two injuries on the top of my head, from which sixteen pieces of bone have been extracted at different times, and which still cause me excruciating headaches at every change in the weather. There is a wound in the fleshy part of my right arm, and one through the fore-finger of my left hand which still gives me trouble; for there are some splinters of bone in it yet. I have a wound also in my right leg, and one in my right shoulder, as well as others too slight to mention. For the latest of them I was given ninety-six pounds—one year's pay as Ensign—for the rest not one single penny, as they were inflicted prior to His Majesty's munificent grant to wounded officers. I must confess that, in a sanguine mood, I had entertained the hope that all these wounds might more than outweigh the offences for which I had been convicted; and the failure of this last shred of consolation almost broke my heart. My eldest child, seeing my grief, and thinking that I still cried for his mother, put his arms round my neck and tried to comfort me, telling me what we had told him, that she had gone away and would soon come back again. We were found in this state by my kind friend, and neighbour, Captain Marshall, of the Bombay Army. He was a friend indeed. His lady, who had a child three days older than mine, took my infant and nursed it with her own. I owe eternal gratitude to these kind people, and I hope that this expression of what I feel may meet their eyes in the distant land in which they dwell.

When Captain Marshall saw the sentence, he walked into another room until he could recover his self-command, but he soon was back, though there were tears in his eyes. "You must cheer up, Shipp," he said. "You have often mounted the breach, and braved the danger. Remember that you have these dear babes to clothe, and feed." He persuaded me to spend the rest of the day at his house, and in the evening, hoping that it might divert me a little, he got together a small musical party, but the weight of my misfortunes pressed too heavily upon me for that. I was best left to myself, and to my motherless children. A month was allowed me in which to wind up my affairs; and then I was to go to Calcutta, and from there to England. The time granted was so short, that I had to sell all my property in the country for a mere nothing. Having disposed of it as best I could, I set out for the Presidency with my small son, and as I had no means of caring for the baby I parted with him to my brother-in-law, J. P. Mellaird Esq, an indigo planter of Tirhoot, where my wife's mother, somewhat recovered from the suffering she had undergone, found refuge also.

It was a dismal voyage down the Ganges, and when I reached Calcutta I was forced to wait some time for a ship. At last I was ordered to place myself under the command of Captain Mathers, of His Majesty's 59th Regiment, and strange to say to proceed home with invalids. It was an order which I was bound to obey, but it came as a final blow, for it made it impossible to take my little boy home with me. The ship was packed with troops; and I could not get accommodation for my son under a thousand rupees, a sum of money which I simply did not possess. I could have got a passage on a small foreign ship, for both of us, on the amount the Company allows for an officer who is being sent home; namely fifteen hundred rupees. So my last comfort was taken from me, and my boy was forced to remain in India with my brother-in-law, where he is to this day.

At the beginning of April 1825 I embarked on the free trader *Euphrates*, Captain Mead commanding. He had no more than twenty-three hands in all, a totally insufficient crew for a ship like ours, with a winter voyage before us. This would have been a harsh prospect for most people, who had been in India as long as I had, and whose nerves had been shattered by the rigours of that climate; but mine, I am glad to say, were still strong, and I was pretty well used to hardship. It was impossible not to think of the future. I left England as a child, without a single friend or relative to bid me goodbye, and I was returning without a soul to bid me welcome. Yet there is something about going home which appeals to every English bosom, and I would be content to live there, even in poverty. But it was distressing beyond measure to leave my children behind, and I could hardly bear to turn away from the river which, a few days before, had carried my son away from me. Places with which I have been associated in the past have always had a deep fascination for me. I remember when I was in England in 1807, and wandering along the lanes behind my old barracks in Colchester, I found my name on a stile, which I had cut there all those years before when I was a little fifer, and I sat there for an hour or more, pondering over it and looking at it again and again. So it is not to be wondered at that I should cling to the spot where I last saw my motherless child.

But the scene on shipboard drove all other thoughts out of my mind, at least for a time. The din of more than two hundred soldiers, and their friends from shore; all up to their necks in a final carouse, rioting in their drink, fighting, falling over one another, blaspheming, singing, fifing, and fiddling, all jumbled together in the confined space; with all their bedding, their parrots, and mynor birds, was enough to drown all else. The next morning we left Fort William where we had been lying, with a fair wind, and water so quiet that I could have wished my heart to be as still; but I was leaving a country where I had spent the prime of life, and the happiest of my days. I soon found that I had to deal with a very queer lot indeed. Captain Mathers was dying when we left, and did indeed die before we reached home; so all the trouble and anxiety of the party fell upon me. There was no means of enforcing discipline, and I can safely say that, with the exception of about twenty of them, a more drunken, disorderly, mutinous set than the fellows I had under my charge never disgraced a soldier's uniform. A voyage to or from the East is always dull and monotonous, even with pleasant companions, and those on the *Euphrates* were anything but pleasant. There were no private passengers, save the wife and little daughter of the Captain who was nominally in charge. A young officer, belonging to the Company's Bombay Artillery, died when we were only a few days out of port, and his body sent over the side. He was little more than a boy. Besides them we had one doctor, and Lieutenant Rock, a Company's officer who was in charge of their troops.

The misery of that passage was indescribable, but perhaps it can be guessed at a little when I say that we had more than two hundred, sorely-injured men on board; some without legs, some without arms, others wretchedly wounded in all parts of the body, twenty of them had only been taken from hospital a week or so before we left. All were huddled together on one small deck; with four women, and four children, and all the beds, bedding, trunks, and boxes, personal possessions, and birds of different kinds which the men were taking home in the hope of making a little money out of them. In this confusion, everyone who could move pushed, and shoved, and struggled as well as he could, to get a better place; treading under foot all those who, from disease or drunkenness, were unable to look after themselves. The stench and the heat in this airless hell-hole was appalling. A good number of the men were drunk for the greater part of their time; where, or how, they got the liquor I never could discover, and nothing that I was able to do could stop them getting it. Discipline was almost impossible, for there was no place of confinement on board, or handcuffs, or any of the usual means of enforcing orders, or of separating the ringleaders from their dupes. Lieutenant Rock, the Company's officer, and I had to risk our lives to prevent open mutiny among the troops. It was a mercy we were not thrown overboard, for they threatened to do so more than once. The most refractory among them knew as well as we did that we had no means of making them obey, so they set all orders at defiance, refusing in the most peremptory way even to clear up their own filth. In the end I was forced to pay a set of fellows, with a couple of extra drams a day, to clean the decks in order to keep off disease, which so often breaks out on shipboard simply from want of cleanliness. That miserable voyage lasted six months; and was one long experience of riot, anxiety, and every misery, with scurvy adding to the general horror. Thirty-eight soldiers, two officers, and one child, died in that short space of time, the men in most cases through drink.

We reached England in October, and made port at Gravesend. The next day my detachment was marched to Chatham, and there drawn up on parade, where I left them in charge of the staff officer at Fort Pitt Barracks. That parade ended my military career, which had lasted more than thirty years, twenty-five of which had been spent on the burning soil of

India. I had no reason to regret that I was parting with the drunken, quarrelsome lot of men that I was leaving, and yet giving up the command of them meant that I was no longer a soldier, and the thought of that bowed me to the earth. And yet I can take pride in the fact that I have performed my duty to my country loyally, faithfully, and I trust bravely. To my fellow soldiers I say farewell. May the banner of England be hoisted in victory wherever it goes, and so long as my eyes can see I will follow the record of your wars, exult in your successes, and drop a tear of pity for those that fall.

End Piece

When he left the army Shipp settled in London. Friends in India had supplied him with introductions, and letters of recommendation, to various people which he was sure would be the means of finding him comfortable employment; but he was given hospitality, and pleasant promises, and nothing else. It was an age of patronage, when even the most distinguished Generals and Civil Servants stood a poor chance of an adequate reward, without the help of highly-placed connexions. Shipp, arriving home without influence and in disgrace, had a bleak future. He hoped that the East India Company might be willing to find him something to do, but they were not. They did, however, grant him a pension of fifty pounds a year; which presumably took the place of the half-pay on which he was supposed to have retired, for nothing more is heard of it. Fifty pounds a year was not much to a man of Shipp's habits. His time in the army had done little to teach him the value of money. It had always been light come light go, and the next campaign would pay all debts. With his background, it was perhaps natural that he should have been more careless in his expenditure than he ought to have been. In the universal tipping of that day, especially, he was very lavish. It gave him the feeling of superiority which he needed.

When his money began to run low he turned to authorship, and published in 1826 *The Shepherdess of Arranville* "a pathetic tale," in three acts. In 1829 his autobiography appeared, and, either because he doubted his own powers, as the compiler of the last chapter of his life says, though that seems unlikely, or at the suggestion of his publishers, he got it worked over by the literary gentleman referred to earlier. It was well received and Shipp was up in the air again, convinced that he was on the way to making his fortune as a writer. He got married a second time, and produced another piece for the stage, *The Maniac of the Pyrenees, or, the Heroic Soldier's Wife*, a melodrama in two acts, but it was not successful. This was followed in 1831 by *The Military Bijou,* a small collection of anecdotes which scraped the barrel out of which the autobiography had come. A more important piece was a letter to Sir Francis Burdett, called *Flogging and its Substitutes, A Voice from the Ranks*, which also appeared in 1831. It expressed Shipp's profound aversion to corporal punishment in the army, and presented a reasoned case against it. Beside having some influence on the agitation against flogging then going on it brought him a gift of sixty pounds from Sir Francis. Only the memoir is of much importance today. It was republished in 1843 when a short chapter was added giving details of Shipp's later life. An illustrated edition, with an introduction by H. M. Chichester, appeared in 1890 and was twice reprinted. It was also issued in a tiny volume in minute print at Wakefield, without a date, but apparently about the middle of the nineteenth century; possibly some reminiscence of Shipp's stay in the town in 1808 still lingered there.

The setting up of the Metropolitan Police in 1829 offered Shipp a chance for the kind of work he was best fitted to do, and he became an Inspector in the Stepney Division under Lieutenant Parlour. The two old soldiers got on well together and when, a few months later, Parlour was made Superintendent of the Liverpool Police he encouraged Shipp to join him. There, as Superintendent of the Night Watch at a salary of two hundred pounds a year, he did good work in breaking up the gangs which had infested the city before the founding of the police force. He once personally arrested a madman who was terrorizing everybody with a carving knife; and foiled an amorous ship's Captain who had lured a girl on to his vessel with the tale that he would marry her at a suitable time and that, in the meanwhile, she would be quite safe as her brother was on board.

In May 1833 Shipp was elected Governor of Liverpool Workhouse; in spite of the fact that there was a large number of candidates and the special vestry had already decided to appoint the Master of St Andrew's Workhouse, Holborn. The post carried a salary of three hundred pounds a year, a handsome residence and various perquisites. Writing was still his hobby, and he published stories of Hindu life in the Liverpool newspapers, a book called *The Eastern Story-Teller* and another with a military theme called *The Private Soldier*. On the 27th of April, 1834, he died of pleurisy, and was considered sufficiently important to be given an obituary in *The Gentleman's Magazine* and *The Annual Register*. His funeral, it is recorded, was attended by a large circle of friends, and all the inmates of the workhouse. There was something fitting in that, for Shipp's life had come full circle. He had begun in a workhouse himself, an orphan boy with no one else to care for him, and ended as a Workhouse Master with all those years of hardship and adventure in between.

As often before he was in debt when he died, but there were still friends to come to the rescue. One of them, a gentleman who held a bill of sale on all Shipp's property, generously gave the widow back her furniture. Others contributed six hundred pounds to a subscription for her benefit, decided upon at a public meeting and carried through by Lieutenant Parlour. So the widow and her children, we are not told how many, had something to help them along until suitable work was found for her.

Notes

Chapter One

1 There is no record of Shipp's baptism in the Saxmundham registers; they did not record births. A copy of the only entry concerning the Shipp family has been kindly sent me by the rector of Saxmundham. "1786, Shipp. Thomas, son of Thomas Shipp and Laetitia his wife, late Laetitia Knowles, Spinster, was privately baptized Septb 15th 1786." This is puzzling, for Shipp only refers to one brother, who was older than himself. Possibly the infant after being baptized, died also. His father is said to have been a marine.

Chapter Two

1 War Office records show that John Shipp was enlisted in the 22nd Regiment of Foot on the 17th of January, 1797.
2 To show that he was a new recruit.
3 A slang word inviting ridicule for something.
4 He must have been twelve if he was born in 1785. Shipp always counted his age from 1785, and yet sometimes says that he joined the army at ten, sometimes at nine. The age for boy recruits was between ten and sixteen. Shipp was tall for his age, and the parish authorities may have put his age on a bit in order to get rid of him, and this led to confusion in his reckoning later on.
5 The soldier stationed in front of the troop at their drill, to show them the motions and the timing.
6 In 1766, when Gibbon the historian was there, Hilsea Barrack was a square of low ill-built huts, with low ceilings and no ventilation. Windows were kept closed, so as to keep the men warm. The place was continually wet and dirty, with typhus and smallpox endemic.

Chapter Four

1 Sir John Barrow, who was in South Africa about this time, says that the two boy regiments were sent to the Cape to take the place of seasoned soldiers who had been transferred to Madras. They arrived ravaged by disease, "a parcel of weakly boys unfit to carry a musket," and local volunteers had to be enrolled to provide some security. Yet when the ships had been properly cleaned, and the crew refreshed, they carried other troops to their destination without losing a single man. After two years in Africa the boys became fine soldiers, fit for service in any part of the world. *Travels into the Interior of Southern Africa*, Sir John Barrow. London, 1804, p. 157.

Chapter Five

1 Yet provisions were very cheap. Meat twopence a pound. Bread a penny to twopence a pound. Vegetables of all kinds cheap and abundant. Good wine was threepence a pint. One of the soldiers' grievances was that they were not allowed to buy it in bulk and so get it cheaper.

2 The Graaf-Reinett (Shipp's Graaf-Reynett) area had got thoroughly out of hand. The Boers were in rebellion against the British Government at the Cape and the Native tribes, always at war with the settlers, made the most of the opportunity to rob, burn and murder everywhere. On the 29th of July, 1799, the Landrost reported that Hottentots and Kafirs were in possession of nearly the whole district of Graaf-Reinett. *History of South Africa*, Theal. London, 1915. Vol. 1, p. 60.

3 The Boers referred to leopards as tigers, the wolves were probably jackals.

4 Barrow's picture of the Boers at that time is unflattering. "By indolent habits, excess of food and fondness for sleep, they become no less gross in their persons than vulgar in their manners. I believe there is no country in the world that affords so large a proportion of unwieldy and

bulky people. I am certain there is none where the animal appetites are indulged with less restraint.'' Barrow, op. cit., p. 103.

5 Continual warfare with the Natives, and the dangers of a pioneer life, took such toll of the male population that the Boers often found it difficult to get husbands for their daughters. Men, frequently of German extraction, who were discharged or deserted from the Dutch army, were much sought after; and so a promising young fellow like Shipp would also be welcome. Desertions were so common that the severest measures had to be taken to stop them.

6 The Americans had captured the greater part of the Eastern carrying trade, and had more ships at the Cape than any other country except Britain.

7 Fort William, named in honour of William the Third, was founded in 1700, when the area which afterwards developed into Calcutta was bought from the grandson of Aurungzebe. The most famous incident in its history was its capture by Siraj-Uddaula, in 1756, and the imprisonment of 146 of the garrison in the Black Hole, a detention room for disorderly soldiers, measuring eighteen feet by fourteen with only two small air holes. Only twenty-three came out alive. This took place on the 20th of June. In the following January Clive retook both Calcutta and the fort. For the fascinating story see *The Black Hole of Calcutta*, Noel Barber. London, 1965.

Chapter Six

1 Gerard, first Viscount Lake of Delhi and Laswaree (1744–1808), was one of the most successful of British Generals in India. After serving in the American and French wars he was sent to India in 1800, as Commander-in-Chief and second member of the Council. At this time he was in command of the army operating against the Mahrattas in the north, Major-General Wellesley commanding in the south; between them they broke up the

Mahratta confederacy. Though not a planner, like Wellesley, he had an instinct for the pitched battle. Brave, loyal to his subordinates, a strict disciplinarian but careful of his troops, he was much loved by them as Shipp emphasizes later on.

2 Lake had just won his great victory at Laswaree (the 1st of November, 1803), with the loss on his side of eight hundred killed and wounded.

3 Byannal, i.e. Bianna Pass, which lies between two ranges of hills on the route from Agra to the territories of the Rajah of Jeypore then under British protection.

4 The Mahratta were Hindoo mountain tribes, inhabiting a great part of Western and Central India. Under Sivaji (1627–80), they withstood the Moghul Emperor and came to be the ruling power in the Deccan. Sivaji's descendants continued to be held in great respect as the offspring of the gods, but real power passed to the Peishwa, originally the chief minister, with his capital at Poona. Subsidiary chieftains established principalities of their own; Raghoji Bhonsla in Nagpore, Damaji Gaekwa around Baroda, Tukoji Holkar in Malwa on the northern bank of the Narbudda river, Mahaji Scindia in large tracts immediately south of Agra, and Delhi. A good deal of Shipp's fighting was done against these last two families. Though independent these chieftains owed a limited allegiance to the Peishwa as head of the Mahratta confederacy. In 1802 Holkar drove the Peishwa from Poona, who placed himself under British protection. Scindia and Bhonsla allied themselves with Holkar. Sir Arthur Wellesley attacking from the South, won a great battle at Assaye (the 3rd of September, 1802), Lake from the North won an equally important battle at Laswaree (the 1st of November, 1803), and took Delhi. Bhonsla and Scindia made their peace with the British. Lake defeated Holkar at Furrukabad (1805), in Shipp's first campaign, and made his peace with the British (the 7th of January, 1806). This particular Holkar was Jaswant Rao Holkar, a picturesque ruffian who had managed to survive the feuds and misfortunes which had killed off his two half-brothers, who were the legitimate

heirs, and another brother illegitimate like himself. He lost an eye by the explosion of a matchlock, and referring to the Hindoo belief that one-eyed men are evil, said, "I was bad before but now I shall be the high priest of rogues." Vicious, cruel, untrustworthy, but with courage and some humour he was an adept at controlling the plundering hordes which made up his army. He was mad for the last three years of his life, and died on the 20th of October, 1811.

5 Ameer Khan, a Pathan soldier of fortune at the head of a horde of undisciplined marauders, who accepted him because they needed a leader of sorts, and obeyed him as much as they felt inclined. An association with Jaswant Rao suited them, as it gave them the appearance of a legitimate army and Ameer Khan was as loyal to the Holkars as he was to anybody.

6 Pindaree, said to be a nickname given them because of their fondness for a fermented drink called pinda. They were robber bands, working in groups of two to three thousand under a chosen leader. They were used by the Mahratta leaders, and paid with the opportunity to plunder. Some of the more outstanding managed to establish themselves as hereditary chieftains in parts of Central India. Shipp describes these robber bands in some detail later on, but generally calls any of the enemy horse Pins. For their history see *A Memoir of Central India,* Malcolm. London, 1824. Vol. 1, Chap. x.

7 *Paul Pry*, a three act comedy by John Poole, first performed at the Haymarket in 1825, when Liston had a tremendous success in the name part which he "filled with a thousand little absurdities." Paul Pry became as popular a character as Mr Pickwick, prints and statuettes of him were sold everywhere. The humour lies in the main character always "wanting to know."

8 He probably means Siva, the main deity of the Mahrattas, who was called Maha Deo, the great god.

9 The British troops were in a savage mood, because Holkar had recently sent back some of his prisoners with their noses and right hands cut off.

10 He had joined Holkar against the British at the siege of Delhi.

11 The Governor and Company of Merchants of London trading to the East Indies, was incorporated in 1600. It united with some other companies, and in 1708 became The United Company of Merchants of England trading to the East Indies. The Company, with growing supervision and assistance from the Crown, administered the British possessions in India until 1858. These possessions were organized in three Presidencies: Madras, Bombay, and Bengal. The Company had its own armies, but was assisted by the forces of the Crown. There was a good deal of friction between them, because the King's troops regarded themselves as being in a much superior position to the Company's men.

12 William Monson (1760–1807). He was a man of extraordinary bravery, but unsuccessful in independent command. In June, 1804, he was sent with a strong force in pursuit of Holkar, aiming to link up with General Murray's forces from the East, and so crushing the Mahrattas between them. Murray failed to meet him, and Monson was forced to retreat but not in any "masterly" fashion. It was the rainy season, but he had advanced without any means of crossing water and with few supplies. He neglected opportunities of fighting with advantage, and was irresolute all through. His retreat cost him twelve British officers killed, two drowned, two missing, five wounded and nearly half the five battalions he had started with. The men Shipp mentions had deserted at a critical point in the retreat in face of the enemy and were in any case subject to the death penalty.

Chapter Seven

1 A detachment of men appointed to lead an assault or to attempt some other desperate task. The Dutch phrase from which it comes "verloren hoop", that is, lost troops, makes its meaning clear.

2 The rupee was generally reckoned at 2/-. A crore was ten million.
3 Gabions were wicker, or woven wire, cylinders filled with earth. Fascines were long faggots.

Chapter Eight

1 A shell at this period was an iron ball filled with explosive. The fuse passed through a wooden tube inserted in the shell. There were holes in the tube at intervals down its length, corresponding to the time at which the burning fuse was to reach and detonate the explosive. All the unwanted holes were stopped with clay. If this was done carelessly, or the clay dropped out, the shell exploded at the wrong time and was generally disastrous.
2 Ginjall, a long matchlock turning on a pivot and throwing a two-pound ball.
3 The Rajah paid an indemnity of two million rupees and allied himself again with the British.
4 Shipp undoubtedly gives the real cause of the failure. In a paper on the *Bombardment of Fortified Places* addressed to Lord Moira, the Governor General, in 1814, Lord Metcalf argued that the British power in India rested solely on military superiority, and therefore the army should have the finest equipment possible, particularly mortars and shells, as these were the best means of reducing fortified places. He attributed the failure at Bhurtpore "partly to the difficulties opposing the attack, partly to the firmness and activity of the defence, and partly to the presence of a large enemy army under the walls which embarrassed our operations, and partly to the want of confidence on the part of our troops after the first attack." This last remark is only partly true. The men did their utmost but were asked for the impossible. Lake was criticized for attempting to take so strong a place "with a rush and a cheer" but he had little else. The failure at Bhurtpore had repercussions all over India, for it proved that the British were not invincible. Eventually, on the 18th of June, 1826, Lord

Combermere took the place without much trouble, but he was abundantly supplied with artillery.

5 Ensign, the lowest rank of commissioned officer in the infantry. The pay was ninety pounds a year.

6 The practice of officers purchasing their commissions in the army was not abolished until 1871.

Chapter Nine

1 Canon G. W. J. Oram, Vicar of Aldeburgh (Shipp's Aldborough) tells me that the burial register of his church contains the following entry. "Ship [*sic*] Thomas, married man; aged 52 years, was buried April 10, 1806—consumption". This was in all probability Shipp's father, an assumption strengthened by the fact that John heard the news from an Aldeburgh man.

2 According to the *D.N.B.* he owed about two hundred pounds.

3 Quaker, a dummy gun about two feet long.

4 Flogging was the punishment for many crimes, both civil and military. In the army it was inflicted by drummer boys, but as Shipp has pointed out these could very well be grown men; in the navy it was the boatswain, and a heavier cat was used. In both services there were many officers who would go to great lengths to avoid inflicting it, but there were also sadists who got a horrible enjoyment out of it. In 1812 the Duke of York forbade regimental courts martial to inflict more than three hundred lashes on any man, for any fault. There was a growing agitation against the practice, in which Shipp himself took part, declaring in his pamphlet that for "one devil it drove out it drove fifteen in" and vigorously denying the statement that the soldiers themselves did not think it degrading. Supporters of flogging claimed that a soldier's life was so hard, and the men so brutalized, that no other punishment was available. It was, however, less and less used, until the Army Act of 1881 substituted other punishments; the navy dropped it in 1879, but in the

form of birching it was not removed from the civil code until 1948.

5 The *Warren Hastings* had been captured off the Cape of Good Hope by the French frigate *Piedmontese*, and Captain Larkins roughly treated. The *Piedmontese* was afterwards taken by H.M.S *St Fiorenzo*. William Hickey tells the story at some length. *Memoirs*. London, 1948. Vol. iv, p. 429.

6 Sir Claude Martine Wade, afterwards distinguished himself by being the first British officer to force the Khyber Pass and enter Kabul.

Chapter Eleven

1 "Conductors are assistants given to the commissary of the stores, to receive or deliver out stores to the army, to attend at the magazines by turns when in garrison, and to look after the ammunition wagons when in the field." Military Dictionary, 1778. Quoted *N.E.D.*

2 The men of the 87th had an Erse battle cry, "Faugh a Ballagh", clear the way, which got them the nickname of the Old Fogs.

3 The Ghurkas, who are the dominant race in Nepal, are descended from those Rajputs and Brahmins who were forced out of India by the Mohammedan conquests. They moved into the lower Himalayas, dominated the original inhabitants, who are of mixed Mongol stock, and established a strong military state. Their encroachments on districts protected by Britain led to war in 1814. Of the four columns sent against them only one, that led by Major-General, afterwards Sir David, Ochterlony, had any success. The one under General Gillespie suffered a severe reverse, the General himself being killed. Unused to mountain warfare the British Commanders, except Ochterlony, made frontal attacks on stockades and heavily defended passes, and suffered accordingly; he relied on artillery and flanking movements. Ochterlony's success led to a pause in the war but, as the Ghurkas refused to ratify a treaty, he

was ordered to continue his attack. It was at this point that Shipp came into the campaign.

Chapter Twelve

1 British soldiers were only given two meals a day, breakfast at 7.30 and dinner at noon. In India, when the army was on the march, breakfast seems to have been put off until the first part of the route had been covered, and the troops halted for a rest. It was a sociable meal and one which Shipp obviously enjoyed, and frequently mentions. Dinner was taken when the march was over.

2 David Ochterlony (1758–1825) was born in Boston, Massachusetts, and joined the Company's Bengal Army in 1777 in which he had a brilliant career. He was a man of great energy and intelligence, with a good knowledge of India and its peoples. After his final success against the Ghurkas, in 1816, he continued to give outstanding service both as a diplomat and a soldier, taking an important part in the reconstruction of the government of Central India. He was created a baronet and K.C.B. in 1815, the first of the Company's generals to receive such an honour. In his later days he was well known in Delhi society as a dignified old man with a large harem. He died in 1825, of a broken heart, because the Governor General refused to support him in an important matter of policy without an independent inquiry.

Chapter Thirteen

1 The Ghurkas fascinated Shipp. He is always willing to praise his enemies when he can, but generally with a good-humoured appreciation of courage he hardly expected to find, but the fighting qualities of the Ghurkas struck him as quite out of the ordinary, an opinion which many others have echoed since. He speaks of their "gloomy religion," they are mainly Hindoos though many are Buddhists of a kind.

2 Major-General Marley, advancing on Katmandu in 1814, threw out two posts, one at Summanpore under Captain Blackney with 300 men, the other under Captain Sibley at Pursah with 350 men. The Ghurkas attacked the posts on the 1st of January, 1815. Blackney was completely surprised, and within ten minutes he and his second in command were killed, and his men in full flight. There were 125 casualties. Sibley had more warning, and made a better fight, but his men after holding out two hours and exhausting all their ammunition broke and fled. Casualties at Pursah were more than 250, including Sibley and a dozen European gunners. Their bodies lay unburied more than a year later. See page 137.

Chapter Fourteen

1 Little perhaps compared with some of the battles on the Indian sub-continent, but important in its results. It determined the campaign, which was itself instrumental in bringing about a peace with the Nepalese which has never been broken to the present day.

2 There is a story about this dog in another of Shipp's books, *The Military Bijou*, where it is described as belonging to the regiment.

3 This seems to have been the Raj Gurru, or High Priest, a powerful official in the Ghurka state with great wealth and an eminently sacred person.

4 *Tom Thumb the Great*, a very popular farce by Henry Fielding. It opens with a ludicrous scene between Doodle and Noodle, two courtiers of King Arthur. Doodle: "Sure such a day as this was never seen! The sun himself on this auspicious day, Shines like a beau in a new birthday suit", and so on. To which Noodle replies, "This day O Mr Doodle is a day, Indeed a day we never saw before" and similar nonsense.

5 The Treaty of Sagauli, signed in March 1816, provided that the Nepalese should withdraw from the disputed territories, and accept a British resident at Katmandu.

6 The Nepalese thought that any attacking army must approach along it, and had made it impregnable. So sure were they that they neglected Ochterlony's march up the gully, described by Shipp, until it was too late.

Chapter Fifteen

1 Lord Hastings, the Governor-General, was attempting to bring something like order into the chronic anarchy of Central India. Local chiefs had set themselves up as independent Rajahs, built themselves strong forts and harboured banditti to support their claims. The most important of these was the Rajah of Huttras, whose fort was reputed to be impregnable. Hastings determined to make an example of him. He knew that the fort could defy anything but heavy artillery, which the government had hitherto been unwilling to supply in any quantity as guns and their transport were expensive. He organized a siege train of 42 mortars which, arriving with speed and secrecy, in his own words "reduced the place in 15 hours". Shipp proves however that this applies only to the fort, the town took longer.

2 Congreve-rockets, called after their inventor Sir William Congreve, were first used in the attack on Boulogne in 1806. "They may be employed for every purpose of the usual light and heavy ordnance," throwing anything from "the 8 inch explosive rocket, weighing nearly three hundredweight, to the six-pound shell rocket which is the smallest used in the field". Their range was from one to three thousand yards. Rees, *Cyclopaedia*. London, 1819.

3 Mohur, a gold coin worth about fifteen rupees, also a seal or a gold ring.

4 Carcass, from French *carcasse,* a skeleton, was an early form of incendiary bomb. It consisted sometimes of iron ribs covered with pitched cloth, sometimes of iron like a shell, with three or four holes for the fire to blaze through. The shell of that day was round. The filling was a composition of mealed powder, saltpetre, sulphur, broken glass,

pitch, shavings of horn, turpentine, tallow and linseed oil. Earlier types were oblong, or oval, but these were too erratic to be used in Europe, though Shipp's account suggests that they were still used in India. Rees, *Cyclopaedia*. London, 1819.

Chapter Sixteen

1 This was Dowlet Rao Scindia. Like Holkar he made use of the Pindarees. Danger from Holkar forced him into an uneasy alliance with the British, which he was always willing to break if he could do so with advantage. His troops were often unpaid, and mutinous, and as oppressive as the freebooters they were supposed to be putting down.

2 *The Heir at Law* was a very popular farce by George Colman the younger. Its humour is in the often worked vein of the man in low life, in this case Daniel Dowlass, a chandler, who suddenly finds himself a lord. It was first performed at the Haymarket, with the famous comedian Dicky Suet in the part of Lord Dubberley. *Bon Ton, or High Life below Stairs*, by David Garrick, first performed in October 1775. It is a farce on the follies of high society, centring round Lord Minikin, a fop and a fool. "A more lively, pleasant or agreeable petite piece is hardly to be pointed out on the English stage." *Biographica Dramatica,* 1817.

3 The Baggage-Master could grant many favours, and would expect to be paid for them. Shipp's superiors were giving him the chance to make his fortune.

Chapter Seventeen

1 Lord Hastings, the Governor-General, was his own Commander-in-Chief. To wipe out the Pindarees, whose centre of power lay north of the river Narbudda, he planned a concentric movement. An approach was to be made on their northern and eastern flanks from Bengal, southward from the Deccan, and westward from Gujirat.

The vast distances involved, and the lack of communications, made it a most difficult operation. The Northern Army was to be under his own general command, and the Southern under Sir Thomas Hislop. The Northern Army, where Shipp served was divided into four divisions, and two corps of observation. The centre division, under General Brown, was to advance southward towards Gwalior. The right division under General Donkin, at Agra, was to overawe Scindia and the Ameer Khan. The left, under General Marshall, at Kalinjar (Shipp's Callenger) was to co-operate with the southern Army on the Narbudda and close the enemy's eastern escape route. The reserve, under Sir David Ochterlony, was to cover Delhi and act in Rajputana. Fortescue, *History of the British Army*. London, 1923. Vol. xi. Chaps. vii to xi.

2 Lord Hastings made his headquarters with the centre division of the Northern Army, the division itself being under Brown's command.

Chapter Nineteen

1 The devastation caused by the Pindarees was incredible, it took generations to recover. Out of 3,710 villages in Holkar's territory, 1,663 lay deserted, in 1817. Out of 351 villages in the state of Dhar, 315 had been abandoned. Tigers had fed so long on unburied human bodies that they overran the country, and "literally fought with the returning inhabitants for the fields." Malcolm, *Central India*. London, 1824. Vol. ii, p. 232.

Chapter Twenty-One

1 Paun, or Pan, is the leaf of the Piper Betel, rolled up with a little of the areka nut, a little cardemom, cachu and unslaked lime, sometimes a small quantity of tobacco is added to make the mixture more pungent. It was used particularly by Native women, and was offered to guests and visitors. When chewed it became bright scarlet.

2 No doubt they would have felt obliged to die with him.
3 India at this time was full of adventurers, both French and English, who were anxious to make their fortunes and, with luck, to carve out independent principalities.

Chapter Twenty-Two

1 Lac, i.e. 100,000.
2 Shipp, even if he knew, is not very precise about the reasons for the attack on Asseerghur, and is vague on its topography. Appa Sahib, the Rajah of Nagpore, who had been dethroned by the British, was stirring up trouble, and with Cheeto, the last of the Pindaree chiefs of any consequence, had taken refuge in Asseerghur. The fort itself was built on a huge, isolated rock, and defended by a lower fort which could only be approached through a walled town on the western side. General Malcolm, with forces from Madras and Bombay, was to take the town and lower fort, General Doveton the upper one. Malcolm took the town on the 18th of March, with little loss, though there was a dangerous counter-attack, as Shipp describes. The lower fort was taken on the 29th of March, without opposition. General Doveton was forced to wait for the heavy guns which Shipp and his friends were bringing up from Saugar, which did not arrive until the 3rd of April. On the 8th of April overtures for the surrender of the place were made. When the British marched in the garrison was found to be almost without gunpowder. Appa Sahib escaped to Lahore, and Cheeto's dead body was found in the jungle. He had been killed by a tiger.

Chapter Twenty-Three

1 Sir John Malcolm (1769–1833), entered the Company's service in 1782. He was distinguished as a soldier, administrator and diplomat, as well as being a man of letters. He was an authority on Persian affairs, and twice led missions from India to that country, where the Shah called him his

"favourite foreigner." He was a man of great personal charm, famous as a raconteur, and with a rare understanding of oriental life and thought. In this campaign he both commanded an army, and acted as political agent. He was feeling disappointed and resentful just then, at being passed over for the Governorship of Bombay, which he had been led to expect, but people in London influential with the Company were against him. After a short retirement in England he was at last given the Governorship in 1827. He served in it for four years, dying in England in 1833.

2 Sir John Malcolm said that the heat and glare from the rock had become unendurable, and cholera had also broken out.

Chapter Twenty-Four

1 This was Mulhar Rao, a son of Jaswant Rao. Though he had managed to survive the intrigues, and murders, consequent on his father's madness and death, he was always in danger and had no great reason to be cheerful.

2 Oujein was one of the most ancient of the sacred cities of India. It was said to have been overwhelmed by a rain of earth, but in Malcolm's opinion had been buried by a rise in the nearby Seepra river. At the time of Shipp's visit, the modern city, about two miles from the ancient one, had ceased to be the capital of Scindia and was falling into decay, though some of the Rajah's family still lived there.

3 The row which destroyed Shipp was of the sort that could so easily blow up among men who had been too long in India, and had too much time on their hands. At a court martial at Gazeepore on the 6th of July, 1823, he was charged with unofficer-like and ungentleman-like conduct, which consisted in making "various gross and unfounded charges against Major Browne his superior officer." Shipp had bought a horse at Calcutta, under the impression that it was the sort of animal Browne wanted. Some rather involved racing and horse buying transactions were

going on between Browne and Shipp at the time, in which a man called Chisholm was involved. Browne at first repudiated the Calcutta purchase, but paid for it in the end very reluctantly. The affair was gossiped about, and Shipp came to believe that Browne, in an unauthorized meeting of the officers of the regiment, had "endeavoured to prove that I had literally swindled him out of the price of a horse, 1200 rupees" to the great injury of his reputation in the regiment. Angry at what he thought was going on behind his back, Shipp complained of Browne's conduct to the officer commanding the regiment, Colonel Miller, who told him that he was mistaken. Stubborn as ever, Shipp made the same complaint to the Commander-in-Chief, who also told him that he was wrong, and advised him to withdraw his accusation against Browne. But Shipp persisted, and the court martial followed. In the meantime Colonel Miller, who had been his friend and might possibly have been able to smooth things over, died, and Major Browne was actually in command of the regiment. It is hard to see what induced Shipp to be so reckless; but no doubt his many wounds, and his long stay in India, were having their effect upon him, and coming up from the ranks he perhaps felt that it was more necessary for him to be persistent, in what he thought was a point of honour, than others would have been. And so he threw away his career.

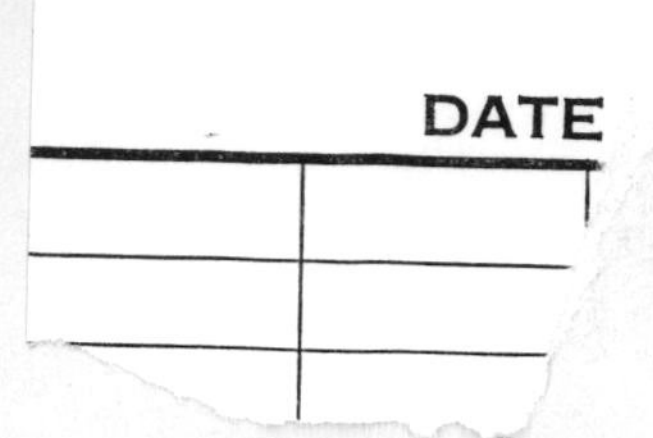
DATE